SOUTHERN LITERARY STUDIES

Fred Hobson, Editor

The Southern Inheritors of Don Quixote

THE SOUTHERN INHERITORS OF
DON QUIXOTE

Montserrat Ginés

Louisiana State University Press   Baton Rouge

MM

Copyright © 2000 by Louisiana State University Press
Manufactured in the United States of America
First printing
09   08   07   06   05   04   03   02   01   00
5   4   3   2   1

Designer: Barbara Neely Bourgoyne
Typeface: Minion
Typesetter: Coghill Composition, Inc.
Printer and binder: Thomson-Shore, Inc.

A portion of the chapter "Honor for the Sake of Honor: The Windmills of Yoknapatawpha"
appeared previously as "Don Quixote in Yoknapatawpha: Faulkner's Champion of Dames"
in the *Southern Literary Journal,* 27, no. 2 (Spring 1995), 23–42. It is reprinted with
permission.

Library of Congress Cataloging-in-Publication Data

Ginés, Montserrat.
    The Southern inheritors of Don Quixote / Montserrat Ginés.
        p.   cm. — (Southern literary studies)
    Includes bibliographical references (p.   ) and index.
    ISBN 0-8071-2589-X (alk. paper)
        1. American fiction—Southern States—History and criticism.   2. Cervantes Saavedra,
    Miguel de, 1547–1616.   Don Quixote.   3. Cervantes Saavedra, Miguel de,
    1547–1616—Influence.   4. Picaresque literature, American—History and criticism.   5.
    American fiction—Spanish influences.   6. Southern States—In literature.   7. Space and time
    in literature.   8. Idealism in literature.   I. Title.   II. Series.
PS261 .G56   2000
863'.3—dc21   00-028728

To Louis D. Rubin, Jr.,
and
my children,
Benjamí and Clara

The horse of Don Gaiferos in his headlong gallop leaves a vacuum behind him, into which a current of hallucinating air rushes, sweeping along with it everything that is not firmly fixed on the ground. There the soul of Don Quixote, light as thistledown, snatched up in the illusory vortex, goes whirling like a dry leaf, and in its pursuit everything ingenuous and sorrowing still left in the world will go forevermore.

—José Ortega y Gasset, *Meditations on Don Quixote*

CONTENTS

PREFACE

The reluctance to confront reality and the tragicomic results of seeking to assert one's individuality in the face of the hostile world are traits readily associated with Don Quixote, but certain writers of the American South have shown themselves to be particularly sensitive to these same attitudes. The presence of the spirit of Don Quixote in southern literature is a phenomenon not of influence but of confluence. Don Quixote's ideal is largely embodied in noble-spirited, idealistic, self-deluding characters who embark on absurd quests and unfeasible undertakings. This ideal is so intrinsic to the literary imagination of southern writers that any attempt to demonstrate a conscious imitation of Cervantes becomes a question of secondary importance.

The writers considered in this study were all innately sympathetic to the idea of tilting at windmills. The futile quest to right the world's wrongs, often in complete disregard of the compromise that reality imposes, was powerfully attractive to them. However differently they expressed the discord between the ideal and the real, their fiction includes basic elements of the Quixote motif: the attempt to reinstate the chivalrous ethic and conceptions of honor in a commonplace, business-oriented world; the struggle to resist a shifting, pluralist interpretation of the world; and the absurd predicament of heroes or heroines who, disconnected from reality, stand alone with their dreams before the world.

This study covers approximately one hundred years of literary production, starting at the turn of the century with Mark Twain and continuing with James Branch Cabell, William Faulkner, and the more contemporary authors Eudora Welty and Walker Percy. I do not mean to imply that the

Quixote motif in southern literature is found exclusively in the works of
these writers, but I would maintain that it figures quite prominently in the
works of the authors here considered.

Although there are works dealing with Cervantes' influence on Mark
Twain, as well as isolated references to quixotic aspects of William Faulkner's oeuvre, a study of this nature, dealing with the subject both in general
terms and as a genuine phenomenon, has not been attempted until now. I
hope that this work will provide a new perspective on southern literature
while at the same time reminding us of the power of art to capture universal themes beyond the boundaries of time, place, and distinct literary traditions.

I would like to express my deepest gratitude to Louis D. Rubin, Jr., to
whom I owe both the subject and the focus of this work. I would especially
like to thank him for all the help and encouragement he has given me since
I first wrote to him from the other side of the Atlantic. At the time, he
knew no more about me than my name, which appeared on the letter
heading. Once the work was under way, he never ceased to offer his assistance, reading sections of the manuscript and making valuable suggestions.
I hope that I have managed to include all of his suggestions in the finished
text. Above all, it is his spirit of good will and generosity that has influ-
enced me most. Not everyone who sets out enthusiastically on such an undertaking is fortunate enough to be able to count on a helping hand such
as he extended to me. Even though this work has reached completion
rather later than I would have wished, I trust that what is contained among
its pages will meet with his approval.

Likewise I would like to express my gratitude to Fred Hobson, who, in
spite of being a very busy man, very willingly and sincerely took me under
his wing when I arrived from Barcelona with my project as a visiting
scholar at the University of North Carolina (UNC) at Chapel Hill. He very
kindly read my work in progress and gave me the benefit of his comments,
in addition to the decisive support of publishing a section of Chapter 3 in
the *Southern Literary Journal.*

I would also like to thank Laurence Avery, head of the English Department at UNC when I was working on the present book, for accepting my
two applications to be a visiting scholar. His kindness and helpfulness
made my own task much easier. Thanks also to Charlotte McFall and Nina
Wallace for their constant support and assistance; to the staff of Davis Library for their highly professional help at all times; and particularly to

Mitch Whichard and Jean Greene, who unfailingly provided me with a space where I could work; to my friend, the irreplaceable William Ilgen, without whose help and wise advice my visits to Chapel Hill would never have been so fruitful and enjoyable. To Eleanor Ilgen, my sincerest thanks for reviewing one of the chapters of my manuscript. Her acute attention to detail improved my writing considerably. Her friendship did the rest.

Other people in Chapel Hill helped immensely in many ways. My work may well have been impossible without Argentina Granada and her daughters, who cared for my children and sometimes even for me. To all the good friends I have in North Carolina go my thanks for their kindness during my stays there.

In Barcelona I am indebted to the Universitat Politècnica de Catalunya, which granted me the sabbatical that enabled me to carry out my task in the conditions required for its successful completion; to my colleagues in the English Department for the innumerable times they have gone out of their way to help; and to Carmen Franquesa, the department secretary, for her patient and efficient assistance in the preparation of the final manuscript, the bibliography, and much more. I would especially like to thank Jennifer Palmer, Neil Moore, and Joann Welsh, UNC graduate students in the Departments of Linguistics and Roman Languages, respectively, in Barcelona on a one-year exchange, who helped me in the final revision with their patience and excellent linguistic judgment.

A special mention for Jeff Palmer, writer and personal friend who lives in Barcelona, to whom I owe the translation of parts of the manuscript that were originally written in Spanish, as well as a close and detailed reading of the work as a whole. The help he has given me has been invaluable. Talent can receive no adequate repayment, but I hope to be equal to his generous friendship.

Last, but not least, I wish to thank the Board of Editors of Louisiana State University Press; John Easterly, Executive Editor; and George Roupe, Editor. Mr. Roupe's editorial suggestions were always on the mark and greatly facilitated the process of completing this book.

ABBREVIATIONS

CY   *A Connecticut Yankee in King Arthur's Court.* Vol. 9 of *The Works of Mark Twain.* Edited by Bernard L. Stein. Berkeley: Published for the Iowa Center of Textual Studies by the University of California Press, 1979.

HF   *Adventures of Huckleberry Finn.* Vol. 8 of *The Works of Mark Twain.* Edited by Walter Blair et al. Berkeley: Published for the Iowa Center of Textual Studies by the University of California Press, 1988.

TS   *The Adventures of Tom Sawyer.* Vol. 4 of *The Works of Mark Twain.* Edited by John C. Gerber, Paul Baender, and Terry Firkins. Berkeley: Published for the Iowa Center of Textual Studies by the University of California Press, 1980.

FOE   *Figures of Earth: A Comedy of Appearances.* Vol. 2 of *The Works of James Branch Cabell.* New York: R. M. McBride, 1927.

JG   *Jurgen: A Comedy of Justice.* Vol. 6 of *The Works of James Branch Cabell.* New York: R. M. McBride, 1928.

RGN   *The Rivet in Grandfather's Neck: A Comedy of Limitations.* Vol. 14 of *The Works of James Branch Cabell.* New York: R. M. McBride, 1929.

FiU   *Faulkner in the University: Class Conferences at the University of Virginia, 1957–58.* Edited by Frederick L. Gwynn and Joseph L. Blotner. Charlottesville: University Press of Virginia, 1959.

GDM   *Go Down, Moses, and Other Stories*, by William Faulkner. New York: Random House, 1942.

LA   *Light in August*, by William Faulkner. New York: Modern Library, 1950.

LiG   *Lion in the Garden: Interviews with William Faulkner, 1926–1962*. Edited by James B. Meriwether and Michael Millgate. New York: Random House, 1968.

Rv   *The Reivers*, by William Faulkner. New York: Random House, 1962.

SF   *The Sound and the Fury*, by William Faulkner. New York: Random House, 1956.

TM   *The Mansion*, by William Faulkner. New York: Random House, 1959.

Twn   *The Town*, by William Faulkner. New York: Random House, 1957.

GA   "The Golden Apples." In *The Collected Stories of Eudora Welty*. New York: Harcourt Brace, 1980.

LB   *Losing Battles*, by Eudora Welty. New York: Random House, 1970.

LG   *The Last Gentleman*, by Walker Percy. New York: Farrar, Straus & Giroux, 1966.

The Southern Inheritors of Don Quixote

INTRODUCTION
The Southern Inheritors of Don Quixote

All is possible. All is in doubt. Only an old hidalgo from the barren plain of La Mancha in the central plateau of Castile continues to adhere to the codes of certainty. For him, nothing is in doubt and all is possible.
—Carlos Fuentes, *Don Quixote; or, The Critique of Reading*

The first question that all those who undertake a study of the literary prototype Don Quixote must ask themselves is: What exactly are the phenomena that Cervantes portrays in his deranged knight? Throughout the critical history of Cervantes' work, *Don Quixote* has been the subject of many interpretations. Certain features, however, make up the essence of the character. Above all, Don Quixote embodies an ideal as chimerical as it is indestructible—that the knightly function can be revived in a crass present. It is chimerical because, by definition, it belongs to the world of fantasy, and as such is unattainable in historical reality. It is indestructible insofar as it lies deep in consciousness itself, impervious to criticism and consequently rejecting all attempts to verify its authenticity. Likewise, Don Quixote is defeat, vain undertakings, perpetual testimony to failure and misfortune, all of which has made of him a "symbol of the toil and perplexities of the will to excellence in this world."[1] He is also the first self-

---

1. Fernando Savater, *Instrucciones para olvidar el "Quijote" y otros ensayos generales* (Instructions on how to forget *Don Quixote* and other general essays) (Madrid: Taurus, 1985), 21. All translations of excerpts from this book are mine.

deceiving modern hero, the first to take on the world single-handedly in his own ridiculous solitude. *Don Quixote* abounds with irony, misunderstandings, and paradox, reflecting the ambiguous and many-sided gaze of its creator, who, while appearing to mock everything, actually mocks nothing, providing us in the end with a portrait of a loser, ironic but also full of dignity and affection. A host of characters throughout the history of literature have followed in the old hidalgo's footsteps.

The historical background for Don Quixote's follies is furnished by an autocratic Spain sunk in economic and social decline, but still absorbed in its dreams of grandeur. In Cervantes' Spain an old hidalgo could very well be living in penury while still preserving the bearing and air of breeding of the person he had once been. The reading of books of chivalry carries Don Quixote back to a heroic and knightly order of things for which he still yearns, and which Cervantes mockingly reflects through the mad hidalgo's dress, his grandiloquent speech, his self-proclaimed mission to right all wrongs, his vain nostalgia for a golden age—in short, his idealized, one-track vision of the world. Cervantes sends his derided knight on a journey through the coarse inns and taverns of La Mancha, where he encounters a plain and unadorned reality, divested of heroism and romanticism. Wherever the feverish aspirations of his knight come to grief, the author's irony comes to the fore, but always with sympathy for his character's fruitless efforts to grapple with the imponderables of reality and historical time.

Cervantes' literary archetype has gone beyond cultural frontiers to take abode in the literature of many countries, either for reasons of literary mimesis or because of a simple confluence of vision: Gustave Flaubert, whose *Madame Bovary* faithfully recreates the wanderings of the Knight of La Mancha's unbalanced imagination, pertinently said that he "traced [his] origins to the book that he knew by heart even before [he] learned how to read: *Don Quixote*." The English novel of the eighteenth century bears Cervantes' mark, and among the world's greatest novelists, Dostoevski, Stendhal, Joyce, Melville, and Flaubert himself have also reworked Don Quixote's characteristics in some of their books.[2] We also find instances of

2. Gustave Flaubert, *Correspondance II, 1847–1852* (Correspondence II: 1847–1852) (Paris: L. Conard, 1926), 442: "Je retrouve tous mes origines dans le livre que je savais par coeur avant de savoir lire: *Don Quichotte*." Likewise, Fyodor Dostoevski reveals his debt to *Don Quixote* in the genesis of Prince Myshkin in his novel *The Idiot*; see Ludmila B. Turkevich, *Cervantes in Russia* (Princeton: Princeton University Press, 1954), 124–25.

Don Quixote's influence in American literature from the beginning of the nineteenth century. But it is in the literature of the American South where, from the end of the nineteenth century, the clash between the ideal and the mundane world that so exemplifies the Manchegian knight has most consistently arisen. Certain southern writers have been particularly sensitive to the fundamental themes of Cervantes' novel: the insoluble discord between the real and the ideal and the attempt, at once grotesque and dignified, to affirm one's individuality in complete disregard of common sense and against all the demands of historical reality.

Within the context of American society as a whole, historical, economic, and social factors shaped the culture of the South, giving it a distinct character, and these factors provided extraliterary underpinnings sensitive to the Quixote spirit. First, the institution of slavery ensured that the traditional hierarchical structures of a rural society remained preeminent over the democratizing social ethic that has been the cornerstone of the American ideal since the Declaration of Independence. Furthermore, the patriarchal foundation of southern society and the emphasis it gave to the notions of honor, chivalry, and the importance of lineage over work and money were the cultural factors that set the South apart from the general work ethic that was the totem of society in the North. In much the same way, the experience of defeat and its corollary, economic penury and loss of prestige and social position among the ruling class, gave rise to a sense of loss, frustration, and decline that created in its wake a climate favorable to the romantic harking back to the past and attitudes that tended toward the unrealistic and the fantastic. All these elements are at the root of the myth of the Lost Cause, which Frank E. Vandiver describes as "the first American resistance against the organization-State, against racial indistinction, against mass and motor—in other words, against the modern world." As a consequence, the South remained remote from the typically American culture of "success," as C. Vann Woodward has pointed out: "Southern history, unlike American, includes large components of frustration, failure, and defeat. It includes not only an overwhelming military defeat, but long decades of defeat in the provinces of economic, social, and political life."[3]

3. Frank E. Vandiver, "The Confederate Myth," in *Myth and Southern History*, ed. Patrick Gerster and Nicholas Cords (Urbana: University of Illinois Press, 1989), 149; C. Vann Woodward, *The Burden of Southern History* (Baton Rouge: Louisiana State University Press, 1960), 19.

Although the comparison may not be immediately apparent, I would like to touch briefly on certain similarities between the situation in the American South at the end of the nineteenth and the beginning of the twentieth centuries and conditions in Cervantes' Spain. That a literary paradigm such as Don Quixote so deeply rooted in a particular cultural and historical context as the old hidalgo in the reality of Spain should reappear so frequently in the literature of another time and place—in southern fiction in this case—is a fact worth noting. I believe this points to a conjunction of historical and literary factors that are similar in both societies and that set in motion aspirations that are also similar, leading to a like response when brought face-to-face with the fleeting nature of existence.

As Spain passed from the sixteenth to the seventeenth century, it went through a period of isolation from the rest of Europe. This situation was brought about by the enormous discrepancy between its imperial dreams (a legacy of the Emperor Charles' time, but still intact during the reign of his successor) and the reality of a country on the verge of economic ruin, suffering a deep structural and social crisis. The obsession with having a good name and coming from a noble line, the rejection of the values of trade and commerce, and the scorn felt for both work and money created a climate of chronic uncertainty, driving a breach between the ideal and reality that was without precedent in the European consciousness. The historian Pierre Vilar describes Cervantes' time as a descent from "splendor" to "decline," and contends that the "definite crisis of the Spanish power" and "the first great crisis of doubt suffered by the Spanish" can be placed between 1598 and 1620. He goes on to make the following assessment of Cervantes' novel: "In the decline of a society worn out by history, in a country that has carried its inner contradictions to the furthest possible extent . . . there emerges a masterpiece that captures in images the tragicomic contrast between the mythical structures and the reality of human relationships."[4]

Drawing a comparison between Cervantes' situation in Spain at the end of the sixteenth century and his counterparts in the rest of Europe, Carlos Fuentes states that Cervantes "must wrestle between the old and the new with far greater intensity than, say, Descartes. And he certainly cannot face

---

4. Pierre Vilar, "El tiempo del 'Quijote' " (The time of Don Quixote), in *El "Quijote" de Cervantes* (Cervantes' *Don Quixote*), ed. George Haley (Madrid: Taurus, 1980), 17, 29. My translation.

the world with the pragmatic assurance of Defoe. Robinson Crusoe, the first capitalistic hero, is a self-made man who accepts objective reality and fashions it to his needs through the work ethic, common sense, resilience, technology and, if need be, racism and imperialism." Compared with the pragmatism and the resources that Robinson Crusoe had for dealing with the world, Don Quixote is a reflection of "the most ludicrous failure in practical matters in recorded history."[5] Fuentes places Quixote and Crusoe at opposite poles as literary archetypes representative of the Hispanic and the Anglo-Saxon worlds respectively. Writers of the American South, however, found little in common with the "Anglo-Saxon" archetype. And neither did Defoe's hero attract the literary imagination of the majority of the twentieth-century American writers; however, those from the South were the first to find in the paradigm of Don Quixote resonances that were very close to their own world. Many southern writers showed an innate sympathy toward the essentially quixotic attitude of tilting against windmills, of upholding concepts of honor and chivalry, however outmoded they appeared to be in a makeshift, materialistic, and secular world. This attitude stemmed from the conflict between an inherited tradition and the values of the modern society in which those writers were brought up. The inherited tradition was based on a patriarchal ethic in which the individual's sense of honor and his worth in the community were the very touchstone. Modern values ushered in the democratization of society and cultural uniformity, both consequences of the South's incorporation into the world of industrial capitalism. Fully aware of the futility of their characters' endeavors, these authors viewed their quixotic strivings with irony and often with humor, but theirs is also a vision full of affection, sympathy, and understanding.

Before I pursue further the distinctive manifestations of quixotism in southern fiction, I need to clarify two important points. First, the worldview that generated Don Quixote's progeny in southern literature was that of the privileged, white, educated elite of southern society. And it is from that vantage point that these writers engaged their literary imaginations in quixotic characters and situations. Second, the pervasiveness of the Quixote theme in southern literature is a phenomenon inscribed in the literary

5. Carlos Fuentes, *Don Quixote; or, The Critique of Reading* (Austin: Institute of Latin American Studies, The University of Texas at Austin, 1976), 45–46; originally published as *Don Quijote o la crítica de la lectura* (Mexico City: Editorial Joaquín Mortiz, 1976).

sensibility of Southern Renaissance writers, since it entails a vision fixed at the crossroads between tradition and modernity. From there these writers recreated in all their complexity the myth that resists both change and the march of historical time and the self-deception and fear of loss that all change involves. They attempt to combine the old and the new by means of irony and humor as antidotes to obstinacy, boastfulness, and nostalgia. They unhesitatingly support modernity, but mistrust fin-de-siècle American industrial capitalism as much as they mistrust the reversion to a tradition that denies historical change.

With his mixture of self-deception, disproportion, and nobility of spirit, Don Quixote, struggling against a recalcitrant world resistant to his dreams, is an idealistic and tragicomic hero, and Cervantes' purpose in exposing the excesses to which such a pursuit of the ideal world can lead when divorced from reality is both burlesque and satirical. Here is a scenario that fits exactly these southern writers' perceptions of the world and their dissatisfaction with it. Their intellectual development distances them from the cultural inbreeding that invariably lies behind any exclusive nationalism or regional patriotism, endowing them with an ironic perspective on the myths underlying that culture, but without converting them to the pragmatic mentality so typical of twentieth-century America. On the contrary, they are contemptuous of the worship of "success." These southern writers are suspicious of a culture that rewards and venerates only the triumphant, preferring to follow the tenets of honorable conduct. It is hardly surprising, then, that they choose Don Quixote as their literary prototype when they wish to depict their characters' aspirations toward transcendence. Rash, excessive, or immoderate behavior; impulsive acts; the stubbornness of the "I" before the world—all that Don Quixote represents—are for them well-known traits, "sins" of their own cultural background. But these writers also share with Cervantes a further ironic and paradoxical vision: the splendor and misery of the soul in irreconcilable conflict with itself as it goes off in pursuit of excellence.

While all these writers reflect in their fiction the quixotic motif from varying perspectives, the greatest difference is to be found in the work of the only woman analyzed in this study, Eudora Welty. All the male writers have their roots in a culture that had made of the past an age unsurpassed and of the Civil War an heroic exploit. For them, the quixotic stance is founded on a notion of honor, the chivalric ideal, the longing for heroism in the grand manner—concepts frequently giving rise to outmoded, fruitless, and pathetic behavior. This is not so in Eudora Welty's case. She also speaks to us of lost battles, of stubbornness and tilting at windmills, but instead of historic grandeur her heroines' ideals are inspired by a more personal passion. The fact that Eudora Welty, a born Mississippian from Jackson, was not raised in a genuine southern family—her father came from Ohio and her mother from West Virginia—may account in some measure for her lack of literary interest in the southern chivalric ideal and the impact of the Civil War. Also, female sensibility has never shared the same perception of heroism or of the ideal as male sensibility.

For Eudora Welty, the unattainable ideal is not to be found in a romanticized past or the grandeur of the knightly ideal. The impossibility of realizing one's dreams has more to do with habit and atavism. The aspirations of personal development of her heroines are often thwarted by the tyranny of daily routine or inhibited by fear of the unknown so common in the self-preserving communities such as those in which Welty's heroines live. Miss Lotte Elizabeth Eckhart in *The Golden Apples* and Miss Julia Mortimer in *Losing Battles* do not entertain romantic dreams. They have individual passions that turn into crusades teeming with quixotic zeal. Their immoderate pursuits are to bring knowledge and art to bear on narrow-minded communities that forbid the realization of individual dreams. But their efforts come to nothing; they are doomed to misunderstanding and ostracism. Far from being discouraged, however, they learn how to live with defeat. Although failure is their lot, they refuse to give up their aspirations to the very end. They lose the battle but never their dignity or their faith in their undertakings. Their sense of honor is closely bound up with their self-esteem, on which others invariably trample. It is a sense of honor bound up even with despair.

Honor, lineage, and reckless courage acquire quixotic dimensions in Mark Twain's world. In this light he portrays his southern aristocrats, anachronistic or self-deluded in their dealings with the world. But while Twain pokes fun at the South's chivalrous pretensions and its literary preferences for the works of Walter Scott and the like, he also pays tribute to the world of romance through the character of Tom Sawyer—who, like Don Quixote, sought to embellish life with the fantasies of literature—and also through his own memories of boyhood and youth on the banks of the Mississippi River. Mark Twain brilliantly brings Don Quixote and Sancho Panza to life again in the shape of Tom Sawyer and Huckleberry Finn, the most memorable partnership in American literature. They not only reproduce the characters from Cervantes' novel but also establish a genuine dialogue between the ideal—as romance and thirst for heroism—and the ineluctable force of the real transposed into the common sense of the ordinary folk of the American frontier among whom the author moved in his youth. Much of Twain's own life experience, as well as his complex and many-sided personality, has gone into the development of this dialogue. Don Quixote and Sancho Panza reappear in *A Connecticut Yankee in King Arthur's Court*, a book written in the burlesque style. Here, the ideal is embodied in the superstition, ignorance, and backwardness of those who still proudly uphold the tenets of medieval chivalry. The real appears as the pragmatism, now synonymous with progress, that bursts upon medieval obscurantism in the shape of the harbingers of twentieth-century capitalism. Ironically, however, it is the Connecticut Yankee himself who performs the quixotic act: after setting out on his adventure as a convinced representative of modernity, he ends up under the spell of the very world he sought to redeem.

Don Quixote, mounted on an old nag and armed with nothing but a lance, challenging windmills that regard him impassively from a distance, is a constant presence in the events of William Faulkner's Yoknapatawpha County. From the many situations and attitudes in which one encounters the predisposition or mood that animates Don Quixote's adventures in Faulkner's novels, one may very well infer that the Knight of La Mancha became part of Faulkner's subjective landscape as a permanent point of reference. Faulkner loved *Don Quixote*. In Cervantes' character he recognized a path that has been trodden time and again by human beings in their hapless journey through life as they strive to bridge the gulf separating dream from reality. Faulkner regarded history as the expression of a natural force of life forever looming over the unsuspecting individual and the individual as a being striving uselessly to resist it. His vision, however, was never deterministic. He firmly believed that the concept of honor and dignity equipped people to struggle against the overmastering power of destiny. In Faulkner, this conviction of the honorableness of the species stems from the purest ethics of chivalry and is founded on the belief that certain nonpragmatic ideals and values point the way to what human beings ought to be, revealing their capacity as spiritual beings. Perhaps human beings can never reach the heights to which they aspire. Perhaps reality never reflects in just measure their desires for perfectibility. But perhaps, also, the potential inherent in the longing for perfection can free them from the chains of circumstance, allowing them to see themselves as they would like to be, as they would like the world to see them, and even to go so far as to clutch at heroism in the pursuit of such a chimera. This feeling emanates from many passages in Faulkner's work, passages in which his characters abandon common sense and embark obstinately on foolish pursuits or emerge as self-appointed righters of wrongs and embrace in solitude a moral crusade to which they cling as if to an indelible mark of identity. The inability of many of Faulkner's characters to impinge upon the present, their alienation from the world around them, and their clumsiness and ineptitude in action are consequences of the admiration the author felt for praiseworthy but vain undertakings that reveal human beings' strivings for dignity and excellence.

William Faulkner followed the footsteps of the disinherited Knight of La Mancha—his delusions of grandeur, his idealization of the past, his moral idealism, his stubborn refusal to resign himself to the dictates of the real world—across the rugged terrain of his heartland, Mississippi, a region doubly ill-starred, on the one hand by history, which subjected it to the desolation of a war and to the humiliation of defeat, and on the other by the delusions of those who thought they could divert the course of time and events and thereby prevent its entry into the modern world. In Faulkner, idealization of the past reflects the twofold vision of the quixotic utopia. On one hand, the past is a mythical time in which heroic action was possible, as perceived by Gail Hightower in *Light in August*. On the other, the past is an Arcadia of over-spilling nature, longed for by Isaac McCaslin in *Go Down, Moses*, a rural paradise now plundered by the predator man. While showing understanding for those of his characters who have inherited the burden of the past, at the same time Faulkner regards with skepticism their retreat from the real world.

In the moral idealism of the last descendants of Yoknapatawpha gentry, who wish to right the wrongs of the world and defend virtue single-handedly, Faulkner brings Don Quixote to life at his best: in their fustian manners, their obstinacy, their neglect of the claims of actuality, and their sterile nostalgic outlook, which is often a consequence of the heroic ideal portrayed in his work. Who better than Don Quixote as a means of debunking such an ideal and the pretension to tragic grandeur that stems from the fallacy that all old times were better times? But Faulkner must also have gleaned from the pages of *Don Quixote* that the heart is not always bereft of power, for exclamations of success are sometimes hollow, whereas failure is frequently redolent of sincerity and often carries a message of hope. Accordingly, Faulkner depicts his "champion[s] of dames" (as one character refers to Quentin Compson), who spring to the defense of honor when it neither asks nor wishes to be defended, as engaging in a praiseworthy conduct, but comical and sad. Quentin Compson in *The Sound and the Fury* and Gavin Stevens in *The Town* and *The Mansion* represent this type. Other victims of the soul-sickness of moral idealism are Isaac McCaslin in *Go Down, Moses* and Horace Benbow in *Sanctuary*. Faulkner portrays them as losers, derided and self-deluded heroes, prey to their own incorrigible idealism, while never leaving us in any doubt about the respect they deserve in their attempts to achieve excellence.

But when Faulkner shows us the comical, bizarre, and even hazardous nature of certain quests on which his errant knights embark, then the county of Yoknapatawpha becomes as prosaic as the barren plains of La Mancha. Equipped with steed and squire, but bereft of adventurous deeds to perform and wrongs to right, Faulkner's knights pursue glory in the mirages of the mind, serving an abstract ideal that exempts them from having to come to terms with a crass reality. Flem Snopes' materialistic code and his lack of scruples are brittle, but the irony with which V. K. Ratliff describes Gavin Stevens' quixotic reactions to Flem's success is an example of Faulkner's objectivity toward his characters' absurd behavior.

A compromise between the ideal and the real is beyond the reach of most characters in Yoknapatawpha County. They most readily succumb to the romantic appeal of the ideal and draw no benefits from their struggle in life. (Only the stubbornness of a few poor whites provides a means of bringing about some improvement in their circumstances.) The Sancho Panzas of this world yell themselves hoarse trying to make common sense prevail, but in vain. Not the Ratliffs, not the Edmondses, not the Ameses or the de Spains nor all the custodians of actuality against whom Faulkner sends his deluded knights to do battle can do anything to stamp out the "fastidious ideal." Faulkner faithfully reproduces the spirit of Cervantes' book by revealing human nature's irrepressible tendency to idealism, as well as its devastating effects when the ideal is divorced from all sense of reality. But, like Cervantes, Faulkner regards his characters' misguided ventures with sympathy and understanding, allowing us insight into his divided loyalties.

A further affinity with Cervantes' *Don Quixote* in southern writing is found in the fiction of James Branch Cabell. In Cabell the ideal of chivalry, which had such an influence in his native Virginia, is debunked and treated with an irony equaled only by Mark Twain. Cabell exposes the deceits behind the South's chivalrous-heroic pretensions and the damage caused by those who were motivated by them, without ever denying the human mind's propensity to idealization. In *The Rivet in Grandfather's Neck*, chivalry and the renunciation implicit in courtly love are presented as quixotic whims and fickleness. The result is always a sterile act that does nobody any good but exempts the protagonist from the more human and banal aspects of love. In *Jurgen* and *Figures of Earth* Cabell's use of parody is his most fertile means of discrediting the absolutes of justice, heroism, and love, which Don Quixote was so determined to reinstate. Cabell's process of debunking is so ferocious that in the end nothing is left standing. Justice is not something dispensed according to one's deserts, but rather the self-given right to have our desires gratified. Love is anything but romantic sublimation; it is eroticism, vanity, fleeting pleasure, and, finally, boredom. Heroism, understood as courage and lofty ideals, amounts to little more than the human need to place virtue outside of oneself in order to preserve its purity, and is, in turn, never a reality that the hero takes upon himself. But for all his broadsides of parody and debunking, Cabell does not confine himself to scorning the human desire for pleasures greater than those that life ordinarily may offer. The urge to dream, the flight into fantasy, is perhaps the only resort left to human beings in their condition of uncertainty. But he also warns us not to entertain any sterile hopes of ever satisfying our longings. For, beyond our capacity to dream, we will always be led back to ourselves as the object of our own imaginings. We must always be setting out, like Don Quixote from La Mancha, on that journey to nowhere.

In *The Last Gentleman* Walker Percy casts an ironic but sympathetic eye on the last vestiges of the chivalrous ideal played out against the backdrop of contemporary America. He poses the question of how much exactly is left of the values of honor and chivalry that characterized the South in the past but have since become obsolete in the modern world. Percy likewise explores the possible consequences of these values when they are carried to excess. From this point of departure, we follow the fortunes of his gentleman through an ironic tale of maladjustment between his own actions and attitudes, more suited to a chivalrous-heroic conception of the world, and the social conventions that surrounded him. The result is a combination of Quentin Compson and a character that could almost be called chaplinesque—an awkward and absurd figure akin to Don Quixote inasmuch as he attempts to impose his own interpretation of life on the ineluctable world of facts, against which he is constantly banging his head.

Percy is a suitable culmination to this study of the southern heirs of Don Quixote. Through the romantic disposition of his last gentleman, he rebukes the southern heroic ideal for its denial to accept the commonplace, what he calls "everydayness." But he also resents the loss of some fine qualities of the old ethics swept away by the process of cultural homogenization experienced by contemporary American society. The alternative, Percy implies, is not to be found in the stoic attitude that stems from a self-satisfied belief in its high ideals. On the contrary, it lies rather in a healthy skepticism toward all kinds of searching for the transcendental. The only real truth is that which springs not from the world as we ideally interpret it but from our own relationship with the world as it is. And this truth will always be a partial truth, since it is personal and bears the fruit of individual experience. This is how Williston Bibb Barrett, the "last gentleman" to appear in the literature of the American South, seems finally to understand it.

It would be misleading to suggest that the Quixote theme is restricted to the group of writers considered here or that it is not congenial to other sensibilities in southern literature. Although I do not intend to go beyond the scope and focus of the present study by hinting at themes not central to it, it seems appropriate to conclude by briefly pointing out other possible approaches to quixotism in other southern writers, as a way of suggesting that the theme might be followed up—or at least addressed—from a different viewpoint and time span.

Also, as I have stated before, I refer to the quixotic traits of southern fiction as reflections of an outlook on the southern past, the southern community, and southern mores that are characteristic of white southern writers of a particular period of time and circumstances. It seems unlikely that any black southern writer would have the same perspective on the past, feel the same ambiguity or uneasiness about the present, or express the same sort of irony toward his or her own ambivalence that a white southern writer would. African American concerns about history and the role of human beings in it are inevitably different. In that respect, Ralph Ellison's *Invisible Man* provides a good example of the contrast between the two kinds of experience.

The ordeals of the protagonist of Ralph Ellison's *Invisible Man* as he attempts to attain an identity as a full human being in white-dominated

America are nothing if not quixotic, although they spring from an experience entirely different from that of, say, a Quentin Compson or a Will Barrett. The journey of Ellison's Invisible Man is quixotic and so is his endeavor, but Ellison's protagonist is marked racially as an outsider, whereas Don Quixote is not. Rather, Don Quixote is the upholder of values and beliefs of a well-established society, albeit a passé society whose values and beliefs no longer make sense. When Louis Rubin points to the appropriateness of the quixotic motif as a way of grasping the estrangement of Ralph Ellison's Invisible Man, as well as the absurdity of his endeavor, he is referring to a sort of quixotic journey, one that fully expresses the contemporary urge for identity. Seen as "a protest against ideological confusion . . . against a world in which [one] cannot define [one's] human identity to [one's] own spiritual satisfaction," the adventure of Ellison's protagonist across the plains of anonymity, his effort to transcend this anonymity and have "his own individual humanity" recognized—this adventure, given the time and place, is totally quixotic.[6]

In fact, Will Barrett's pilgrimage and that of Ellison's Invisible Man have many things in common. The voyages share the episodic form, the protagonists' naive faith in the power of the journey, tragicomic characterization, and self-deceit. Both heroes feel the urge for identity, they are both "underground men" in the midst of their cultures (the Invisible Man's alienation is from both white and black culture), and they both face mock battles and chaplinesque encounters and are baffled by a reality they fail to comprehend. In the end, they both have to come to terms with disillusionment. But if the manner of the quest is similar, its substance is not. A black man and a white member of the privileged class in the South must necessarily undertake different sorts of journeys. They both wish to alter their given reality, but from opposite positions in the American social scheme: Percy's protagonist travels north to south to retrieve the essence of his privileged white southern identity; Ellison's protagonist travels south to north, away from his racially doomed fate. Will Barrett's penchant for searching the past for meaning that can make sense of the present is unquestionably southern. The Invisible Man's quest after his own humanity chronicles the futile revolt of a black American who seeks to amend his fate, and, as such, his voyage is entirely racially oriented.

6. Louis D. Rubin, Jr., "Don Quixote and Selected Progeny; or, The Journeyman as an Outsider," *Southern Review* 10 (January 1974): 35, 55.

The "visibility" that Ellison's character seeks is an entirely quixotic objective, especially at the time in which the novel is set. It is quixotic inasmuch as Ellison's hero strives against imponderables; however, the windmills he confronts are authentic giants. The Invisible Man's wish to become "human" is not granted, but his endeavor, unlike that of Cervantes' knight, is not divorced from the possibilities and the difficulties of his time. In Ellison's novel there is the basis for an investigation of the Quixote motif that speaks of vision more than "distorted" vision, of "being denied" more than "denying." The Invisible Man stands halfway between Camus' absurd hero and Cervantes' sorrowing knight, on the vortex where reasonableness and illusory ingenuity collide, as a true representative of Don Quixote's "selected progeny."

I

MARK TWAIN'S
SEARCH FOR IDENTITY

"I know who I am," replied Don Quixote, "and I know, too, that I am capable of being not only the characters I have named, but all the Twelve Peers of France, and all the Nine Worthies as well, for my exploits are far greater than all the deeds they have done, all together and each by himself."
— Miguel de Cervantes Saavedra, *The Adventures of Don Quixote*

I didn't see no di'monds, and I told Tom Sawyer so. He said there was loads of them there, anyway; and he said there was A-rabs there too, and elephants and things. I said, why couldn't we see them, then? He said if I warn't so ignorant, but had read a book called *Don Quixote*, I would know without asking.
— Mark Twain, *Adventures of Huckleberry Finn*

Mark Twain was well acquainted with Cervantes' work, particularly with *Don Quixote*. The full range of episodes in Twain's novels that echo episodes in *Don Quixote* are proof of his indebtedness to Cervantes. Moreover, to anyone acquainted with Mark Twain's oeuvre there is no question that the writer must have felt enthralled by Cervantes' burlesque treatment of chivalry, as shown in the well-known passage of *Life on the Mississippi* in which he praises *Don Quixote* for having "swept the world's admiration for the mediæval chivalry-silliness out of existence." Twain ponders Cervantes' *Don Quixote* as opposed to the "pernicious work" done by Walter Scott's novels, which, Twain declares, contributed to restoring romantic notions, particularly in the South, where, he writes, "the nineteenth century is curiously confused and commingled with the Walter Scott Middle-Age sham civilization." (In a display of literalness, he actually sinks the *Walter Scott*, the shipwreck Huck and Jim board in *Adventures of Huckleberry Finn*, in the Mississippi River.) He goes so far in his invectives as to attribute the backwardness of the region to "the Sir Walter disease" and to charge "Sir Walter" himself with having had "so large a hand in making Southern character, as it existed before the war, that he is in great measure responsible for the war."[1]

Twain's fictionalized account of his own brief involvement in the Civil War shows the extent to which he despised fraudulent chivalry. Discussing "The Private History of a Campaign That Failed" and Twain's experience with the Marion Rangers in the Civil War, Daniel Aaron ponders the fact that while Twain chose to "present himself and his companions as if they were Tom Sawyer and his carefree gang (his way of justifying his ambiguous relation with the war), he also stripped the war of idealism and just cause, and portrayed its participants as 'bumpkins and fanatics who pointlessly murdered each other.' " One could argue that Twain saw the Civil War as a quixotic undertaking, considering how many of its participants thought of it in terms of high-minded ideals of chivalry and warfare. War, like Twain's Marian Rangers themselves, is burlesquely represented by soldier Dunlap, whom Twain describes as "young, ignorant, good-natured,

1. Mark Twain, *Life on the Mississippi* (1883; reprint, New York: Heritage Press, 1944), 271–73. Further references to *Life on the Mississippi* will be to this edition. For Mark Twain's acquaintance with Cervantes' *Don Quixote* see Edward Wagenknecht, *Mark Twain: The Man and His Work* (Norman: University of Oklahoma Press, 1967), 44; Minni M. Brashear, *Mark Twain, Son of Missouri* (Chapel Hill: University of North Carolina Press, 1934), 35, 223, 235n; E. Hudson Long and J. R. LeMaster, eds., *The New Mark Twain Handbook* (New York: Garland, 1985), 146; and J. DeLancey Ferguson, *Mark Twain: Man and Legend* (Indianapolis: Bobbs-Merrill, 1943), 45. Twain's indebtedness to *Don Quixote* has been the subject of several research works over the years; see Olin H. Moore, "Mark Twain and Don Quixote," *PMLA* 37 (June 1922): 324–46; E. H. Templin, "On Re-Reading Mark Twain, " *Hispania* 24 (October 1941): 269–76; George Santayana, "Tom Sawyer and Don Quixote," *Mark Twain Quarterly* 9, no. 2 (1952): 1–3; Arturo Serrano Plaja, *"Magic" Realism in Cervantes: Don Quixote as Seen Through "Tom Sawyer" and "The Idiot,"* trans. Robert S. Rudder (Berkeley: University of California Press, 1970); J. H. Harkey, " 'Don Quixote' and the American Fiction Through Mark Twain," (Ph.D. diss., University of Tennessee, 1968); and Stanley T. Williams, *The Spanish Background of American Literature*, vol. 1 (New Haven: Yale University Press, 1968).

well-meaning, trivial, full of romance and given to reading chivalric novels." The burlesque scenery of the Marian Rangers as it appears in "The Private History," with its misadventurous, self-deluded army band, ultimately suggests, in Aaron's view, a "seriocomic attack on militarism and war." The war was a deceitful pursuit that exacted the most terrible cost. The death of a stranger, accidentally shot down by Twain's militia, was all it took for Twain to desert, or, in his own words, "to retire from this avocation of sham soldiership while I could save some of my self-respect." The dreadful scene of this absurd death, Twain recalls, "took the romance all out of the campaign, and turned our dreams of glory into a repulsive nightmare."[2]

In spite of the evidence that Mark Twain borrows from Cervantes' *Don Quixote*, what concerns us here is not so much proving an influence as showing how Twain's congeniality with the Spanish author can be related to the particulars of time and place and personal idiosyncrasy from which Twain's life and work sprang. Twain was born into a world in which traditional society and industrial society collided head on, where the marks of the first were still strongly felt even as the second was growing steadily. Twain's fascination with chivalric values, which he debunked and esteemed with the same emotional vehemence, has been rightly connected with the resilience of chivalric ideals in the American imagination in the final decades of the nineteenth century in both the North and the South,[3] but Twain's approach to the chivalric is also bound up with the quixotic paradigm. If chivalric values in Twain's fiction work against the reality principle, yielding futile or anachronistic behavior—his southern aristocrats are good examples of such an attitude—they also come to represent the possibility of romance, heroism, and glory as an alternative to life as it is. The character of Tom Sawyer in *The Adventures of Tom Sawyer* and the author's own experiences on the idyllic Mississippi of his youth, as described in *Life on the Mississippi*, explore this longing more deeply. The quixotic motif so common in Twain's fiction appears to be essentially related to Twain's concern with personal identity, a central aspect of his literary imagination.

2. Daniel Aaron, *The Unwritten War: American Writers and the Civil War* (New York: Alfred A. Knopf, 1973), 136–37; Mark Twain, "The Private History of a Campaign That Failed," in *The American Claimant and Other Stories and Sketches* (New York: Harper & Brothers, 1917), 275, 279, 271.

3. See John Fraser, *America and the Patterns of Chivalry* (Cambridge: Cambridge University Press, 1982).

Mark Twain's family sprang from decaying gentility, holding onto concepts of assigned status and social privilege that were not consonant with their actual wealth or circumstances. Twain had firsthand knowledge of quixotic inadequacy as the son of John Marshall Clemens, whose lack of affluence never affected the pride he felt in being, first and foremost, a Virginian. Arthur G. Pettit describes Twain's father as "a dignified and austere Whig descended from a long line of Virginian landowners and slaveholders. . . . [He] considered himself an authentic throwback to the ethos of the previous generation, a leftover Jeffersonian stranded in the backwash of the Mississippi frontier." Hinting at how inadequate John Clemens' talents were to the kind of frontier life he was bound to in Florida, Missouri, Dixon Wecter observes, "Here, in the midst of these honest, kindly, lazy, half-literate rustics who chewed tobacco, drank hard liquor and loved to wrestle, but who seldom saw a book or magazine, the talents of a hard, cold, precise intellect were singularly wasted."[4]

John Clemens' aristocratic pretension, his demeanor of a past splendor, shared by so many other Virginians of his time and condition who headed to the border South in search of better opportunities, carries unequivocal quixotic connotations, as it showed an utter disregard for the actualities of his new milieu. Their new destinations, whether the actual frontier or established communities with less tradition than Clemens' native Virginia, were certainly not places where caste and its prerogatives would affect in any significant way the life of those who came to live there, but Virginians like Clemens never renounced their pretensions. Twain was keenly aware of the discrepancy, and thus he wrote of Hannibal: "It was a little democracy which was full of liberty, equality and Fourth of July, and sincerely so, too; yet you perceived that the aristocratic taint was there. It was there and nobody found fault with the fact or ever stopped to reflect that its presence was an inconsistency."[5] The collision of aspiration and reality, one of the hallmarks of Twain's humor, is primarily a legacy of the years he spent in Hannibal and of his wanderings on a steam packet and in river towns. The pathos emerging from this collision revolves around the pretension to role and status which is wholly incongruous with the shifting, democratic ways

4. Arthur G. Pettit, *Mark Twain and the South* (Lexington: University Press of Kentucky, 1974), 14; Dixon Wecter, *Sam Clemens of Hannibal* (Boston: Houghton Mifflin, 1952), 50.

5. *The Autobiography of Mark Twain*, ed. Charles Neider (New York: Harper & Brothers, 1959), 28. Further references to *The Autobiography* will be to this edition.

of life in mid-nineteenth-century America. The inability of a Tom Sawyer to conform to the slow pace of a small river town brings to mind the life experience of Samuel Clemens. A true heir to his father's rejection of the frontier homogenizing process, young Samuel Clemens could never bring himself to accept his given circumstances, which afforded him neither distinction nor high purpose.

In *Life on the Mississippi* we learn of young Samuel Clemens' "permanent" ambition to become a master pilot, "the only unfettered and entirely independent human being that lived in the earth."[6] He fulfilled his dream, but, ironically, the same river that responded to his claims of heroism and romance and accepted him among its peers also furnished him with an antagonistic kind of experience. It brought him into contact with the vernacular language and experience he was later to put to work so brilliantly in *Adventures of Huckleberry Finn*. It might be said that Mark Twain borrowed from Southwestern humor as Cervantes borrowed from Spanish picaresque. Frontier humor supplied Twain with the appropriate language to play off the vernacular against the genteel in an unprecedented tête-à-tête between these antithetical sets of experience and values. The result was Tom Sawyer and Huckleberry Finn, a duo more reminiscent of Don Quixote and Sancho Panza than any other ever produced by American literature.

Doubtless there is a similarity between the burlesque mood of Twain's oeuvre and that of Cervantes' *Don Quixote* (*A Connecticut Yankee in King Arthur's Court* is a prime example), but there is also a strong parallel between the literary imaginations of the two authors regarding the problem of personal identity. Identity was the rock upon which Don Quixote foundered, but it is also the greatness of Cervantes' character: "I know who I am," says Don Quixote in reply to the laborer and neighbor Pedro Lozano, when the latter tries to will him back to his real identity, "and I know, too, that I am capable of being not only the characters I have named, but all the Twelve Peers of France and all the Nine Worthies as well."[7] By having his lunatic old knight utter these words, Cervantes touches upon the problem of identity in an unprecedented way. He not only raises the conflict between what one is and what one wishes to be, but he also reflects such im-

6. Twain, *Life on the Mississippi*, 90.

7. Miguel de Cervantes Saavedra, *The Adventures of Don Quixote*, trans. J. M. Cohen (London: Penguin, 1950), 54. Further references to *Don Quixote* will be to this edition.

balance in the distorting mirror of his protagonist's imagination. In many of his novels Twain approaches the problem of identity in much the same way. He exposes with poignancy, with humor, and at times with discouragement both the wish to transcend actuality and the deluded perception that humans have of the world and of themselves. This concern with identity has its most light-hearted version in the character of Tom Sawyer, through whom Twain recreates the longings of his own childhood as a visionary young boy, obsessed with literary identities that exceeded his own. It reappears forcefully in *A Connecticut Yankee* with the blackest undertones, where the protagonist's visionary undertaking reflects Twain's own conflicting loyalties between democratic and aristocratic creeds and, ultimately, his yearning for older values that had become obsolete in entrepreneurial late-nineteenth-century America. It is also conspicuous in most of his southern aristocrats, who quixotically uphold their identities, unaware as they are of how obsolete their notions of honor and caste have become.

Twain's strivings to find a literary voice followed the intricate path of his personal conflicts. Henry Nash Smith detects at an early period of Twain's career, while the writer was working as a reporter for various newspapers, his uneasiness with high culture and his efforts to find a literary outlet for the tensions between the vernacular and the genteel that encompassed his life. "In an effort to solve this problem," Smith observes, "Mark Twain introduces into the dispatches to the Union a fictitious character called Mr. Brown, possibly suggested by Cervantes' Sancho Panza, as a mouthpiece for deflationary lowbrow remarks in the manner of Simon Suggs or Sut Lovingood." The attempt proves unsuccessful, however, because it lacks "Cervantes' integrated over-all conception (and his confidence in the reader's grasp of the difference in rank between Sancho and Don Quixote)"; as a result, "the humorous tradition offered no way of managing the Mr. Brown character through an extended narrative."[8] Twain later overcomes this shortcoming in his twin creations of Tom Sawyer and Huckleberry Finn. Nowhere else in his fiction is the conflict between culture and materiality, always latent in his work, so brilliantly addressed. By dramatizing the two opposed kinds of experience through the comradeship of two boys who strongly depend on each other, Twain emulates Cervantes' accomplishment. When he attempts to integrate the

---

8. Henry Nash Smith, "How True Are Dreams?: The Theme of Fantasy in Mark Twain's Later Work," *Quarry Farm Papers* 1 (1989), 9–10.

conflict in the struggle of a single character, as in *A Connecticut Yankee,* the result, on the whole, is not nearly as satisfactory.

The quest to integrate culture and sentiment can be seen as the driving force of Mark Twain's literary imagination, springing from the writer's own struggle to come to terms with his multifaceted self. Albert Bigelow Paine quotes the author's account of a recurring dream that suggests Twain's life-long battle with personal identity: "Sometimes in that dream I am dressed like a *tramp* instead of being with my night clothes. . . . I take hold of some man and whisper to him, 'I am Mark Twain;' but that does not improve it, for immediately I can hear him whispering to the others, 'he says he is Mark Twain' and they look at me a good deal more suspiciously than before, and I can see they don't believe it, and that it is a mistake to make that impression."[9] Samuel L. Clemens, Mark Twain, was a man inhabiting a personality he had never been totally sure was his own. He was by nature a humorist, a born deflator of the genteel tradition. Yet, much as he was intellectually in flight from it, he could never really break free from the tradition of respectability he so often rebuked. He cherished an egalitarian doctrine, but he felt a veiled admiration for aristocratic distinction. He was fond of the chivalric spirit while at the same time celebrating the new pragmatic order that was destined to put an end to it. He directed his implacable satire against the world of social rank and the absurd code of honor of his southern upbringing, but he retained from that same world a longing for personal definition and simplicity of life that he found lacking in the America of his mature years. He finally found a voice for these conflicting forces in his own life experience in the character of imaginative and scheming Tom Sawyer—the youth Twain really was—and that of uncomplicated and straightforward Huckleberry Finn, whom he admired but could never be. The balance between the romantic and the realistic side of human experience that Tom and Huck's comradeship symbolizes is never to be found again in his fiction. It was only through this charismatic companionship that Twain was able to find for his concern with identity a literary outlet that matched his talent.

Discussing the southernness of Mark Twain's experience during his Hannibal years, Louis D. Rubin has pointed out that while, geographically speak-

---

9. Albert B. Paine, *Mark Twain: A Biography: The Personal and Literary Life of Samuel Langhorne Clemens,* 3 vols. (New York: Harper & Brothers, 1912), 3:1368–69.

ing, Hannibal, Missouri, is not part of the South, it "was settled by southerners, it was linked economically to the river and was dependent upon the trade up and down the river, it was a slaveholding community, and when the war broke out it was largely secessionist in sentiment." The southern migrants to the border South brought with them a social and cultural array of attitudes and beliefs, particularly a marked obsession with social rank and the privileges it confers. The remnants of this "aristocratic taint" seem quaint in Twain's fiction when seen against the shifting ways of frontier life or the framework of the new bourgeois, democratic America. The aspiration to distinction of a once-privileged class, now in decline but still holding onto its former prerogatives, is often made to appear quixotically absurd. Dixon Wecter provides a real-life example of such an attitude in his portrait of John Marshall Clemens, when the family moved from Florida, Missouri, to their new destination of Hannibal: "The stiff-necked pride of Clemens the Virginian, no less than his invincible hope, impelled him to quit Florida in the same spirit as that in which he had left Fentress County—being as his son wrote, 'not a person likely to abide among the scenes of his vanished grandeur and be the target for public commiseration.' " John Marshall Clemens' pretension to a social rank that no longer matched his actual circumstances and his loyalty to the values of an already declining world are easily discernable in Twain's fictional aristocrats.[10]

Twain's southern aristocrats are obsessed with good name, high breeding, and a rigid code of honor, all of which are no longer consistent with the ways of the world around them, but to which they cling with quixotic obstinacy. Yet, however much they are portrayed as being absurd and anachronistic, impractical, grandiloquent, or self-deceiving, they are also noble-spirited, honorable, and uncompromising in their concern for their own reputations. The aristocracy of Dawson's Landing, in *Pudd'nhead Wilson*, and Colonel Grangerford, in *Adventures of Huckleberry Finn*, are good examples. The Howards and Driscolls of Dawson's Landing are First Family Virginians, for whom honor is first and foremost: "The F.F.V. was born a gentleman; his highest duty in life was to watch over that great inheritance and keep it unsmirched." To watch over his good name was one of his "unwritten laws," and "if he swerved from it by so much as half a point of the compass it meant shipwreck to his honour." Judge York Leicester Driscoll, Dawson's Landing's first citizen, is depicted as a man "just and generous . . . respected, esteemed, and beloved by all the community," but for whom "to be a gentleman—a gentleman without stain or blemish— was his only religion," so much so that he refuses to look beyond himself when matters related to his honor and good name are at stake. "You cur! You scum! You vermin! Do you mean to tell me that blood of my race has suffered a blow and crawled to a court of law about it?" he fumes to his nephew Tom Driscoll when he learns of Tom's intention to resort to the courts to redress one such offense. The scene in which Judge Driscoll takes his nephew's place in the duel against one of the twins is not unlike one of Don Quixote's battles. The bullets are more likely to hit the bystanders than the contenders. "We all got hit 'cep' de blon' twin en de doctor en de seconds," says Roxana, the slave woman who spies on the encounter. "De Jedge didn't git hurt, but I hear Pudd'nhead say de bullet snip some o' his ha'r off." The farcical tone of this passage provides a playfully ironic comment on the defense of honor with excessive zeal. Pembroke Howard, "another Old Virginia grandee," is mockingly described as "an authority on the 'code,' and a man always courteously ready to stand up before you in the field if any act or word of his had seemed doubtful or suspicious to you, and explain it with any weapon you might prefer, from brad-awls to artillery."[11]

Twain's portrayal of the Grangerfords in *Huckleberry Finn* provides a further example of how an exaggerated sense of honor is made to appear not only absurd and anachronistic but also painful and bloody, as the feud between this clan and the Shepherdsons attests. Yet the Grangerfords' world, passé and ossified as it may be, holds a strong attraction for Mark Twain. Although we may attach some irony to Huck Finn's assessment of Colonel Grangerford's aristocratic breed when he says that to be well born is "worth as much in a man as it is in a horse," the characteristic straightforwardness of the boy suggests the author's veiled admiration. He is "a gentleman all over," says Huck of the Colonel and illustrates his statement with these admiring words: "There warn't no frivolishness about him, not a bit, and he warn't ever loud. He was as kind as he could be—you could

---

11. Mark Twain, *Pudd'nhead Wilson: A Tale,* in *"Pudd'nhead Wilson" and "Those Extraordinary Twins,"* ed. Sidney E. Berger (New York: Norton, 1980), 58, 4, 60, 72, 4.

feel that, you know, and so you had confidence" (*HF* 142). As Robert Penn Warren has noted, through Huck's eyes the Grangerfords come across as frontier gentlemen, who "even with their blood-drenched honor, are kind, hospitable, dignified, totally courageous, and even chivalric in their admiration of the courage of the Shepherdsons."[12]

The longing for chivalric values, or yearning for a time of integrity, is evident in Colonel Sherburn's encounter with the angry mob that has come to lynch him. Through the bitter, raging Colonel Sherburn, Twain gives an indictment of the "average man":

> Do I know you? I know you clear through. I was born and raised in the South, and I've lived in the North; so I know the average all around. The average man's a coward. In the North he lets anybody walk over him that wants to, and goes home and prays for a humble spirit to bear it. In the South one man, all by himself, has stopped a stage full of men, in the day-time, and robbed the lot. Your newspapers call you a brave people so much that you think you *are* braver than any other people—whereas you're just *as* brave and no braver. Why don't your juries hang murderers? Because they're afraid the man's friends will shoot them in the back, in the dark—and it's just what they *would* do. . . . Now the thing for *you* to do, is to drop your tails and go home and crawl in a hole. (*HF* 190)

Through these acerbic words Colonel Sherburn vehemently claims the right to a higher class of being, at odds with the vulgar, unheroic age of his present. Sherburn's shooting of the pathetic Boggs is absurdly bloody, but his quixotic harangue to the mob appeals to our admiration for the daring, unyielding hero. The episode contains no irony whatsoever, only straightforward rage. Colonel Sherburn's rage is the author's rage, revealing his distrust of what the democratic culture has become. But Twain's admiration for these men's boldness and uncompromising self-assurance is ultimately undercut by the devastating consequences of their quixotic follies.

The visionary, irrationally optimistic Colonel Sellers, however, is Mark Twain's best portrayal of a quixotic soul. This is highly ironic, considering that Sellers, alone among Twain's aristocrats, tries hard to be in step with his time. As Wayne Mixon points out, Sellers has come to represent the southerner who embraces the promises of the New South; he embodies one

---

12. Robert Penn Warren, "Mark Twain," *Southern Review* 8 (1972): 475.

of those "flesh-and-blood New South promoters," who "perceives that economic regeneration depends upon sectional reconciliation." His approach to life is "to forget the past, conciliate the South, and proceed with the business of making money,"[13] but his inability to match his dreams of wealth to his real possibilities makes him a helpless idealist and an undisputed failure in practical matters. No undertaking looks too formidable to him, and his castles in the air invariably crumble to ruins.

Colonel Sellers' highly imaginative temperament and his deluded pretense to high breeding and social respectability, completely at odds with his real condition in life, combine to produce a perfect quixotic exemplar: the "legitimate Earl of Rossmore," who calls a cheap boardinghouse room his "premises" (*The Gilded Age*) and a rickety old frame house on his property the "Rossmore Towers" (*The American Claimant*). Lady Rossmore, as Twain ironically calls Colonel Sellers' resigned wife, pinpoints her husband's fantasies thus: "As for the suddenness and capacity in imagining things, his beat don't exist. . . . As like as not it wouldn't have occurred to anybody else to name this poor old rat-trap Rossmore Towers, but it just comes natural to him." But, again, we see Twain's respect for his quixotic hero, as Mrs. Sellers adds, "Well, no doubt it's a blessed thing to have an imagination that can always make you satisfied, no matter how you are fixed." In his autobiography Twain recounts how he found his inspiration in a real-life character, James Lampton, a cousin of Twain's mother, who "floated, all his days, in a tinted mist of magnificent dreams and died at last without seeing one of them realized." When Twain as a young man saw Lampton, he was offered and "ate a basin of raw turnips," which he "washed . . . down with a bucket of water." (This experience presaged the famous scene in *The Gilded Age*.) When Twain saw Lampton again twenty-six years later, he was "old and white-headed," but every bit the man he had always known: "[He] entertained me in the same old, breezy way of his earlier life and he was all there yet—not a detail wanting; the happy light in his eyes, the abounding hope in his heart, the persuasive tongue, the miracle-breeding imagination—they were all there; and before I could turn around he was polishing up his Aladdin's lamp and flashing the secret riches of the world before me. I said to myself: 'I did not overdraw him by a shade, I set him down as he was; and he is the same man to-day'."[14]

13. Wayne Mixon, *Southern Writers and the New South Movement, 1865–1913* (Chapel Hill: University of North Carolina Press, 1980), 91.

14. Mark Twain, *The American Claimant and Other Stories and Sketches* (New York: Harper & Brothers, 1917), 40; *Autobiography of Mark Twain*, 19–20, 22.

The Colonel's most salient feature is the ability of his raving imagination to turn squalor into glamour, a painstaking activity that Twain masterfully renders with a blend of pathos and tenderness. There are many engagingly humorous examples of this; for instance, we read that his clothing, "napless and shiny" with overuse, "had the air of being entirely satisfied with itself and blandly sorry for other people's clothes," and, in an episode fit to stand beside Don Quixote and Mambrino's helmet, the Colonel's prodigious imagination turns a basin of raw turnips into a refined dish. By the same token, when he invents "a stove with a candle in it and a transparent door," one of his contrivances to fight "rheumatism," as he euphemistically likes to call the freezing cold of his family household, he expects it to be his pot of gold at the end of the rainbow. Nevertheless, Twain's fondness for his character is unmistakable: "The real Colonel Sellers, as I knew him in James Lampton, was a pathetic and beautiful spirit, a manly man, a straight and honorable man, a man with a big, foolish, unselfish heart in his bosom, a man born to be loved; and he was loved by all his friends, and by his family worshiped."[15]

Squire Hawkins in *The Gilded Age* is yet another character who sees fortune materialize before his very eyes, in the same way that Don Quixote saw giants in broken-down windmills. The character, who is said to have been modeled after Twain's own father because of his reluctance to sell land in Tennessee, is just as absurd as his friend Beriah Sellers in his dreamy aspirations. The illusion that one day fortune will finally smile on him never deserts him and is his touching way of turning his back on a dismal life. His Tennessee land will, in time, reap all the wonders of America's ensuing prosperity. "Pine forests, wheat land, corn land, iron, copper, coal—wait till the railroads come, and the steamboats! We'll never see the day, Nancy—never in the world," he tells his wife, who exhibits a Sancho Panza attitude, half blind respect, half disbelief of her husband's reveries, "but they'll ride in coaches, Nancy!" he concludes, speaking of the wonders awaiting their children. Hawkins' fantasies are as grand as his conviction is firm. "I've been watching," he mutters to his wife. "I've been watching while some people slept, and I know what's coming." Betrayed by their

15. See two different editions of *The Gilded Age*: Mark Twain and Charles Dudley Warner, *The Gilded Age: A Tale of Today*, 2 vols. (New York: Harper 1901), 1: 86, 91; and *The Adventures of Colonel Sellers, Being Mark Twain's Share of "The Gilded Age,"* ed. Charles Neider (New York: Doubleday, 1965), 50, 54; *Autobiography of Mark Twain*, 19.

own natures, Twain's entrepreneurs are burlesquely yet tenderly depicted as parodies of aspirant tycoons, quixotic souls in constant flight from the drab reality of their lives.[16]

No American fictional hero has been more consistently associated with Don Quixote than Twain's preadolescent Tom Sawyer. Yet the relevance of quixotic Tom to Twain's imagination has been on the whole overlooked. Most studies center on Twain's use of the Quixote model as a consequence of the writer's admiration for Cervantes' novel. But in addition to the direct literary influence, Tom Sawyer reflects so many aspects of Twain's own personality that one can hardly fail to see in Tom's quixotic longings, fancies, and aspirations the creative energy that went on to shape the writer's literary imagination.

Tom is steeped in literature and romance. He reads books with an obsessive zeal, seeking to embellish his existence, clamoring for a life instilled with the substance, vigor, and heroic intensity of fiction, as did old Don Quixote. But how can an American lad be compared with an old, lunatic Spanish hidalgo who cannot tell a herd of sheep from an army and who makes a fool of himself by drifting off course so completely as Cervantes' knight does? Yet Tom Sawyer may well bear comparison with Don Quixote, in spite of the gap separating the characters. Books fill both their heads with desire for an adventurous life. Tom's romantic mind, his ceaseless scheming, his punctiliousness in subjugating actuality to the dictates of romance are in their own way as extraordinary and disproportionate as Don Quixote's.

Tom Sawyer and Don Quixote diverge only when faced with the dichotomy between literature and life. Don Quixote chooses the first, and by that choice, by excluding himself from the hazardous process of living, he is defeated from the very outset of his journey. He encounters defeat in every corner of his exuberant imagination. Tom Sawyer, on the other hand, avoids quixotic disillusionment because he has a firm grasp on reality. Tom

---

16. Twain and Warner, *Gilded Age,* 2: 22, 20, or Twain, *Adventures of Colonel Sellers,* 6, 5. John Clemens' grand expectations on the 100,000 acres of land he purchased in East Tennessee are recorded in his son's autobiography: "My father's dying charge was: 'Cling to the land and wait; let nothing beguile it away from you. . . . Whatever befalls me, my heirs are secure; I shall not live to see these acres turn to silver and gold but my children will' " (*Autobiography of Mark Twain,* 19–22).

does not renounce what gives him his greatest delight, namely, being the hero of his own story. At the close of *The Adventures of Tom Sawyer* he has fulfilled his dream manifold by finding a treasure, becoming a hero in his village, and rescuing a damsel in distress.

Tom Sawyer knows the importance of the audience, not only as a way of deriving pleasure when he is publicly revered but also as a means of escaping the ordinary and climbing the ladder of success and status in life. Don Quixote's career follows the ascetic pattern of medieval chivalry, while Tom seeks glamour through romance. In many respects Tom's stance is justified. The pathetic picture of old and impoverished Don Quixote, with his anachronistic chivalry, is as emblematic of the illusory dreams of glory of seventeenth-century Spain as Tom Sawyer's exuberant youth and dreams of success are emblematic of prosperous and all-promising nineteenth-century America. Don Quixote's fantasies are destined never to transcend the barren locale of his hometown. Tom's longing for romance and heroism provides a way out of Hannibal and into the world to realize the promise of America. Louis D. Rubin summarizes Tom's world of boundless possibilities by remarking that "for Tom Sawyer, life on the Mississippi has indeed been a place where all things are possible, where a man can change the world."[17] Tom's prospects are those dreamed of but forever denied to Alonso Quijano. Tom Sawyer and Don Quixote both seek adventure as a way of escaping their inauspicious lives, they both go in quest of glory and aspire to the heights of romance, and they both wish to alter their given realities, but only Tom succeeds in realizing his dreams, when in the course of his adventures, fiction actually overlaps with life.

"The sun rose upon a tranquil world, and beamed down upon the peaceful village like a benediction" (*TS* 57) we read at the opening of *The Adventures of Tom Sawyer* of the small Mississippi river town of St. Petersburg, but such peacefulness is precisely Tom's greatest source of restlessness. Tom is in constant flight from his milieu, from the never-ending, monotonous school day, from the tedious pace of the town. Daydreaming becomes imperative for him, the essence of his personality, his means of making his existence tolerable. Tom's most cherished dream, the substance of all his reveries, is to be the object of public worship. Underlying this

---

17. Louis D. Rubin, Jr., "Tom Sawyer and the Use of Novels," in *The Curious Death of the Novel: Essays in American Literature* (Baton Rouge: Louisiana State University Press, 1967), 96.

aspiration are a refusal to accept a mediocre fate and a revolt against the world that treats him unjustly and ignores his singularity.

Becky Thatcher figures prominently among Tom's offenders. It is because of his failed courtship with Becky that he climbs to the summit of Cardiff Hill in a melancholic fit and broods over his hapless fortune. Tom dramatizes his feelings with fantasies of revenge and gratifying prospects of glory. He determines to desert his friends and family and go away, "ever so far away, into unknown countries beyond the seas—and never [come] back any more!" Among his plans of flight he entertains thoughts of becoming a soldier and "return[ing] after long years, all war-worn and illustrious," or an Indian buffalo hunter, who would "come back a great chief . . . and sear the eyeballs of all his companions with unappeasable envy," or a pirate, who "at the zenith of his fame" with unaccountable delight "would suddenly appear at the old village and stalk into church all brown and weather-beaten . . . and hear with swelling ecstasy the whisperings: 'It's Tom Sawyer the Pirate! the Black Avenger of the Spanish Main!' " (*TS* 87–88).

There is little doubt that Tom Sawyer's fantasies reflect young Samuel Clemens' aspirations as a youth during his Hannibal years. The longing for celebrity and the wish to flee from a dull life, as he perceived his own in such a small community, were the two greatest incentives of his adolescent years. Mark Twain's autobiographical account of his wretched feelings at the sight of some fortunate boys who preceded him in his ambition of becoming a master pilot on a steam packet on the Mississippi leaves no doubt about Tom Sawyer's similarity to his creator: "By and by one of our boys went away. He was not heard of for a long time. At last he turned up as apprentice engineer or 'striker' on a steamboat. This thing shook the bottom out of all my Sunday-school teachings. That boy had been notoriously worldly, and I just the reverse; yet he was exalted to this eminence, and I left in obscurity and misery."[18]

In *Life on the Mississippi* Mark Twain relates how he decided that one day he would leave Hannibal and never return unless it be as a hero. Later he would become an apprentice on a steam packet and tour the Mississippi, where he encountered real-life adventures. Yet, ironically, and in consonance with his true talent, he found his glory not in the toils of life but in the travails of fiction by becoming a successful professional fantasist.

---

18. Twain, *Life on the Mississippi*, 31.

Before life took its toll of lost faith and vigor on the funniest man in America, he turned his eyes to his childhood for inspiration, only to find his old longings and dreams intact. He turned full circle to where his imagination had first taken flight, and he conceived Tom Sawyer, a youngster with a prodigal imagination who turns Cardiff Hill into Sherwood Forest, Jackson's Island into a pirate shelter, McDougal's Cave into bandit headquarters, and blue-eyed Becky Thatcher into his lady in domnei. Next to him he places his squire and companion, Huckleberry Finn, an artless boy with a great heart who approaches life in the same uncomplicated way as Sancho Panza. Huck Finn's dealings with actuality leave him little room for reveries since his life is a permanent adventure of survival.

The dialogue between Tom and Huck is a constant re-creation of the exchanges between Don Quixote and Sancho Panza, and it dramatizes the relation of the ideal and the real in the same way. The two dispute each other's authority, but they travel in good comradeship. Tom always tries to force his arguments upon Huck, who invariably acknowledges the bookish authority of his friend, patiently tolerates his extravagances, and little by little sees his fascination for his friend grow. Critics of *Don Quixote* have referred to the progressive impact of the ingenious Don Quixote upon the prosaic Sancho as *quixotization*. Huck's fascination for his extremely imaginative companion takes on the same quality. Tom's fantasies gradually impinge on Huck to the point that he incorporates features of Tom's personality, particularly when he is not the object of Tom's dominating character and leadership. In *The Hero's Task*, Fernando Savater describes the hero's friend as someone "who is fascinated not so much by the hero's ideals but by the hero himself, even when they seem to embody opposed options in life." Savater argues that Quixote's attraction for Sancho is splendidly unfolded at the end of the novel when the hidalgo "recovers" his right mind and abjures his previous undertakings. His squire practically reprimands him and reminds him that "the maddest thing a man can do in this life is to let himself die just like that, without anybody killing him." In the same passage Sancho tries to cheer his master by suggesting that promising new adventures await him if he can only gather enough strength to be the valiant knight he has always been.[19] Like Sancho's fondness for Don Quixote, Huck's fondness is for Tom Sawyer himself, not for the con-

---

19. Fernando Savater, *La tarea del héroe* (The hero's task) (Madrid: Taurus, 1983), 119, my translation; Cervantes, *Don Quixote*, 937.

tent of Tom's imaginings, which do not speak to Huck at all. We learn from the narrator of *The Adventures of Tom Sawyer* that "Huckleberry was filled with admiration of Tom's facility in writing and the sublimity of his language" (*TS* 100). It is an admiration no less heartfelt than that of Sancho toward his master.

We also see Huck's devotion when we find him imitating Tom several times throughout *Adventures of Huckleberry Finn*. For example, he harangues Jim ("I read considerable to Jim about kings, and dukes, and earls, and such" [*HF* 93], he says, proudly borrowing from Tom Sawyer's unmistakable style) and is every bit as unsuccessful in getting Jim to grasp his arguments as Tom normally is with him. We see Huck also imbued with Tom's frame of mind when he hatches a plan to simulate his own drowning in the river as a way of escaping from his miserable life under Pap's wild rages and beatings. The plan seems so crafty to him that he feels it could have been devised by Tom himself. "I did wish Tom Sawyer was there," he says, greatly satisfied with his own skill, yet acknowledging his friend's greater talent in these matters: "I knowed he would take an interest in this kind of business, and throw in the fancy touches. Nobody could spread himself like Tom Sawyer in such a thing as that" (*HF* 41). Huck's metamorphosis into an apprentice of Tom Sawyer is also evident in his growing taste for adventure. In the shipwreck episode, he tries to persuade Jim to board the shipwreck and experience an adventure, thus turning his back on common sense. At Jim's reluctance to acquiesce to his plan, he readily evokes Tom Sawyer's spunk as a model to follow: "Do you reckon Tom Sawyer would ever go by this thing? Not for pie, he wouldn't. He'd call it an adventure—that's what he'd call it; and he'd land on that wreck if it was his last act. And wouldn't he throw style into it?—wouldn't he spread himself, nor nothing? Why, you'd think it was Christopher C'lumbus discovering Kingdom-Come. I wish Tom Sawyer *was* here!" (*HF* 81). In fact, taken as a whole, Huck and Jim's adventures and misadventures along the Mississippi are carried out very much in the manner of Don Quixote and Sancho Panza's, with Huck playing Tom's usual role (Don Quixote) and Jim playing Huck's (Sancho). The absurdity of Jim's flight from slavery with only the helping hand of a poor white boy, their dismal encounters with civilization on shore, and the hazardous drifting itself toward an uncertain destination are all permeated with the quixotic spirit.

Yet Huck's quixoticism lies elsewhere, at the core of his moral stance. When he refuses to hand Jim over to his persecutors, when he turns a deaf ear, not only to the heavily prejudiced society he lives in, but also to his own biased conscience, he performs a most genuine quixotic act. Roger B. Salomon has referred to Huck's resolve as a "quixotic absurdity" because, he says, "in the light of our more sophisticated *adult* knowledge, he is jousting with windmills, though they are for him very real, his courage very touching and his moral instincts sound." Furthermore, if we agree with Mario Vargas Llosa that "Don Quixote personifies the liberality of the mind against the sordidness of the real world, against the meanness of common sense, incarnate in pitiful Sancho Panza, who, conversely, due to his unfailing pragmatism, has become the symbol for spiritual vulgarity, conformity, and cowardice," we must conclude that Huck's stance in helping a runaway slave in his flight to liberty is more akin to Don Quixote's than to Sancho's. Finally, his decision "to light out for the Territories"— his idealistic flight to the West to escape Aunt Sally's "sivilizing" hand—is also absurdly romantic. "Twain knew that there is no escaping the real world," as Robert Penn Warren puts it; unavoidably, Huck will run into "buffalo-skinners, railroad builders, blue-coated cavalry, Robber Barons," and so forth. And because Twain knows all that, Warren remarks, "we might take Huck as the embodiment of the incorrigible idealism of man's nature, pathetic in its hopeful self-deception and admirable in its eternal gallantry, forever young, a kind of Peter Pan in patched britches with a corncob pipe stuck in the side of his mouth, with a penchant for philosophical speculation, a streak of poetry in his nature, and with no capacity for growing up." In Warren's portrayal of Huck Finn, Tom Sawyer's valet comes across as an attractive knightly hero, quixotically challenging maturity, or civilization. Twain once more vindicates romance against the claims of the real world, this time through his most genuinely unconventional hero.[20]

The question remains whether Tom Sawyer's manipulative tendencies could, in principle, run counter to quixotic characterization. According to Edward L. Galligan, Tom Sawyer is a false comedian, a jester, who knows that his comedy is a joke, and is only pretending that it is not. Tom never jousts with windmills, Galligan contends; on the contrary, Tom, "like the

20. Roger B. Salomon, "Mark Twain and Victorian Nostalgia," in *Patterns of Commitment in American Literature*, ed. Marston La France (Toronto: University of Toronto Press, 1967), 89; Mario Vargas Llosa, "El último de los caballeros" (The last gentleman) *Quimera* 56 (1986): 15 (my translation); Warren, "Mark Twain," 482–83.

duke and the duchess [in *Don Quixote*], is only pretending to a Quixotic belief in enchanters"; therefore "he is just playing a game, a nice safe game."[21] Galligan correctly says that Tom's imaginings are not self-deceptive. Tom makes up the caravan of Spaniards and "A-rabs" and performs the theatrics of Jim's escape from the Phelps farm fully aware of their fictional nature. In the grip of his own unrestrained devices, Tom turns histrionic, and his punctilious imaginings become comical. Nonetheless, and for the same reason—the very punctiliousness with which he performs his theatrics—Tom is Don Quixote's peer. When Huck says that Tom "[is] always just that particular. Full of principle," (*HF* 307), he is referring precisely to Tom's obsession with doing things by the book. Tom may come across as a maneuvering, self-centered, and conceited boy, but he is as demanding and as headstrong in his artistic machinations as the raving Don Quixote. Tom wants to see the extraordinary impinge on the everyday, and he resorts to his powerful imagination to make up for what he finds lacking around him: romance, adventure, glamour, and a broader horizon wherein to realize his dreams of glory and renown.

Success is precisely what sets Tom Sawyer most significantly apart from Cervantes' hero. Tom succeeds where Don Quixote fails utterly, namely, in the attempt to match fantasy and life. Tom's romantic illusion of becoming a hero in his own community is wholly realized in *The Adventures of Tom Sawyer*. He becomes the village hero in the small community of St. Petersburg; he marches triumphantly into the church where his funeral is taking place; he receives public recognition for his courage in the cave (thanks to which he and Becky Thatcher come out of the cave alive); and he does find a treasure. Through all these exploits he emulates the deeds of his "authorities," and he is finally allowed a taste of glory. He moves about the town "with a dignified swagger, as became a pirate who felt that the public eye was on him. . . . He tried not to seem to see the looks or to hear the remarks as he passed along, but they were food and drink to him" (*TS* 145). In the end not only have Tom's dreams come true but his imagination has transformed the life of the town, turning the small village into a place of romance and the realistic concerns of its inhabitants into romantic undertakings:

21. Edward L. Galligan, *The Comic Vision in Literature* (Athens: University of Georgia Press, 1984), 57, 62–63.

Every "haunted" house in St. Petersburg and the neighbouring villages was dissected, plank by plank, and its foundations dug up and ransacked for hidden treasure—and not by boys, but men—pretty grave, unromantic men, too, some of them. Wherever Tom and Huck appeared they were courted, admired, stared at. The boys were not able to remember that their remarks had possessed weight before; but now their sayings were treasured and repeated; everything they did seemed somehow to be regarded as remarkable; they had evidently lost the power of doing and saying commonplace things; moreover, their past history was raked up and discovered to bear marks of conspicuous originality. (*TS* 232)

Louis D. Rubin concurs in his interpretation of this passage when he says that "in effect, [Tom Sawyer] has *changed his world*. He has made reality conform to his conception of what it should be. . . . Reality for Tom Sawyer has come to mean pirates, treasure, heroism and glory."[22] Tom's life, up to then anonymous and anodyne, mutates into a notorious and attractive one. He eventually achieves Don Quixote's dream of bringing the realms of reality and fiction together.

Although Tom Sawyer was soon labeled the Don Quixote of American literature, of all of Twain's novels only *A Connecticut Yankee* immediately drew comparisons with Cervantes' *Don Quixote*, because of its burlesque treatment of the world of chivalry. A prospectus for the book issued by Charles L. Webster in 1889 reads: "A keen and powerful satire on English Nobility and Royalty. A book that appeals to all true Americans. It will be to English Nobility and Royalty what Don Quixote was to Ancient Chivalry." William Dean Howells writes of "the delicious satire, the marvellous wit, the wild, free, fantastic humor" of *A Connecticut Yankee* and finds that "at every moment the scene amuses, but it is all the time an object-lesson in democracy." Howells points out the affinity between Twain's and Cervantes' humor, even though, he hastens to say, Twain's is more in accordance with contemporary sensitivity in that it is not "at the cost of the weak, the unfriended, the helpless."[23]

22. Rubin, "The Use of Novels," 90.

23. Charles L. Webster, Prospectus for *A Connecticut Yankee in King Arthur's Court*, by Mark Twain (New York: Charles L. Webster and Company, 1889), reproduced in *A Connecticut Yankee in King Arthur's Court*, vol. 9 of *The Works of Mark Twain*, Appendix E, 541; William D. Howells, review of *A Connecticut Yankee* by Mark Twain, *Harper's* 80 (January 1880): 319, quoted in Henry N. Smith and William M. Gibson, eds., *Mark Twain–Howells Letters: The Correspondence of Samuel Clemens and William D. Howells, 1879–1910* (Cambridge, Mass.: Belknap Press of Harvard University Press, 1960), 626.

In 1884, two years before he actually set to work on the novel, Twain drew the following sketch in his notebook: "Dream of being a knight errant in armor in the Middle Ages. Have the notions and habits of thought of the present day mixed with the necessities of that. No pockets in the armor. Can't scratch. Cold in the head—can't blow—can't get a handkerchief, can't use iron sleeve. Iron gets red hot in the sun—leaks in the rain, gets white with frost and freezes me solid in winter. Makes disagreeable clatter when I enter church. Can't dress or undress myself. Always getting struck by lightning. Fall down, can't get up." This preliminary sketch shows Twain's satirical and burlesque intention in *A Connecticut Yankee*. According to Walter L. Reed, "Twain recreates the older eighteenth-century reading of *Don Quixote* as a satire, the reading made proverbial by Byron in *Don Juan* that 'Cervantes smiled Spain's chivalry away.' Yet, like Byron, Twain sees the melancholy side of this victory of the imagination and records it elegiacally. In *A Connecticut Yankee in King Arthur's Court* he recreates this version of the Quixotic project all over again."[24] The book scorns the world of chivalry by exposing its sham to a modern mind: Arthurianism is a myth, and the world view that nurtured it cannot withstand a critical examination from the point of view of a modern sensitivity. Twain's burlesque aim is directed against the foundations of that myth because it contains the essence of all the offenses perpetrated against the common man in the Middle Ages.

In spite of the satirical component, *A Connecticut Yankee*'s greatest affinity with *Don Quixote* is found in the conflict played out between the ideal and the real. Doubtless, *Don Quixote* is a satire on the romances of chivalry, but, as Edwin Williamson has perceptively observed, "as Cervantes extends and deepens his satire, he makes contact with this core of serious ideals and values that is embodied in Arthurian romance and which forms part of the legacy of medieval Europe."[25] *A Connecticut Yankee* evinces the same paradoxical satire of and respect for medieval ideals.

24. *Mark Twain's Notebook,* ed. Albert B. Paine (New York: Harper & Brothers 1935; reprint, St. Clair Shores, Mich.; Scholarly Press, 1971), 171; Walter L. Reed, *An Exemplary History of the Novel: Don Quixote Versus the Picaresque* (Chicago: University of Chicago Press, 1981), 220, quoting Byron's *Don Juan,* Variorum Edition, ed. Truman Gay Steffan and Willis W. Pratt (Austin: University of Texas Press, 1958), 3:363–64.

25. Edwin Williamson, *The Half-Way House of Fiction: "Don Quixote" and the Arthurian Romance* (Oxford: Clarendon Press, 1984), 207.

Twain set out to scorn Arthurianism, its tenets, and its degrading conditions. The novel is a bleak exposure of ignorance, superstition, and brutality in humankind, attacking not only the evils of the Middle Ages but also those still enmeshed in western civilization. (Scholars have pointed out that Twain's Arthurian England in *A Connecticut Yankee* contains more or less deliberate echoes of the slaveholding antebellum South.) In sum, Twain's violent satire strikes at the pillars of medieval society: Church, nobility, and monarchy are the target of his most devastating barbs. But the same cannot be said of the Arthurian legend, for if at first it is the target of his buffoonery, it soon reemerges as the embodiment of a set of fine values. This ambivalence is conspicuous throughout the novel. For instance, the narrator (Hank Morgan) may mockingly refer to King Arthur's court as a court of "Comanches" or turn knights errant into living bulletin boards and send them about the country to spread civilization, but he also admires the king's knightly nobility, his manliness, and his generosity. In another instance, he sees the king hold the young daughter of a poor peasant woman who is dying of smallpox and then hand the child into her mother's arms, indifferent to the risk he is running, and Morgan deems this an act of "heroism at its last and loftiest possibility" (*CY* 331). Though Morgan refers to the knights of the Round Table as "big boobies" and reports that the whole Round Table seems a little less than a children's "nursery," he perceives "a fine manliness observable in almost every face; and in some a certain loftiness and sweetness that rebuke[s] . . . belittling criticisms." He finds "noble benignity" and "purity of countenance" in Sir Galahad and even "majesty and greatness in the giant frame and high bearing of Sir Launcelot of the Lake" (*CY* 69). Morgan lavishly mocks the puerile, romance-ridden minds of these people, but he feels a strong attraction for the courtesy, loyalty, trustworthiness, and galantry that these same minds exhibit, all of which are qualities we owe to the world of romance.

Like *Don Quixote*, Twain's *Connecticut Yankee* is woven around the conflict between the ideal and the real, but Cervantes' pattern is reversed. If the real, as represented by Sancho, is plain and homespun in Cervantes' book, and the ideal, as personified by Don Quixote, conceited and highly articulate, Twain places the "ideal" on the side of superstition and ignorance, against reason and discernment. In other words, Twain's protagonist preaches civilization against spurious chivalry, whereas Don Quixote seeks to restore chivalry among modern men. The dialogue between the two conflicting sides—previously dramatized through Tom Sawyer and Huckleberry Finn—is now carried on between Hank Morgan and Demoiselle Alisande la Carteloise, whom Morgan nicknames Sandy. Morgan is a Yankee from Hartford, Connecticut, who finds himself marooned, a Robinson Crusoe in Arthurian England. In spite of his dislike for the ignorance, superstition, and heedlessness of its people, he deems the land full of opportunity for someone who, like him, is "a man of knowledge, brains, pluck, and enterprise" (*CY* 109). Alisande is the hopelessly deluded woman he escorts in her foolish quest to release her captive mistress from an ogre's castle, and he learns a few things from her about the follies of knight errantry. The burlesque tone of the book reaches its height when the visions of the two clash violently and are played out against each other. The Yankee's nineteenth-century rationale scornfully undercuts Alisande's fantasies, which reflect the absurd convictions and simple-mindedness of the leading figures of Camelot, such as King Arthur, Merlin, and the entire Round Table.

Alisande and the Yankee set off on a journey that closely mimics that of Don Quixote and Sancho Panza, but the roles are somewhat mixed or reversed. Alisande, the Yankee's squire, shares Sancho's ignorance and shrewdness, yet she is romance-ridden and speaks in rambling prose that parodies the bombastic style of medieval romances. Hank Morgan has Sancho's common sense, but he also shows Don Quixote's wisdom and nobility of purpose. He is out to right the wrongs of humanity's Iron Age, and he is determined to accomplish his objective. His quest may be business-oriented, but his aim is well meaning insofar as it will better the lot of the inhabitants of this gloomy land. The exchanges between the two follow Cervantes' pattern in Don Quixote and Sancho Panza, with Alisande's delusions sharply contrasted to Hank Morgan's accurate perception of reality. Through Alisande's eyes we see a pigsty transformed into a castle and princesses turned into hogs. Through the Yankee's ironic perception we see knights going "holy grailing" or moving about in ridiculous outfits that would befit Don Quixote himself. The ideal is pitilessly mocked, and through his protagonist's efforts, Twain succeeds in devising "surreptitious schemes for extinguishing knighthood by making it grotesque and absurd" (*CY* 247).

As the novel unfolds, it soon reveals its hidden paradox: Twain scorns the illusion-ridden mind of medieval chivalry through a protagonist who is an idealist, a harbinger of a utopian dream. This contradiction comes to the surface in the absurdity of the Yankee's crusade. Twain's Yankee is a

Sancho Panza by experience, but he is Don Quixote at heart. He is a true visionary who blindly believes in the enormous possibilities available to humankind through the advances of civilization and the egalitarian creed. Twain's Yankee entrepreneur is in reality a romantic who, as Walter L. Reed puts it, "exchanges his historical existence for a historical dream." Although he may at first seem antithetical to the high-minded Don Quixote, the Yankee entertains an identical unrealistic aim: to change the world by sheer will. (Don Quixote wants to reinstate chivalry back in his own historical time; Hank Morgan strives to transform Arthurian England into nineteenth-century America.) Also, Twain's Yankee shares the self-deception and obstinacy common to all true dreamers. As Reed observes, "Morgan's historical knowledge, obviously derived from books as well as from his own experience, becomes equivalent to Quixote's chivalric romances. It is a world encoded in Morgan's mind, resisted by other characters and even perceived by the reader as belonging to another order of existence."[26]

Furthermore, in his missionary zeal to put an end to the miseries of the world he has set out to reform, Hank Morgan never feels dismal or disheartened. "Did you think you had educated the superstition out of those people?" Clarence asks on seeing the Yankee's perplexity when he learns that England is at war and his crusade of reform has gone down the drain. "I certainly did think it," Hank answers unhesitatingly. Clarence's reply carries an eloquent authorial comment: "Well, then, you may unthink it" (*CY* 464). In an ironic turn of mind, Twain takes his protagonist's faith in the power of reason to quixotic lengths as a means of conveying his own distrust in it. The events leading to an all-out war in the country are conspicuous examples of just how unreason rules over common sense. The knights reveal Sir Launcelot's love for Guenever to the king out of sheer envy. The king causes havoc in the whole country out of sheer jealousy. The Church takes advantage of the upheaval out of sheer greed. The battle of the Sand Belt, which culminates in the destruction of both Arthurian England and Hank Morgan's American plan, is but a result of men's frail comprehension of their own destinies, which in the final analysis are governed by irrationality, viciousness, and infirmity. But however much Twain views his protagonist's naïveté with irony, he also thinks highly of the moral stance that informs his quest. In a letter to his daughter Clara he shows annoyance at Howard Taylor for failing to grasp the depths of his

26. Reed, *Exemplary History*, 220–21.

protagonist's soul: "He has captured but one side of the Yankee's character—his animal side, his circus side; the good heart and the high intent are left out of him. . . . I told Taylor he had degraded a natural gentleman to a low-down blackguard."[27]

At the heart of the Yankee's paradox lies a deeper conflict, one that engages the writer's imagination fully and creates the quixotic tension in the book. Although he does not suspect it himself at the outset of his journey, Twain's protagonist in fact sets off on another adventure, a more engaging and personal one, that will reverse his loyalties, cause a shift in the tone of the narrative, and introduce a further ambiguity into the novel's plot. The first half of the novel establishes a dichotomy between two opposite kinds of experiences and values. On one hand there is simple-minded medieval chivalry, which the Yankee defines so well when he says that "brains were not needed in a society like that, and, indeed, would have marred it, hindered it, spoiled its symmetry—perhaps rendered its existence impossible" (*CY* 69). On the other, there are knowledge and reason, ushered in by modern civilization. This dichotomy allows a variety of readings. It sets Yankee ingenuity and its gospel, the work ethic, against impractical southern chivalry, the despotism of custom against the emancipating power of reason, and the realm of romance against the irrefutable laws of reality. At first, the former element of each of these polarities undermines the latter by making it look inferior or ridiculous; hence, the satire is firmly secured. But when Hank Morgan allows sentiment to penetrate his life, the boundaries progressively begin to blur, giving rise to the novel's central paradox: What are we to make of the Yankee's missionary quest when he grows increasingly affectionate toward the world he wishes to reform? In other words, how does *A Connecticut Yankee* turn its back on the satirical genre?

Marthe Robert provides a fitting explanation when she argues that "satire assumes a way of seeing and thinking that, for all its caustic bitterness remains essentially optimistic, confident of the final triumph of some kind of order (reason, nature, health, or simple good sense), and it remains, above all, convinced of the authority of its own message." From this it follows that satire works with a "categorical *either/or*"; that is, it rebukes one option in order to offer an alternative. Quixoticism, on the contrary, by remaining ultimately suspicious of its own ideal, assumes "a distressing *and* carried to the limits of the absurd" and maintains that "piety and

---

27. *The Love Letters of Mark Twain*, ed. Dixon Wecter (New York: Harper, 1949), 275.

irony, respect and humor, admiration and criticism, compassion and rigor," are not mutually exclusive pairs. "By its refusal to pose mutually exclusive alternatives," Robert concludes, "quixoticism resolutely turns its back on the satiric method."[28]

In *A Connecticut Yankee* these "disturbing opposites" work their way through the novel, revealing no alternative. Hank Morgan, introduced as the quintessential Yankee, a "practical" fellow, "nearly barren of sentiment" and "poetry" (*CY* 50), becomes more and more sentimentally attached to a land of simple-minded folk who have little to do with his experience. King Arthur's world, in spite of its bleakness and the injustice endured by the majority of its people, is also a place for joy, true feelings, and noble actions. The Yankee marries Alisande, who proves a devoted wife and bears him a loving daughter. He becomes good friends with Sir Launcelot, who proves his devotion with caring and loving attention to Hank's daughter, Hello Central, when she is stricken with a severe illness. There is Clarence, too, his valuable and loyal squire, and King Arthur, whom he comes to admire. When appreciated for their humanity, all these characters seem to shake off their former defects. In Hank's eyes they are now emotionally sound human beings, healthy individuals, and behave accordingly. Hank Morgan persists in his quest to transform their world and continues to make fun of their nonsensical practices, but he feels less hostile and grows more concerned and sympathetic toward those he now perceives very much as his equals.

The novel's shift in tone has been the subject of much speculation in literary scholarship. Daniel Aaron contends that "the transformation of Hank Morgan, liberator, into Morgan, the vengeful 'abolitionist,' midway through the book reflects the author's changing point of view" and that as a result of this shift, "what began as good-humored burlesque of chivalry ended in a ferocious assault against the agencies of industrialism from which he had once hoped so much." The death of two of Twain's daughters, bankruptcy, and increasing emotional distress have been cited as causes of his progressive disillusionment. Henry Nash Smith believes that the inconsistencies in Hank Morgan's characterization have a lot to do with Twain's vivid imagination, which "proves superior to his conscious

28. Marthe Robert, *The Old and the New: From Don Quixote to Kafka*, trans. Carol Cosman (Berkeley: University of California Press, 1977), 25–27; originally published as *L'Ancient et le nouveau: de Don Quichotte à Franz Kafka* (Paris: Grasset, 1963).

contrivance," and therefore, "powerful ironies begin to appear in the narrative."[29] (Smith's view echoes Flaubert's insight on the creative process: "On n'écri pas toujours ce qu'on veut," the French writer once acknowledged, hinting at the power of the imagination over our intellectual reasoning.)

Of all the conjectures about Twain's contradictory turn of mind in *A Connecticut Yankee*, one thing seems clear: in no other novel did Twain weave his own thoughts and contradictions so tightly with the adventures and misadventures of his hero. Because Twain dramatized his own contradictions so well, and because he brought the power of his ironic imagination to bear upon them so forthrightly, we may allow him to depict an unromantic Sancho Panza as the vindicator of a romantic dream and to portray a man who wishes passionately to see romance go up in smoke get caught up in its web. "If man is so limited and so unworthy," Charles S. Holmes aptly asks, "why bother with Utopian social reorganizations?"[30] It is more likely that Twain cast his character as a modern Robinson, but perceived him as a New World Don Quixote, a contumacious idealist unable to find a middle ground between his hopes for human betterment and the reality of human shortcomings. This seems to be the only plausible explanation for the Yankee's relentless pursuit of his dream despite mounting evidence of the chasm separating his world and the Arthurian world. He should have anticipated that his trust in the power and legitimacy of his cause was not enough to make the people of this dark land give up their follies. He had seen too much of their nonsense to put his trust in a fairy-tale ending. But he never considers giving in. Oblivious to harsh reality and rejoicing in how "things were working steadily toward a secretly longed-for point" (*CY* 444) only three years after his arrival, Morgan sees irrationality hardening into a conspiracy against his projected land of dreams. All of England begins preparing for a final assault once the king discovers Guenever's love for Launcelot and is ready to risk all in defense of honor. One has to be a Quixote, Twain seems to imply, to pretend that such atavism of the mind does not exist. Hence, the Yankee's futile endeavors are best explained as an attempt to force sentiment to submit to the laws of reason rather than an effort to enlighten the Dark Ages. The problem is

29. Aaron, *The Unwritten War*, 144–45; Smith, "How True Are Dreams?" 13.

30. Charles S. Holmes, "*A Connecticut Yankee in King's Arthur Court*: Mark Twain's Fable of Uncertainty," *South Atlantic Quarterly* 61 (1962): 469.

that to Hank Morgan's mind romance and reason seem incompatible, as the following words attest: "I was a champion, it was true, but not the champion of the frivolous black arts, I was the champion of hard unsentimental common sense and reason. I was entering the lists to either destroy knight errantry or be its victim" (*CY* 430). Right after his victory over Sir Sagramour, Hank understands that he has not won, and that he will never win his personal battle.

Mark Twain's world, at a crossroads between the two antagonistic experiences described earlier in this chapter, is the foundation of Hank Morgan's radical view. For Henry Nash Smith, "Like most of his countrymen, Mark Twain oscillated between enthusiasm for the brave new world of science and technology, and nostalgia for the simple agrarian world that the industrial revolution was destroying before his eyes." John Fraser—who calls Mark Twain "America's own Cervantes"—provides a key to Twain's idiosyncrasy when he observes that "if Twain attacked historical chivalry as strongly as he did, it was partly because he himself was incurably fascinated by the chivalric spirit. And despite his voiced esteem for 'the wholesome and practical nineteenth-century smell of cotton factories and locomotives' his writings are those of someone who adored romance."[31]

Twain's love-hate relationship with the values of chivalry and those of modern capitalism moves toward an impasse in *A Connecticut Yankee*. Hank Morgan's nineteenth-century advances signal the end of irrationality, but at the expense of an entire way of life. Ironically, the very same advances hinder the progress of the Yankee's newly discovered emotional life. Back in his own historical time he becomes a ghostly creature, distressed and melancholy, longing for the simplest emotions. He cries out in anguish for Sandy and his daughter, Hello-Central, and yearns for the world he once despised. The Yankee's quixotic journey verifies Marthe Robert's view that "the idea that a declaration suffices to extinguish the influence of the past is precisely one of the serious delusions that quixoticism attempts to destroy."[32] Hank Morgan does away with the past, but at the price of his soul.

31. Henry N. Smith, "An Object Lesson in Democracy," in *Mark Twain: The Development of a Writer* (Cambridge, Mass.: Harvard University Press, 1962), 157; Fraser, *Patterns of Chivalry*, 46, quoting *Life on the Mississippi*, Stormfield Edition of *Writings of Mark Twain* (New York: Harper, 1929), 333.

32. Robert, *The Old and the New*, 27.

The human cost of quixotic illusion is much greater in Twain's *A Connecticut Yankee* than in Cervantes' *Don Quixote*. Through his mad knight, Cervantes makes a commentary on the harmful effects caused of an illusion-ridden mind, and so it befalls his knight to lose his wits and waste his life. By having him acknowledge his folly, however, Cervantes allows his knight the prospect of a serene death. "There is nothing in the book that suggests premeditated satire upon faith and enthusiasm in general," observes George Santayana on Cervantes' standpoint in *Don Quixote*. "There is no bitterness in his pathos or despair in his disenchantment; partly because he retains a healthy fondness for this naughty world, and partly because his heart is profoundly and entirely Christian." At the end of his days Don Quixote deplores the fact that he has discovered too late the absurdities and deceits of "those detestable books of chivalry," but his Christian faith makes him give praise to God for having recovered his judgment and for finally freeing him "from the misty shadows of ignorance." Hank Morgan is also made to witness his own delusion, but his end *does* suggest the "premeditated satire upon faith and enthusiasm" that Santayana finds not present in *Don Quixote*.[33] Morgan fails to find a compromise between the two disparate sides of his existence. He dies a stranger to himself, as his final words attest. In an effort to reach out to Sandy and retrieve her from the vanishing vapors of the dream, he fancies his present to be in the distant Middle Ages and his past in the "remote unborn age" of his real historical time:

> I seemed to be a creature out of a remote unborn age, centuries hence, and even *that* was as real as the rest! Yes, I seemed to have flown back out of that age into this of ours, and then forward to it again, and was set down, a stranger and forlorn, in that strange England, with an abyss of thirteen centuries yawning between me and you! between me and my home and my friends! between me and all that is dear to me, all that could make life worth the living! It was awful—awfuller than you can ever imagine, Sandy. (*CY* 492–93)

The book's ending reflects Twain's disillusionment and profound distrust in progress as the panacea for human freedom. Mark Twain's Yankee thinks he can defeat atavism single-handedly, only to find himself knocked

---

33. George Santayana, "Cervantes," in *Essays in Literary Criticism of George Santayana*, ed. Irving Singer (New York: Charles Scribner's, 1956), 118; Cervantes, *Don Quixote*, 935.

sprawling for his pains. He struggles to impose reason upon sentiment only to find himself the victim of both. In the final event, he loses two battles. He fights against the incorrigible irrationality of history and is defeated. He challenges sentiment, which he rejects as a puerile pastime, a nuisance, and loses that battle too when sentiment creeps into his life. His doom is commensurate with the absurdity of his quest. The novel ends with his mind irreparably split between who he is and who he wishes to be. Twain's distrust in the possibilities of improvement for humankind grew ever greater in the latter stages of his literary career. After *A Connecticut Yankee* his voice turned bitter, the humor of his earlier work increasingly absent from the books that followed, until "the gap between the real and the ideal, at first merely humorous, grew into a chasm that laughter could no longer bridge."[34] Virtually at one with the protagonist in his most quixotic novel, Twain never reconciled himself to the two worlds that encompassed his experience.

34. Rubin, "Post-War Scene," 63.

2

JAMES BRANCH CABELL
Quixotic Love—The Exercise of Self-Deception

Then Rudolph Musgrave noted, with a delicious tingling somewhere about his heart, that her hair was like the reflection of a sunset in rippling waters,— only many times more beautiful, of course,—and that her mouth was an inconsiderable trifle, a scrap of sanguine curves, and that her eyes were purple glimpses of infinity.

—James Branch Cabell, *The Rivet in Grandfather's Neck*

Her name is Dulcinea; her country el Toboso; a village in La Mancha; her degree at least that of Princess, for she is my Queen and mistress; her beauty superhuman, for in her are realized all the impossible and chimerical attributes of beauty which poets give to their ladies; that her hair is gold; her forehead the Elysian fields; her eyebrows rainbows; her eyes suns; her cheeks roses; her lips coral; her teeth pearls; her neck alabaster. . . .

—Miguel de Cervantes Saavedra, *The Adventures of Don Quixote*

James Branch Cabell's oeuvre has been considered in comparison with some of the greatest achievements of world literature: Byron's *Don Juan*, Goethe's *Faust*, Shakespeare's *Troilus and Cressida* and Homer's *Odyssey*. There remains for us here to present Cabell's literary affinity to Cervantes' *Don Quixote*. Although this study does not deal with matters of influence, it is nevertheless interesting to consider Cabell's own reflections on Cervantes' novel. All in all, he thought the book did not warrant the worldwide acclaim it had received. In *Beyond Life* he acknowledges Don Quixote as "one of the great characters of fiction" and praises the humor of Cervantes' book and the unrivaled character-drawing in Sancho Panza, but he does not think very highly of the book's plot and development: the reader's joyous anticipation "of a jaunt through old-world Spain in company with these two immortal types of humanity" (Don Quixote and Sancho Panza), he laments, wanes "long before the end of the fourth chapter." Cabell goes on to complain that "the essayists have written much more entertainingly about Don Quixote than Cervantes ever did." His opinion stands in sharp contrast to that of his friend and champion, the literary critic of the Chicago *Tribune*, Burton Rascoe, who considered *Don Quixote* one of the "titans" of world literature. In fact, when Rascoe raised *Jurgen: A Comedy of Justice* to the ranks of literary excellence by comparing it to Cervantes' *Don Quixote*, Cabell let the compliment pass unacknowledged. He told Rascoe in a letter that he thought highly of his book *Titans* and that he agreed with him with a few exceptions, among which he mentions Rascoe's praise of Cervantes' novel. Yet, curiously enough, the qualities Burton Rascoe found in the creator of *Don Quixote*, "his sub-acid comments, his calm force of understatement, his bland affirmation of what we know, sometimes with anguish, to be the reality of life," are all qualities typical of Cabell's prose.[1]

In what way is Cabell's literary imagination related to *Don Quixote*? The southerners who tried to make nineteenth-century middle-class rural society into the equivalent of Walter Scott's chivalric milieu were mainly engaged in a quixotic venture; however, they were completely serious in thinking they could do so. (William Gilmore Simms's romances of antebellum South Carolina or Thomas Nelson Page's rehabilitation of the chivalric myth in the postwar South are examples of this attempt.) Cabell was keenly aware of the quixotic nature of such chivalric fiction and wrote with mingled amusement and admiration about it. *The Rivet in Grandfather's Neck*, *Jurgen*, and *Figures of Earth*, expose the main tenets of the world of chivalry—personal risk, quest for justice, ideal love, integrity, and heroism—to the "bleaching" test of reality. Cabell's nexus with Cervantes is to be found in the way this Virginian author creates a stark contrast between chivalric delusion and harsh reality in order ultimately to undermine heroic grandiloquence, arrogance, and vainglory and to depict human beings' futile strivings to escape the human condition.

1. James Branch Cabell, *Beyond Life: Dizain des Demiurges*, vol. 1 of *The Works of James Branch Cabell* (New York: R. M. McBride, 1927), 216; Burton Rascoe, *Titans of Literature: From Homer to the Present* (New York: G. P. Putnam, 1932), 238.

Cabell, like Cervantes, mockingly contrasts what is familiar and commonplace with what is remote, exotic, and singular; however, contrary to the pervading high burlesque of *Don Quixote*, he roots his material in the conventions of the low burlesque. His protagonists handle the world of illusion as skillfully as the Manchegian knight; that is, they are aware of its deceits yet are unwilling to do without them. Don Quixote's confession to Sancho that Dulcinea is a creation of his imagination and therefore perfect, regardless of what she might be in real life, is paralleled in Cabell's fiction. "I imagine all I say to be true, neither more nor less," the mad knight tells the baffled Sancho, "and in my imagination I draw her as I would have her be, both as to her beauty and her rank; unequalled by Helen, unrivalled by Lucretia, or any other famous woman of antiquity, Greek, Barbarian, or Roman. Let anyone say what he likes, for though the ignorant may reproach me for it, men of judgment will not condemn me."[2] Cabell's heroes are every bit as aware as the Manchegian knight of the delusional nature of their longings, and with far more discernment they manage to live in the present while retaining the dream. Cabell is closest to *Don Quixote* in his obsession with appearances, with the conflicting perceptions we have of the world and ourselves in it. In his novel, Cervantes tells us that reality lies not in what things are but in how we perceive them when shaped and massaged by our imagination and our dreams. Thus, a squalid inn becomes the castle of an enchanted princess; the dust kicked up by two herds of sheep may hide the cavalcade of two hostile armies; and a hapless, pathetic, raving knight is miraculously blessed with the dignity of a hero speaking with the disillusioned wisdom of an ancient philosopher. Cabell, in turn, brings all his virtuosity to bear in depicting the same viewpoint as Cervantes. He contends that what we perceive as real is made up of both the materials of reality and the figurations of our dreams. Our fellow men and women are both visible figures and a more shadowy perception of our consciousness; the latter remains more alien to us, more difficult to fathom or decipher. Others will always seem almost wholly figures of our imaginings, shadows sketched by our own desire or neglected by our indifference.

Cabell's attraction to the world of appearances arises from his distrust of the reliability of our vision. His irony stems from such disbelief, which, in turn, may have evolved from an acute awareness of the disparity between the ideal and the real in the world in which he lived. As Edgar E.

2. Cervantes, *Don Quixote*, 210–11.

MacDonald has pointed out, the Richmond in which Cabell grew up "still felt the tragic glamour of having been the capital of the Confederacy. It was a city that lived half in a romanticized dream of the past and half in a struggle to survive in an unglamorous present. While the aristocrats built the legend of the War of Secession as the last great chivalric war, a war of ideals, a rising and moralistic middle class was gaining political power and imposing its mores on society." In *Let Me Lie* Cabell tells us that in postwar Richmond it was common practice to embellish facts with the imagination. Lies or half-lies displaced a rigorous, objective, historical scrutiny of the war and of the past in general. "Your elders were not telling any lies, either in private or upon memorial days, about their technically unstained and superhuman heroes, or at least not exactly," he writes of his childhood reminiscences. "It was just that grown people told only a part of the truth." That hidden or unrevealed side of the truth emerges constantly in Cabell's fiction, and it is used to dismantle such illusory notions as pure beauty, disinterested love or heroic generosity. At times, it collides head on with fantasy in a clash of gross proportions, as in *Jurgen*, where the author's devices of travesty are fully at work. At times, an amused irony substitutes for gross burlesque, as in *The Rivet in Grandfather's Neck*. But invariably the concealed truth reveals human flaws and weaknesses. Cabell's main preoccupation is the difficulty human beings have discerning between what is real, what appears true to our perception, and what is made up of the stuff of our dreams. This concern is manifest in his heroes' lack of self-assurance—as Jurgen's obsession with contingency attests—or in their retreat into the self—as portrayed in the character of Rudolph Musgrave. Most of Cabell's heroes show an uneasiness with time and change.[3]

Cabell's "acidulous skepticism" about the possibilities of human happiness takes on burlesque connotations when it is aimed at the South's unrealistic notions of itself. His prose is an assault upon "deep thoughts" and the deluded vision of the world held by those who sustain them, namely, the premodern literary southern milieu that preceded him.[4] Cabell reveals to us

3. Edgar E. McDonald, "Cabell Criticism: Past, Present, and Future," *Cabellian* 1 (1968–1969), 21; James Branch Cabell, *Let Me Lie: Being in the Main an Ethnological Account of the Remarkable Commonwealth of Virginia and the Making of Its History* (New York: Farrar, 1947), 156.

4. H. L. Mencken applied the term "aciduluos skepticism" to Cabell's writings. See H. L. Mencken, *James Branch Cabell* (New York: R. M. McBride, 1927), 11. Burton Rascoe calls *Don Quixote* "a book which was in the main an assault upon 'deep thoughts' " (*Titans of Literature*, 228). On this premise he compares *Jurgen* with *Don Quixote*.

his distrust of grand ideals in the words of his "romanticist" character John Charteris, who voices Cabell's own thoughts and obsessions and says, "The true secret of romance" is "to induce the momentary delusion that humanity is a superhuman race, profuse in aspiration, and prodigal in the exercise of glorious virtues and stupendous vices" (*RGN* 134). Dreams and ideals often supplant each other in Cabell's fiction so that sometimes the boundary between the two appears vague, but it is evident that Cabell was more interested in dreams, understood as deluded apprehensions of the world, than he was in ideals, viewed as constructions imposed upon us and alien to our experience. Cabell's estrangement from his social milieu and its ideals is conspicuous in his letters and memoirs. In the terrain of fiction, Cabell's own alienation is paralleled in Jurgen's alienation from the chivalrous court of Glathion, a parody of southern society: "All the while he fretted because he could just dimly perceive that ideal which was served [there], and the beauty of this ideal, but could not possibly believe in it" (*JG* 99). Jurgen constantly confronts ideals that are "a loveliness perceived in twilight, a beauty not clearly visioned" (*JG* 99) and that therefore remain unreal.

James Branch Cabell's birthplace, Virginia, and particularly Richmond, as the intellectual center of the region, played an important role as a guardian of the ideal of chivalry in the South. Rollin G. Osterweis observes that while the cult of chivalry was "common to the planter class in every section" of the South, it "permeated Virginia with particular intensity." Osterweis also points out the relevance that Walter Scott's chivalric romances had in shaping the aspirations of the Virginia gentry: "The fusion of the tradition of the Virginia gentleman with those medieval notions, best exemplified in the writings of Walter Scott, was the most important single factor in the evolution of the cult of chivalry in the Old Dominion." The defeat of the Confederacy enhanced and perpetuated the myth of the "Lost Cause," which came to symbolize a crusade against the advent of a fragmented world heralded by a business-oriented North. "Like all lasting myths," Frank E. Vandiver says of the Confederate myth, "this one had enough validity to sound good. The Lost Cause came on to the present as the last American resistance against the Organization State, against racial indistinction, against mass and motor."[5]

The inadequacy of the myth when seen against the middle-class reality

5. Rollin G. Osterweis, *Romanticism and Nationalism in the Old South* (New Haven: Yale University Press, 1949), 82; Vandiver, "The Confederate Myth," 149.

of the postwar South, particularly that of Virginia and its prosperous, commercial-minded capital, is the subject of Cabell's ironic scrutiny in his book of memoirs, *Let Me Lie*. His irreverent, mocking, but indulgent grasp of his fellows' foibles when it came to concealing discrepancies between fact and fancy in matters of Virginia's past can be called Cervantesque. In *Let Me Lie*, Cabell looks humorously on his contemporaries' penchant for fabricating the legend that suited their claims to chivalry and preserving the tenets of their world untouched. For a period of time southerners shared in one of the most enduring myths of the history of mankind, the cosmology of chivalry, by self-deceivingly isolating their material realities from their spiritual needs. Virginians, Cabell observes of his contemporaries, mapped their past according to some glamorous notions of heroism and chivalry that were more akin to the Waverly novels than to the realities of late-nineteenth-century Virginia. "They were creating," he remarks of these notions, "in the same instant that they lamented the Old South's extinction, an Old South which had died proudly at Appomattox without ever having been smirched by the wear and tear of existence. They perverted no facts consciously; but they did omit, from their public utterances or from their printed idyllic narratives, with the tact of a correctly reared person, any such facts as appeared undesirable—without, of course, ever disclaiming these facts." Cabell penetrates the very fabric of the myth in which the Old South's chivalric aspirations, enhanced by the episode of the war, were being liturgically recreated. He writes humorously that "there were not in Richmond any such old-time things as falchions and guerdons and varlets. Richmond was a progressive and up-to-date city which had rearisen triumphantly, like a phoenix from out of its ashes." Richmond, he adds, "was not at all like Camelot or Caerleon upon Usk; and so you found it kind of curious that the way in which your elders talked, upon platforms, reminded you of your *Stories of the Days of King Arthur*, by Charles Henry Hanson, with Illustrations by Gustave Doré." Cabell observes the Confederacy with a mild, amused irony. He refers to the Confederate generals as the "more prominent knights of the Confederate Round Table," and half-mockingly, half-affectionately he deems General Robert E. Lee a quixotic type. Lee's most heroic gesture, Cabell seems to imply with a touch of irony, was his rejection of worldly success and his refusal to rent out his celebrity, taking over the presidency of a "poverty-stricken and obscure and dilapidated Washington College, in the gaunt hill town of Lexington, Virginia, at the gaunt salary of $1500 a year." Reportedly, General Lee's avowed purpose was "to accomplish something for the benefit of mankind and the honor of God," to which Cabell is quick to add, "Miguel de Cervantes might have ascribed this same phrase to the Knight of La Mancha."[6] The general's attitude can be seen as quixotic, yet his impractical and inflated gesture receives from the writer a salute of admiration.

When Jurgen, as the self-appointed, travestied Duke of Logreus, visits the chivalrous court of Glathion, where "love-making" was "everywhere in vogue" once the war had "satisfactorily ended" and "by way of diversion, gentlemen hunted and fished and rode a-hawking and amicably slashed and battered one another in tournaments" (*JG* 78), we have no doubt that Cabell is parodying the foibles and deceits of Virginian gentlefolk. But it is the worship of women that absorbs his attention most. According to his biographers, as a young man, Cabell went through a traumatic episode of unrequited love, which caused him considerable emotional trouble in the years to come. Later, he may have compounded his painful experience by attributing the causes of his setback to a social context that nurtured absurd and damaging romantic notions, notions that went to the head of an extremely sensitive youth.[7]

Cabell's commentary on human beings' gift for myth-making, on their futile desires to escape from actuality into a world of romance, and on the antidotes necessary to protect themselves from attacks of self-delusion is fully Cervantesque. But the Cabellian quest may be better defined as the attempt to undo everything that the Manchegian knight sought to achieve, namely, to preserve his imagined, unreal world from the drab, unwanted touch of reality.

The Rivet in Grandfather's Neck is the first of Cabell's novels to appear with a Cervantesque label: "James Branch Cabell in this book has done something Cervantesque—there's no other word for it—in smiling a false chivalry away. And it's deadlier for that the writer does it with mockery of the courtier grace of which his victims have ever been enamoured in life

6. Cabell, *Let Me Lie*, 153–54, 147–48, 168–69.

7. For discussions of Cabell's unfulfilled love for Gabriella Moncure as a source of inspiration throughout his fiction, see Edgar McDonald, "Charles Washington Coleman and Gabriella Brooke Moncure, 1862–1955," in *James Branch Cabell and Richmond-in-Virginia* (Jackson: University Press of Mississippi, 1993); and Edgar McDonald, "Cabell in Love," in *James Branch Cabell: Centennial Essays*, ed. M. Thomas Inge and Edgar E. McDonald (Baton Rouge: Louisiana State University Press, 1983).

and in literature, and with the hurtfullest thing of all in a wound-inflicter—pity. A romanticist exposing romanticism's hollowness and sham; such is Mr. James Branch Cabell in this cavalier comedy of acid satire." These are the opening lines of a review of *The Rivet in Grandfather's Neck* published in *Reedy's Mirror*. But it was Cabell himself who, unintentionally, drew the most accurate assessment of the book's affinity with Cervantes' *Don Quixote*. In *Preface to the Past* he wrote: "The book is a comedy of limitations, it is a comedy of neo-chivalry; but it is also a comedy of words which serve as fetishes, as anodynes, and as intoxicants, in the while that reality is resolutely not faced." These limitations, which are not imposed by outside forces but are part of human nature itself, render our dreams hopeless; both in the familiar Lichfield and in far-off Poictesme, human beings are trapped in their human nature, however much they may try to escape it. Cabell's "neo-chivalry" is the same old code of southern chivalry but played against the backdrop of a modern stage and with thoroughly modern characters. Words are used to shield oneself from truth, to hide from genuine emotions. Colonel Musgrave, the "social triumph of his generation" (*RGN* 283), as he ironically likes to call himself, is the champion of this neo-chivalry encompassed by words and limitations. His grandiloquent pose, verbosity, and taste for grand ideas, all aimed at suppressing human fallibility, have unmistakably quixotic undertones.[8]

Rudolph Musgrave is a descendant of Don Quixote. In the first place, he is a faithful servitor of the chivalric code, a code no longer in accord with a modern utilitarian setting. But above all, he has consciously chosen to conduct his life by this code in order to avoid any possible friction with crucial truths about life and himself. Colonel Musgrave's foible is that he must make an artistic performance of his acts. He is possessed not by the appeal of any extraordinary deeds but by his own oratorical conceit, his "highly oratorical, post-prandial-sort-of words which serve him as a narcotic to ease him out of human living." He has a preference for gesture above authenticity, causing him to lose touch with himself and eventually doubt the veracity of his exploits.[9]

---

8. William M. Reedy, review of *The Rivet in Grandfather's Neck*, by James Branch Cabell, *Reedy's Mirror*, quoted in Carl Van Doren, H. L. Mencken, and Hugh Walpole, *James Branch Cabell: Three Essays* (Port Washington, N.Y.: Kennikat Press, 1967), 30; James Branch Cabell, *Preface to the Past* (New York: R. M. McBride, 1936), 192.

9. Cabell, *Preface to the Past*, 191.

Cabell describes *The Rivet in Grandfather's Neck* as a story "about the adventuring of a genuine, deep, and wholly honest chivalry, as it deals with words; with words which ignore that reality whose place they have usurped."[10] It is a Cervantesque announcement, indeed, but Cabell did not have to draw on *Don Quixote* to produce his most Cervantesque piece. Time and place provided him with genuine material. Colonel Musgrave's nostalgic tirades on the uniqueness of the southern past echo those elders who talked nostalgically on platforms in Cabell's memoir, *Let Me Lie.* "We were born masters of a leisured, ordered world," Rudolph Musgrave meditates in the quiet of Matocton, "and by a tragic quirk of destiny were thrust into a quite new planet, where we were for a while the inferiors, and after that just the competitors of yesterday's slaves" (*RGN* 86). These words, with which Colonel Musgrave tries to justify the men of his generation, have a drabber counterpart in those of his wife, Patricia Stapylton, a character who displays a more realistic view of the world. They "clung to their old mansions, and were ornamental," says the narrator, paraphrasing Patricia's thoughts, "and were, very certainly, profoundly self-satisfied; for they adhered to the customs of yesterday under the comfortable delusion that this was the only way to uphold yesterday's ideals" (*RGN* 268). Patricia speaks with the moral authority of Cabell's own voice when she says, "These people—for the most part a preposterously handsome race—were the pleasantest of companions and their manners were perfection," yet she admonishes firmly, "nobody is justified in living without even an attempt at any personal achievement" (*RGN* 268). Rudolph Musgrave is depicted as the epitome of this race, and his life a jewel in the art of self-delusion.

Rudolph Musgrave's portrait bears a remarkable resemblance to the Spanish hidalgo Don Quixote. Musgrave is a middle-aged, conceited, headstrong gentleman, well bred but holder of a meager fortune who considers money a not "altogether suitable subject for a gentleman's meditations" (*RGN* 66), and loves great words and high sentiments. Cared for by a spinster sister, he expects his Dulcinea to come walking through the door at any moment. The fact that his Dulcinea is not a high-born lady but crossbred Patricia Stapylton is but a trifle to him, for "in the women he loved," we are told, "there was much of his own invention" (*RGN* 76). Like every incorrigible romantic, his devotion begins at the very moment he meets his love. He becomes Patricia's enamored suitor until custom ex-

10. *Ibid.,* 193.

hausts what romance had launched—and that happens to him sooner than it happens to other people; it happens, this time even before his actual marriage with Patricia takes place.

But deep inside, Colonel Musgrave is more enamored of gesture than he is of women. He plans his acts carefully so as to make them "colorful" and ornaments them with rhetorical finery to create the right effect. What Rudolph Musgrave enjoys most is "the performance of a picturesque action" (*RGN* 6). The following is a telling example. From the opening pages of the book we learn that Colonel Musgrave has a special devotion for Anne Willoughby—now the wife of John Charteris, a romance writer of some fame—and that devotion makes him capable of a knightly action that dignifies him. He takes the blame for Anne's husband's affair with Clarice Pendomer to prevent his beloved Anne from knowing the truth. But eventually the chivalric gesture of "having acted as a hero in permitting himself to be pilloried as a libertine" (*RGN* 6), while providing him with the opportunity of a neat performance, does not reach the melodramatic heights he expects, for in the end neither he nor his pretended paramour is ostracized by Lichfield society. Cabell's comic outlook on his character's foibles is fully evident in his depiction of Colonel Musgrave's crafty tactics, so theatrical and skillfully planned, but the irony with which the narrator refers to the protagonist's chivalric motives is deliberately lighthearted and sympathetic. Rudolph Musgrave is never made to seem a fool. He is always conscious of the role he is performing and shows no intention of renouncing it. He is well aware that his life and those of his coevals have already been mapped out for them sometime in the past by his ancestors, who, as John Charteris puts it, "squeezed life dry as one does an orange, and left us the dregs" (*RGN* 251).

Consequently, the only tolerable choice that remains to him is to emulate the noble deeds and grand passions of the past as best he can. Colonel Musgrave at least does not believe that life for him can turn out otherwise. He is out of reach of the present, and not only does he know it, but he is quite satisfied with it. He wishes his actions to have no influence on his life, and to that end chivalry serves him well. There is a significant passage in the book that perfectly illustrates Colonel Musgrave's "neo-chivalry." Rudolph Musgrave learns that his sweetheart Patricia, younger and more worldly than he, has her heart set on another man, whom she has been seeing secretly, a certain Joseph Parkison, younger and also more able to cater to Patricia's tastes than Musgrave. The Colonel reacts to this knowledge not with rage, jealousy, or self-pity but with a contained delight, as if he had deliberately prepared himself for it. In the farcical scene that follows, we are first led to believe that he feels duty bound to relinquish Patricia Stapylton to his inferior rival. For a moment he is tempted to renounce duty for Patricia's youth and fortune, but finally neither money nor moral uprightness influence the Colonel's decision. It is his insuperable urge for colorful gesture that finally pushes him into chivalrously acquiescing to Patricia's feelings. Once his mind is made up to this honorable resolve, he gives one of his most memorable performances. With a matchless audience of Lichfield's very best society and in a grandiose Tom-Sawyerish manner, Colonel Musgrave announces Patricia Stapylton's engagement to her younger suitor. Afterward, we are told, he returns "homeward not entirely dissatisfied" (*RGN* 85). In the solitude of his room he "fill[s] a glass with the famed Lafayette madeira of Matocton," and drinks to his fine quixotic gesture, and to a more intangible notion, "To this new South that has not any longer need of me or of my kind" (*RGN* 87). In the passage that follows, it is easy to make out the author's voice, tolerant and sympathetic toward his protagonist's self-exculpatory confession of the cause of his being out of touch with the world:

> We couldn't meet the new conditions. Oh, for the love of heaven, let us be frank, and confess that we have not met them as things practical go. . . . A man who has not been taught to swim may rationally be excused for preferring to sit upon the bank; and should he elect to ornament his idleness with protestations that he is self-evidently an excellent swimmer, because once upon a time his progenitors were the only people in the world who had the slightest conception of how to perform a natatorial masterpiece, the thing is simply human nature. Talking chokes nobody, worse luck. (*RGN* 86)

Colonel Musgrave is as obstinate as Don Quixote in resisting reality's interference to his design. He wishes to remain the ultimate romantic, lest any contact with facts should remind him of how defective human dreams are when acted out in the flesh. He has in Anne Willoughby a veritable Dulcinea, the unattainable love, as a life-long protection against any real possibility of deception. He perceives her as different from any other woman he has known. In a way, he perceives that he might have loved her if he had tried, but he will not allow himself to put his feelings to the test of reality. It would simply be out of character. His seeming courtesy and generosity are aimed at keeping "Helen" forever untouched and the tenets of his world intact.

We learn that Anne Willoughby is happily married to novelist John Charteris—or at least she wants to think she is—and that somewhere in the past, before this marriage, she and Colonel Musgrave had tested their feelings for one another. Why Anne deserted Rudolph Musgrave for John Charteris is never made clear in the novel, but one may assume that Colonel Musgrave did his very best to turn her away from him. Most of all, the Colonel enjoyed protecting her, as when he gladly played the rogue in the case of John Charteris' affair with Clarice Pendomer, by supplanting Charteris' identity, arguing that "the truth would have killed Anne." Also, by means of his contrived exploit, the Colonel "had enjoyed a picturesque action" (*RGN* 6). He has one more chance to make a fine gesture when he succeeds in preventing his wife, Patricia, from running away with Anne's promiscuous husband. Charteris will take revenge by speaking badly of him to Anne, "and the Colonel knew that she would believe them all" (*RGN* 263). But he likes to see himself as Anne's champion and reasons that it was for Anne's happiness that "he had played." The true motive for Colonel Musgrave's ultimate pursuit, however, is to be found once more in the terrain of gesture: "He had won the game; he had played it, heartily and skillfully and successfully; and his reward was that the old bickerings with Patricia should continue, and that Anne should be taught to loathe him" (*RGN* 263). Thus, Anne Willoughby remains Colonel Musgrave's "chosen lady in domnei for a long while," Cabell explains. "Throughout some thirty-five years of his life he thus remained Anne Willoughby's adoring and despairing servitor, at a convenient distance, until a plaguy chance removed any further need for that despair with which his adoration was blended inseparably" (*PTP* 190). For, he continues, stretching irony to the extreme, "of all calamities, his lady in domnei was preparing to marry him." After Patricia's death and John Charteris' murder the path is cleared for Colonel Musgrave and Anne Charteris finally to marry. But Colonel Musgrave will not have it that way. After all these years of vigilantly watching his dame from afar, the prospect of marriage is for him "a bit too much like being proffered ice-cream soda for breakfast during the remainder of one's life-time" (*PTP* 190–91). He will not marry Anne. On the contrary, he will strut his best rhetorical finery to prevent it. His chance meeting with Anne at her husband's tombstone provides the setting for the Colonel's finest performance. His words, a mixture of insight, regret, and self-complacency, are uttered with a light, controlled irony. He admits he has never allowed any true feelings to emerge when he tells her, "I don't think I can word just what my feeling is for you" and then adds sincerely, "Always my view of the world has been that you existed, and that some other people existed—as accessories" (*RGN* 299). Anne and these "accessories" nurture those delusions that make up his identity and his world view.

But Rudolph Musgrave's most overt quixotism lies in his resounding defeat, for after all, he has been defending his dame against nothing. Anne has known all along the part she has played in this comedy of limitations. She is aware that she never loved her husband, that she has just been "his priestess—the priestess of a stucco god" (*RGN* 296). She also knows that she has played Dulcinea to the only man who swears he has loved her. Just as Don Quixote has to believe in Dulcinea in order to believe in himself, Colonel Musgrave's illusory Anne is instrumental in helping him keep the tenets of his world afloat. And he has retained a frozen image of his dame since the time, long ago, when he thought he loved Anne Willoughby. Considering that this conscious self-delusion is firmly lodged in his mind, preventing the real woman from emerging out of his reverie, one is able to see him as a true brother to Don Quixote. The real Anne has lived at a great distance from the Anne of Musgrave's imagination: "This woman had tasted of tonic sorrows unknown to Rudolph Musgrave, and had got consolation too, somehow, in far half-incredible uplands unvisited by him." Yet Rudolph Musgrave's vain renunciation yields him an irresistible delight, that "she lived, and was so exquisite, mainly by virtue of that delusion which he, of all men, had preserved; Anne Charteris was of his own creation, his masterpiece" (*RGN* 288). It is finally left to Anne, the worshiped dame, to reveal the authenticity of Rudolph Musgrave's chivalry, the truth of his quixotic stance: "My friend, remember that I have not thanked you. You have done the most foolish and—the manliest thing I ever knew a man to do, just for my sake. And I have accepted it as if it were a matter of course. And I shall always do so. Because it was your right to do this very brave and foolish thing for me. I know you joyed in doing it" (*RGN* 299).

On his deathbed, Colonel Musgrave confronts failure with dignity. He does not, after all, think he has made a fool of himself. He is convinced that humans are afraid of rising too high—thus his fascination with the little china people who "climbed to the very top of the chimney, where they could see the stars, before they decided to go back and live upon the parlor table under the brand-new looking glass." The Colonel has learned that the heights of human desire are, like the stars to the little china people, "disconcertingly unconcerned when you have climbed to them" (*RGN* 185). Only disenchantment awaits us in the kingdom to come; therefore we may as well "slink home again," as "it is the nature of all china people" (*RGN* 186) to do. Colonel Musgrave is Cabell's mouthpiece regarding mortal limitations and the ways humans devise to evade them. Many of his thoughts, particularly in the last section of the book, exhibit a calm but unswerving skepticism regarding the futility of men's aspiration to the heights of fulfillment. "You heard of other people being rapt by splendid sins and splendid virtues, and you anticipated that to-morrow some such majestic energy would transfigure your own living, and change everything," Rudolph Musgrave broods over his old yearning that life be filled with the intensity of passion, "but the great adventure never arrived, somehow; and the days frittered away piecemeal . . . until at last you found that living had not, necessarily, any climax at all" (*RGN* 316).

When Don Quixote takes to the road, fantasy encroaches upon reality in a manner unprecedented in world literature, revealing the central role of the imagination in shaping our views of reality. Cervantes laughs at how Don Quixote brings to life the intangible matter of dreams; James Branch Cabell follows Cervantes in showing us how men and women weave their own delusions to suit their personal dreams and how fervently they cling to them. Rudolph Musgrave wastes his life adhering to notions of a faded chivalry. But Cabell casts no judgment on him. On the contrary, his standpoint coincides more and more with that of his protagonist as the book draws to a close. Artificer of his own glory, Rudolph Musgrave carries within his own soul his dreariest enemy, the awareness that most of his life has been but a prop to illusion. But in a change of mind redolent of his moral courage and insight, he turns to the only enduring reality he has ever been sure of—his life with Patricia Stapylton. Serene and unassuming, he speaks his last word, which may serve as the book's epitaph, a word of wisdom on the romantic pull of living: "For you and what you meant to me were real. That only was real—that we, not being demigods, but being just what we were, once climbed together very high, where we could glimpse the stars—and nothing else can ever be of any importance" (*RGN* 318). What Cabell champions in Colonel Musgrave's bygone chivalry is not the vanity of heroism but the uprightness of a loyalty aware of its limitations, and ultimately, the relevance and legitimacy of illusion. That is the writer's most forceful and practically only conviction, one that appears in full force in *Jurgen* and *Figures of Earth*.

In *Jurgen* and *Figures of Earth* Cabell addresses the myth of knighthood in its southern version even more incisively than in *The Rivet in Grandfather's Neck*. In a debunking, demythologizing style reminiscent of Twain, he tells the story of two discredited heroes, Jurgen and Manuel, who undertake a voyage away from their daily existences and into fanciful lands to explore unaccountable marvels and emotions unknown to men. Yet they "circumvent" neither "destiny" nor "common sense"[11] as they would have wished but return home wholly unrewarded for their strivings. The two stories have much in common in structure, content, and purpose and in their echoes of the impractical exploits of Don Quixote. Worked into an intricate braid of appearances and facts never taken at their face value and constructed with the elements of a burlesque of chivalry, these stories easily bear comparison with Cervantes' novel. Cabell clearly thought of his tales as a commentary on the role that illusion plays in people's lives. Through these tales he mocks the tenets of a world—his own—made up of fanciful notions, not so much because this world's codes are at odds with the modern stance, but because they are univocal, simplistic truths and, as such, misleading. Yet Cabell is not ready to afford an alternative to the beliefs he so mercilessly stigmatizes. Cabell is not so much a satirist as he is, in the words used by Burton Rascoe to describe Miguel de Cervantes, a master in "the spirit of mockery." Like his character Jurgen, Cabell does not know what to make of this world "wherein nothing is certain" (*FOE* 47). We would do well, he seems to say, if we wrapped ourselves in our illusions while reality forges relentlessly on its way.

Inasmuch as Don Quixote is the knight of faith, who "both pawns and pledges his life to the restoration of the world of unified certainty,"[12] Jurgen and Manuel are his parodies. They may have dreams, but they lack the Don's faith and ideals. They are doubtful as to the purpose of their quest, suspect their own identities as questers, and deflate all truths they encounter on their way. ("How can any of us know anything?" Jurgen wonders

11. Jurgen's journey is prefigured by Nessus, the centaur who accompanies him to the garden between dawn and sunrise, where time is an everlasting present, and anticipates a voyage that will "circumvent both destiny and common sense" (*JG* 10).

12. Fuentes, *The Critique of Reading*, 37.

while he laments being robbed "of the zest which other persons apparently get out of living" [*JG* 319, 321]). Jurgen's and Manuel's stances differ from that of Don Quixote in yet another respect: whereas Cervantes' knight seeks to breathe life into the constructs of his raving imagination, Cabell's heroes, whose journeys are actually entrenched in fantasy, meet drab reality in fantasy's realm. Thus their attempts to raise their lives to higher summits of fulfillment by skimming over the ordinary prove equally as vain and out of proportion as those of Don Quixote. If with Cervantes' knight it is the encroachment of fantasy into reality that gives rise to parody, with Cabell's heroes it is the intrusion of reality into fantasy that creates the burlesque tension. Cabell pokes fun at his mock heroes of lofty purpose by having them face more down-to-earth paradises; lesser pleasures, minor beauties, and more ordinary satisfactions than those they had wished for await them at the end of their unsuccessful quests.

In spite of the differences in tone and mood between the two novels (*Figures of Earth* is less comic than *Jurgen*, and a melancholy Manuel broods over his destiny more than Jurgen does), the same motive and the same affliction run through the two stories: the deeds of men are foreign to their innermost desires, illusions and appearances reign over reality, and the search for truth is chimerical. There is a significant passage in *Figures of Earth* that speaks eloquently of Cabell's obsession with the distortion of our vision. Illusion-ridden young Manuel and his beloved Niafer, successfully brought back to life by the hero, emerge from the bare and desolate November forest and come upon Manuel's former lovers, Freydis and the Princess Alianora. These two royal ladies, splendid in their beauty and magnificently dressed, are riding toward the coast with their entourage. At the sight of the eccentric couple the two handsome sorceresses, who have stopped for a brief exchange with Manuel, show their bewilderment at "the swarthy, flat-faced, limping peasant girl in brown drugget that [is] with Count Manuel" (*FOE* 167). The same perplexity seizes young Osmund Heleigh when he asks the gallant king of Navarre,

> "But who, sire, was that time-battered grey vagabond, with the rearing stallion on his shield and the mud coloured cripple at his side, that our Queens should be stopping for a conference with him?"
>
> King Thibaut said it was the famous Dom Manuel of Poictesme, who had put away his youth for the sake of the girl that was with him.
>
> "Then is the old man a fool on every count," declared the Messire Heleigh,

sighing, "for I have heard of his early antics in Provence, and no lovelier lady breathes than Dame Alianora."

"I consider Queen Freydis to be the handsomer of the two," replied Thibaut, "but certainly there is no comparing either of these inestimable ladies with Dom Manuel's swarthy drab." (*FOE* 170)

The two extravagant, odd-looking figures whom the knights see have much in common with Don Quixote and his faithful Sancho Panza as they blunder their way through the bare landscape of La Mancha, oblivious to the incongruity of their situation. This mock vision of Manuel "of the high head," side by side with his heart's desire, a plain limping peasant girl, is rendered with a pathos that encompasses the foibles, deceits, and duplicities of mankind with an irony not devoid of compassion. In the Cabellian universe, facts are almost always obliquely addressed. They are parodies, appearances, duplicity, a layered fabric of discrepancies between what things are and what they are expected to be. Thus an erotic journey supplants a chivalric journey; faith mutates into skepticism and liberality into scheming; and erotic pleasure displaces love, dissipation displaces restraint, and so on. The whole chivalric value system is addressed from a burlesque viewpoint.

Manuel and Jurgen set out on their journeys as mock knights-errant. Manuel is a young, spirited, simple-minded swineherd maliciously induced by a wizard into rescuing a certain Lady Gisele d'Arnaye. In truth, the wizard is an impostor, and the captive lady is his high-spirited wife, whom he hopes to get rid of by persuading Manuel to champion a fraudulent cause. Jurgen's beginnings are every bit as unheroic. He is an old, retired poet turned pawnbroker whose lady in distress is none other than his nagging, plain wife, Dame Lisa, who has been carried off by the devil as a favor for Jurgen's kindness. Both of their journeys are punctuated by a series of incongruities that work against the fundamental tenets of chivalry; courtesy, humanity, friendship, hardihood, love, modesty, duty, generosity, loyalty, mercy, and love of freedom are deflated one by one. The two champions are travesties of the chivalric hero and the courtly lover. They are neither faithful nor passionate. They are unromantic and demythologizing and quite reluctant to risk any danger for their chosen ladies. Vain and selfish, eager for pleasure or earthly success, they completely mock the knightly ideal.

But Cabell's most irreverent scorn of the chivalric centers on the keystone of southern chivalry—worship of women—which W. J. Cash calls "downright gyneolatry." Here more than elsewhere, the discrepancies between knightly ideals and facts are rendered with a pathos all Cabell's own. Fair ladies and gallant knights, either in King Arthur's court or in more exotic imaginary lands, act by subverting the conventions of what John Fraser has called "the revised chivalric terms of *Ivanhoe*."[13] Women's coldness is transmuted into undisguised passion, their aloofness or feigned rejection into forthrightness and sexual candor. Cabell's damsels are less interested in "magic than in kisses," as the narrator says of Freydis in *Figures of Earth*. Nor are they prone to romance or vulnerable to Byronic rhetoric. On the contrary, they are naturally down-to-earth and more concerned with pragmatic goals in the manner of Sancho Panza, and also like him they speak the language of particulars. They would rather be Aldonza than Dulcinea. The high-flown comments on their marvels are to them only babble, as Freydis tells Manuel plainly: "I wonder to how many other women you have talked such nonsense about beauty and despair and eternity" (*FOE* 107). They are outspoken (Yolanda, for instance, reacts to Jurgen's sexual advances by urging him to come out "straightforwardly with what [he was] hinting at [that] morning" [*JG* 80]), or they show an all too worldly disposition and an interest in following convention to the detriment of personal freedom when it is to their own advantage. Take the case of Niafer, who values Manuel's reunion with her as long as it can provide her "rubies" in her "coronet," because she has "always fancied them" (*FOE* 166). They have no concern for their good name (princess Guenevere flirts openly with Jurgen on the eve of her marriage to King Arthur, for example) or they are sly, greedy, and ambitious, like Princess Alianora, mistress of duplicity, who schemes to kill her own father as a shortcut to the crown. As for Jurgen and Manuel, they have none of the traits of the gallant or chivalric hero. Jurgen's erotic journey contradicts the whole philosophy of courtly love. As a lover he lacks heroic self-control, and love is not a source of pain to him but a joyous entertainment. Hard as he may try, he can never transform himself into an enamored suitor. Not even the

---

13. W. J. Cash, *The Mind of the South* (New York: Alfred A. Knopf, 1941), 86; Fraser, *Patterns of Chivalry*, 80. Fraser points out the patterns of Scott's revision of the chivalric code, which accorded to women the "center of power" and presented them as an "energizing principle, someone to be rendered the traditional homage paid by gallant men to fair women, whose approval they courted, and whom she, in her turn, was entitled to charm."

magnificent Guenevere or the flawless Helen are capable of driving him "out of [his] head" (*JG* 94), as he himself puts it. In turn, Manuel's grievances with the knightly code are endless. His beginnings are neither heroic nor daring. He is in pursuit of "a fine wife and much wealth and leisure wherein to discharge [his] geas," for which he will egotistically "follow after [his] own thinking and [his] own desires" (*FOE* 8). He is neither generous nor virtuous: he surrenders his beloved Niafer to Grandfather Death, for he does "not value Niafer's life more highly than [he values his] life" (*FOE* 37). He achieves notoriety through trickery: three feathers plucked from an ordinary goose procure him a state, the title of Count of Poictesme, and the hand of Alianora the Unattainable Princess.

How do Jurgen's and Manuel's fantastic journeys compare to the pilgrimage of Don Quixote in purpose, development, and conclusion? Like Don Quixote, Cabell's heroes are uprooted from the mediocrity of the real world and transported to the exciting regions of illusion in search of more fully satisfactory experiences, and, like Cervantes, Cabell describes the futility of his characters' penchant for transcending their human limitations with a fusion of irony and sympathy. Grandfather Death's words to Manuel at the end of his journey reveal Cabell's stance on the fate of humanity. Manuel asks whether his destiny "is that of all living creatures." The lord of oblivion responds, "If you have been yourself you cannot reasonably be punished, but if you have been somebody else you will find that this is not permitted" (*FOE* 290). What it is not permitted is what Jurgen and Manuel have so obstinately attempted in traveling under assumed identities, driven by the delusion that they will shun the limitations of their human condition. Finally, their careers as questers are "the marginal man's career of deception,"[14] as Walter Reed has described *Don Quixote*. Their aims, abstract and transcendent, are by definition doomed to failure.

Jurgen, the poet, undertakes a voyage to the past in quest of a rationale underlying the chaotic existence of things. At times he calls this elusive rationale justice, at times faith, but he finds neither anywhere. The only glimpse of justice he ever has along the way is a "common noun" stamped on the book of the Master Philologist in the kingdom of Cocaigne, just a "grammarian's notion," or what he calls "an ethical ideal of conduct proper to the circumstances, whether of individuals or communities" (*JG* 178–79). But to him that sort of justice can only satisfy the "realist," who

14. Reed, *Exemplary History*, 71.

accepts the world of facts for what it is. Jurgen's ideal of justice is a totally different thing. It does not fall into the realm of ethics. It is a sort of metaphysical justice seeking to redress just one wrong: the impossibility for human beings to fulfill their desires. In a fine passage addressing his newly recovered Heart's Desire in the garden between dawn and sunrise, Jurgen mourns their truncated love and spells out his dissension with the "inequitable process" of living: "We have a splendour for which the world has no employment. It will be wasted. And such wastage is not fair" (*JG* 45–46). Needless to say, Jurgen's cosmic justice keeps eluding him all through the journey, and to discredit his claims to perfection, Cabell mockingly depicts him as a rogue whose personal relation with justice inspires only distrust. We repeatedly see him using his cunning to circumvent obstacles and gain his own advantage. As Cabell tells Burton Rascoe in a letter, Jurgen "goes prattling of and demanding justice in all sorts of places, and inflicting injustice everywhere."[15]

Manuel, the man of action, forges into the future with a wish to embrace the world and not to leave it "unaltered" (*FOE* 11). But medieval Poictesme, with plenty of heroic possibility, leaves him with little chance of fulfilling his dream. His illusions are pitted against disillusioning facts. A mighty champion whose mind is inflamed to a degree little short of that of the valorous Knight of La Mancha, Manuel comes up against the same all too familiar limitations, hampered not by fantastic trappings but by his own punctilious human nature. As Louis D. Rubin remarks, Manuel of Poictesme is denied "all possibility for mortal achievement in deeds—not because of crass times, not because of the absence of the aristocratic possibility, but because of the nature of man."[16] Rubin here singles out the thread of one of Cabell's major themes: humanity's inescapable limitations and incorrigible tendency to illusion.

The dreams that set Jurgen and Manuel in motion, leaving behind the here and now in search of higher levels of fulfillment, unfold quite similarly. In his search for justice Jurgen runs "over the grave of a dream and through the malice of time" (*JG* 10). The dream is an attempt to recapture

15. *The Letters of James Branch Cabell*, ed. Edward Wagenknecht (Norman: University of Oklahoma Press, 1975), 77.

16. Louis D. Rubin, Jr., "Two in Richmond: Ellen Glasgow and James Branch Cabell," in *South: Modern Southern Literature in Its Cultural Setting*, ed. Louis D. Rubin, Jr., and Robert D. Jacobs (Garden City, N.Y.: Doubleday, 1961), 131.

the eternal moment, that "little time of which the passing might be made endurable" (*JG* 25). For Jurgen this means the memory of a certain Wednesday in his youth when his first flame, Dorothy la Désirée, appeared to him as a promise of eternity. The malice of time, which quickly reduces things to the most prosaic grounds of reality, is the irretrievability of the past, in which his Heart's Desire is hopelessly lost to a lifeless image. When Jurgen is allowed to go beyond the barriers of time in the garden between dawn and sunrise, he encounters not Helen, "the delight of gods and men," but an aloof creature. He is bewildered. Faced with the fact that the Dorothy whom he loved in youth is but a stranger to him, he resorts to Nessus, the Centaur who had led him there, for an explanation: "And was that Dorothy whom I loved in youth an imaginary creature?" he asks. Nessus' reply attests to, indeed praises, the extent to which Jurgen's vision is a mental construct: "My poor Jurgen, you were once a poet! She was your masterpiece. For there was only a shallow, stupid and airy, high-nosed and light-haired miss, with no remarkable good looks,—and consider what your ingenuity made from such poor material! You should be proud of yourself" (*JG* 30).

In an attempt to thwart fate and make up for his lack of steadfastness in the past, Jurgen confronts Heitman Michael, the man whom Dorothy had favored over him in their youth. In this confrontation he avoids being "brushed aside by the man's brute strength" and stabs his dagger into the "undefended back of Heitman Michael." Afterward he justifies his act by saying that "the man was stronger than I and wanted what I wanted. So I have compromised with necessity, in the only way I could make sure of getting that which was requisite to me. I cry for justice to the power that gave him strength and gave me weakness, and gave to each of us his desires" (*JG* 51).

By killing his rival, Jurgen changes his destiny, but justice is not yet satisfied, at least not in the way Jurgen understands it. When he returns from the garden to the present, he realizes that his beloved Dorothy is not a lady but a harlot, very much like Don Quixote's Aldonza: "Her flesh roughened under his touch, and her cheeks fell away, and fine lines came about her eyes, and she became the Countess Dorothy whom Jurgen remembered as Heitman Michael's wife. . . . And she was leering at him, and he was touching her everywhere, this horrible lascivious woman, who was certainly quite old enough to know better than to permit such liberties. And her breath was sour and nauseous. Jurgen drew away from her, with a shiver of loathing, and he closed his eyes, to shut away that sensual face" (*JG* 54). Cabell's own comments indicate that the Dorothy of Jurgen's imagination is at least as significant as any "real" character in the novel: "I believe the considerate will note this Dorothy la Désirée, howsoever infrequent her corporal entrances, to remain throughout this narrative its most important character," to which he adds, "this Dorothy is very actually, in the phrase which I do not love, 'the author of Jurgen' " (*PTP* 93).

Throughout his outlandish journey Jurgen is haunted by the romantic image that has molded his life and, ironically, robbed him of capacity for passion. His cast of mind, which ought to be poetical, is incapable of any heights of lyricism, and he humorously acknowledges that instead of acting like an expert gallant he twaddles "like a schoolmaster" (*JG* 352). He goes "romancing through the world" into "lands unvisited by other men" (*JG* 317) where he savors the bounties of beauty, youth, and many indescribable delights, but nowhere does he realize any of his dreams or fulfill any of his desires. Beauty quickly fades before his eyes, those favored by it become a bore, and the ecstasies of sexual delight soon become a monotonous entertainment. When, at the sight of Queen Helen, he is seized by what he deems an extraordinary rapture, he recoils, lest she have "some fault" or "some fleck in her beauty somewhere. And sooner than know that," Jurgen explains, "I would prefer to retain my unreasonable dreams and this longing which is unfed and hopeless" (*JG* 224–25). Confronting his fate in an unusually solemn mood, he recognizes the source of his ennui. Jurgen blames the flawless Helen for having been "a robber that stripped my life of joy and sorrow," saying that the moment when "the memory of your beauty as I then saw it, mirrored in the face of a jill-flirt, . . . enfeebled me for such honest love as other men give women." Then he confesses: "I envy these other men" (*JG* 349).

Manuel, the protagonist of *Figures of Earth*, fares much the same in search of his desire. A rustic, extroverted youth at the onset of his journey, Manuel voices his aim plainly: "I must follow after my own thinking, and after a desire which is not to be satisfied with dreams, even though they be . . . as resplendent as rubies of the Orient" (*FOE* 34). But soon this boundless enthusiasm for the world of facts and his confidence in being able to control his destiny come face-to-face with his human limitations. He cannot get rid of the "geas" he has upon him "to make an animated and lively figure, somewhat more admirable and significant than that of the average man" (*FOE* 75). He makes figures in the likeness of King Helmas, whose wisdom was infallible, of King Ferdinand, symbol of the supreme holiness, and of Alianora, the sovereign of love, but they all remain "obstinately lifeless" (*FOE* 89). Not even the figure of his beloved Niafer comes out to his own liking; although faultless when inert, it limps when he finally succeeds in animating it (*FOE* 16). Cabell's ironic but compassionate view of his hero's shortsightedness is nowhere more perceptible than in the champion's attempt to recover his Dulcinea, the plain kitchen wench Niafer, whose life he had unheroically sacrificed to Grandfather Death in order to save his own. This aspirant perfectionist mistakes windmills for giants as self-deceivingly as the Knight of La Mancha. Cabell remarks humorously on Manuel's confession to Freydis that, to him, "there had never been anybody like Niafer, and it would be nonsense to say otherwise" (*FOE* 120). The narrator's assessment is that "It is possible that Dom Manuel believed this. The rather homely, not intelligent, and in no respect bedazzling servant girl may well have been—in the inexplicable way these things fall out—the woman whom Manuel's heart had chosen, and who therefore in his eyes for the rest of time must differ from all other persons. Certainly no unastigmatic judge would have decreed this swarthy Niafer fit, as the phrase is, to hold a candle either to Freydis or Alianora: whereas Manuel did not conceal, even from these royal ladies themselves, his personal if unique evaluations" (*FOE* 120). What Manuel does not know is that the uniqueness of his Niafer can only exist in the lifelessness of the dream. For when he kisses the earthen image he had made of her to summon her back to life, "all memories of paradise and all the traits of angelhood [depart] from her" (*FOE* 161). Manuel achieves his desire to become a mighty champion, but it costs him his youth and causes him to renounce his pursuit of perfection. He emerges an old man, and Niafer a "swarthy, flat-faced, limping peasant girl" (*FOE* 167). Horvendile's prophesy is then fulfilled: "My wish would be for me always to obtain whatever I may wish for," Manuel had once told him, to which Horvendile replies that he can help Manuel to get his wish, but there is a price to pay, "and it is that with the achieving of each desire you will perceive its worth" (*FOE* 39–40). Horvendile's words ring true with the self-defeating experiences of Cabell's burlesque knights. The accomplishment of a desire inexorably brings about its ruin. (Note how the "occasional exchange of endearments" between Jurgen and Anaïtis is comically rendered "as much a matter of course as their meals, and hardly more exciting" [*JG* 170] or how Manuel's life with

Niafer, after all the agonized longing, furnishes him with neither meaning nor passion.)

In short, Jurgen's and Manuel's romantic aspirations always turn to dust in their hands. Unlike Don Quixote, they do not succeed in keeping the ideal unspoiled by earthly existence: their damsels inevitably turn into Aldonzas before their very eyes. Eventually Cabell's heroes learn how much simpler and wiser it is to eschew "queens and princesses" and "other godlike beings" and compromise with lesser gods, more in tune with human nature. In this regard, Louis Rubin has pointedly remarked that "the legendary trappings of Poictesme do not produce an escapist romance; they only heighten the irony. The incorrigible humanness of the characters triumphs."[17] Cabell's questers cut a figure similar to, if less dispirited than, the romance-mad Manchegian hidalgo in his calamitous roamings, crisscrossing between fantasy and reality. As in *Don Quixote*, unglamorous reality inevitably shatters the expectations held by Cabell's heroes of unending romance and high adventure, but we do not see their plights in the same sympathetic light as we see that of Cervantes' prodigious knight. Depicted primarily as rascals or rogues, they are denied the qualities we find most compelling in the character of Don Quixote—namely, faith and genuine idealism. Yet despite their crassness, their quests reveal a similar yearning to transcend life as it is, and their follies maintain an unflinching grip on their lives.

Both *Jurgen* and *Figures of Earth* offer quixotic conclusions, when outright disillusionment or ironic resignation bring soaring flights of fancy down to earth. *Jurgen* ends with its protagonist, contriver of fabulous, dreamlike love affairs, seeking the company of his nagging, prosaic wife, Dame Lisa, and swearing that "for the sake of no notion would I endanger the routine which so hideously bores me" (*JG* 349). Likewise, by the end of *Figures of Earth*, Manuel, the successful champion, the high Count of Poictesme, confesses that he has become a slave to custom at Niafer's side, whom he ironically refers to as "the archetype and flawless model of all wives" (*FOE* 243). Thus, in the same way that Don Quixote never strays an inch away from his unromantic La Mancha, Jurgen never frees himself from his humdrum marriage, nor Manuel himself from the "unfinished, unsatisfying image" he was trying to create beside the pool of Haranton before he set off in search of wealth and worldly fame. Beauties and con-

17. *Ibid.*, 137–38.

quests are of no avail against the leveling hand of custom and obstinate ennui of men. In short, Cabell's heroes are denied achievement by the sole fact of their mortal flesh.

With the intricate web of burlesque distortions woven around his heroes' adventures, Cabell explores the power of appearances in our perception of the world. Appearances are the shadows of our beliefs, he contends. They are manifestations of our innermost desires, and they make up the substance of our reality until they become objective and credible to our eyes. Cabell's theater of appearances warns us against the delusive character of our vision by having princesses act like mistresses, artful sorceress metamorphose into tender souls, a loving sweetheart turn into a lascivious old woman, and a limping peasant girl embody the ideal of beauty. In this respect, James D. Riemer has perceptively pointed out that in *Jurgen* "Cabell satirizes the power of the human will to attribute objective reality to what is in fact unreal or imaginary" and that his "concerns in *Figures of Earth* enlarge to emphasize the uncertainty and unknowability of the physical world as well."[18] Jurgen comes to suspect the authenticity of his Heart's Desire, Dorothy la Désirée, who has such a strong grip on his life. In turn, Manuel sees all the loves and desires and adventures of his career as the champion of Poictesme drowned in the shadowy waters of the dark stream of Lethe, where he comes with Grandfather Death on the last stage of his journey. Where his companion sees only "ordinary water," Manuel sees a "deceiving water" reflecting the face of a young boy instead of that of the old man he thought he was. This confusing image of himself has accompanied him on his travels ever since he renounced his identity and went on to climb the peak of Vraidex after receiving an illusory summons. The conflict that seizes him is strikingly similar to that experienced by Hank Morgan in *A Connecticut Yankee*: he is uncertain as to the reality of his own being; he doubts his own identity and has lost touch with his soul. In short, his life has become solely the reflection of his dreams. "I am not really a famed champion," he laments, "but only a forlorn and lonely inmate of the doubtful castle of my body" (*FOE* 130).

In the end, Cabell has succeeded in reversing the patterns of gallantry and chivalry, the conventions he set out to parody. Jurgen, the champion

18. James D. Riemer, *From Satire to Subversion: The Fantasies of James Branch Cabell*, Contributions to the Study of Science Fiction and Fantasy, no. 38 (New York: Greenwood Press, 1989), 21–22.

of gallantry, babbles like a schoolmaster, can never really participate in the spirit of the occasion, and sacrifices more promising adventures for the tedious Dame Lisa. Manuel, "a wilful champion . . . who went everywhither with a high head a-boasting that he followed after his own thinking and his own desire" (*FOE* 277), ends up drawing a most demystifying self-indictment of his past deeds and glory, bearing the mark of self-defeat: "I seem to see only the strivings of an ape reft of his tail, and grown rusty at climbing, who has reeled blundering from mystery to mystery, with pathetic makeshifts, not understanding anything, greedy in all desires, and always honeycombed with poltroonery" (*FOE* 288). Through Manuel's grave and regretful recapitulation of his hero's life, Cabell discredits both vainglory and mindless chivalry, attitudes that Manuel has come to represent. Furthermore, Freydis' advice to Manuel that "it is not from any remote strange places . . . that a man must get the earth for this image making" (*JG* 119) is also the author's warning against illusion-ridden minds. Yet his word of caution against deceitful dreams and disregard of reality is counteracted by his clairvoyant vision of humanity's fateful tendency to idealization. Cabell contemplates the chimerical journeys of his heroes with both extreme skepticism and sympathetic understanding. He contends that chivalry and gallantry were, for that portion of the world he knew well, his native Virginia, just as legitimate a way for men to tackle their uncertain destiny on earth as any other. Jurgen speaks for Cabell when he says that he could only "dimly perceive that ideal which was served in Glathion, and the beauty of this ideal, but could not possibly believe in it" (*JG* 99).[19] However, he tolerated and understood the need and the attempt—which he observed with a wry eye—to conform to an orderly world and did not ultimately oppose it. "At all events," Cabell wrote, "Chivalry was a pragmatic hypothesis: it 'worked,' and it served society for a long while, not faultlessly, of course, but by creating—like all the other codes of human conduct which men have ever tried—a tragi-comic mêlée wherein con-

---

19. Likewise, Cabell lends his voice to Guenevere's father, Gogyrvan, King of Glathion, when he tells Jurgen, "Youth can afford ideals, being vigorous enough to stand the hard knocks they earn their possessor. But I am an old fellow cursed with a tender heart and tolerably keen eyes. That combination, Messire de Logreus, is one which very often forces me to jeer out of season, simply because I know myself to be upon the verge of far more untimely tears" (*JG*, 86).

tended 'courtesy and humanity, friendliness, hardihood, love and friendship, and murder, hate, and virtue, and sin.' "[20]

Ultimately, Jurgen's and Manuel's inconsequential journeys emerge as the fastidious protestations of an old, worn-out poet and a punctilious clay artist against the seemingly simple truths that the world of facts is incommensurate with men's aspirations and that men's proclivity for romance is insurmountable. "To spin romances," Cabell states in one of his most frequently quoted passages, "is man's proper and peculiar function in a world wherein he only of created beings can make no profitable use of the truth about himself. For man alone of animals plays the ape to his dreams."[21] Dreams, then, are the only incorruptible stuff of we humans. But we dare not bring them into contact with reality, Cabell warns us, for the very contact "takes the color out of things" (*JG* 318).[22] A disenchanted view of human existence comes across in *Jurgen* and *Figures of Earth* every time the protagonists complain of their lack of zeal or insist on their craving for faith and in their inability to believe in received ideals that others accept gladly. Cabell's heroes face their doom as if they know beforehand that their experiences can never be explained or encompassed by a single truth. To them it comes as a bittersweet realization that no setting that men can envisage for the attainment of fullness or contentment can equal the contents of a wish tainted with myth or desire. Ultimately, they crave the desire more than its object, thus bearing out wizard Marimon's wisdom when he tells Manuel at the start of his journey that "he is wiser that knows the shadow makes lovely the substance" (*FOE* 24). The verses written by the Joker, Academician of Argamasilla, to Sancho Panza could well serve as an epitaph to Cabell's heroes:

> How vain are all the hopes of humankind!
> How sweet their promises of quiet seem,
> And yet they end in shadows, smoke and dream.[23]

20. James Branch Cabell, *Chivalry: Dizain des Reines*, vol. 5 of *The Works of James Branch Cabell* (New York: R. M. McBride, 1928), 6.

21. Cabell, *Beyond Life*, 38.

22. Gaunt and somber Mother Sereda stands for the reality principle in Jurgen's story. When Jurgen first encounters her, she is sorting through colored garments that she intends to bleach. Jurgen understands then and there the extent of her power, "more great than any other power which is in the world" (*JG*, 35).

23. Cervantes, *Don Quixote*, 460.

3

HONOR FOR THE SAKE OF HONOR

The Windmills of Yoknapatawpha

> Because no battle is ever won he said. They are not even fought. The field
> only reveals to man his own folly and despair, and victory is an illusion of
> philosophers and fools.
>
> —William Faulkner, *The Sound and the Fury*

Whenever William Faulkner was asked about his favorite books and authors, he never failed to mention Cervantes' *Don Quixote*. In one interview
he said that "the books I read are the ones I knew and I loved when I was
a young man and to which I return as you do to old friends: the Old Testa-
ment, Dickens, Conrad, Cervantes—*Don Quixote*. I read that every year, as
some do the Bible" (*LiG* 251). At West Point he described the qualities he
found appealing in the character of Don Quixote: "It's admiration and pity
and amusement—that's what I get from him—and the reason is that he is
a man trying to do the best he can in this ramshackle universe he's com-
pelled to live in. He has ideals which by the pharisaical standards are nonsensical. But by my standard they are not nonsensical. His method of trying
to put them into practice is tragic and comic. I can see myself in Don Quixote by reading a page or two now and then, and I would like to think that
my behavior is better for having read *Don Quixote*." [1]

---

1. Faulkner's list of favorites first appeared in Jane Stein's interview, "William Faulkner,"
Paris Review 4 (1956): 28–29; *Faulkner at West Point*, ed. Joseph L. Fant III and Robert Ashley
(New York: Random House, 1964), 94.

The many occasions on which Faulkner mentioned *Don Quixote* leads one to believe that it was for him an essential work, a book he always kept on his bedside table. The fact that he read and reread *Don Quixote* many times and the profusion of quixotic characters and situations in his novels and stories indicate that Cervantes was a considerable influence on him. I believe, however, that these characters and situations owe more to Faulkner's own vision of his world and to his particular concept of human beings in this world than to his personal admiration for Cervantes' novel.

Faulkner's strongest conviction is that human beings can face defeat and by their own efforts turn it into victory. Practically they may fail, but the important thing is to overcome fear and to cleave to "the old verities and truths of the heart, . . . love and honor and pity and pride and compassion and sacrifice," even in the most adverse circumstances. One result of this conviction is that in order to uphold their self-respect and defend what they believe to be right, a considerable number of his characters embark on undertakings full of quixotic resonance without regard for their outcome. Thus, in the same way that Cervantes made his fool from La Mancha a colossus of human dignity, so Faulkner claimed for his Yoknapatawphans the undeniable right of human beings to assert their humanity, affirming the honor of the human species as an uncompromising force for good, to be preserved against all odds and all reverses in fortune.

Faulkner's fictional world portrays in many instances a clash between the values of a society rooted in tradition and those brought about by industrial capitalism. This tension is reflected in those of his characters who, in one way or another, try to impose a moral ideal on what they sense to be a crass reality. But if in such characters Faulkner intended to satirize human idealism, in many instances they also seem to represent the author's own beliefs, enthusiasms, and disappointments.

When Faulkner portrays his characters' struggles to transcend their circumstances, he often depicts them as illusion ridden, impractical, unheroic, or self-defeated, but he also sees them as dignified in their quest. This is one of the greatest similarities between Faulkner and Cervantes. But Faulkner's confluence with the Spanish author is also to be found in the way ideals shatter against an implacable reality that proves cold, distant, and unmoving. Faulkner's quixotic heroes face the world in ridiculous solitude. Invariably, the cause of their unhappiness and misfortune lies not in any external conflict but in the web of their own dreams. Faulkner captures with particular intensity this universal discord between the real and the illusory, between intention and reality, giving it the local habitation of a world he knew well, the American South, populating his fictitious Yoknapatawpha County with a multitude of characters who in their unique ways are reminiscent of Don Quixote from La Mancha. George Santayana's reading of *Don Quixote,* asserting it illustrates that "the force of idealism is wasted when it does not recognize the reality of things,"[2] could very well reflect Faulkner's stance on quixotic illusion. Faulkner casts an ironic eye on the spectacle of his protagonists' unsuccessful strivings to achieve the elusive ideal, but his vision provides compassionate insight into the human soul in pursuit of excellence.

The South where William Faulkner was born and brought up is described by Robert Penn Warren as "cut off, inward-turning, backward looking. It was a culture frozen in its virtues and vices, and even for the generation that grew up after World War I, that South offered an image of massive immobility in all ways; an image, if one was romantic, of the unchangeableness of the human condition, beautiful, sad, painful, tragic— sunlight slanting over a mellow autumn field, a field the more precious for the fact that its yield had been meager."[3] This world provides the material Faulkner uses to construct the legend of Yoknapatawpha: the first patricians, symbols of gallantry and courage and blessed with a strong sense of honor; then their descendants who, trapped within the myth of their forebears and unable to accept their own present, strive in vain to transcend a world devoid of virtue and honor, a world all too made of matter. In the process they become the battered and ridiculed heroes of a period that has no use for their type of heroism. Characters as central to Faulkner's narrative as Quentin Compson, Ike McCaslin, Gail Hightower, Gavin Stevens, and Horace Benbow fall within this category. In their own particular ways they are, like Don Quixote, extreme moral idealists who, in their defense of honor and justice, the past and its heroism, or the pastoral myth of the Golden Age, retreat from the adversities of the present and attempt to escape confrontation with reality. They all share with Don Quixote the solitude of their struggle. The characters who surround them stand apart from these idealists' obsessions, throwing into relief the unreality of their lives. Faulkner's idealists are spiritually estranged, subject to anachronistic or ineffectual behavior, and find solace only in an illusory world.

2. Santayana, "Cervantes," 119.

3. Robert Penn Warren, "Faulkner: Past and Future," in *Faulkner: A Collection of Critical Essays*, ed. Robert Penn Warren (Englewood Cliffs, N.J.: Prentice-Hall, 1966), 3–4.

In *Utopia and Counterutopia in the "Quixote,"* Cervantes scholar J. A. Maravall contends that in *Don Quixote,* Cervantes wanted to create a counterutopia that would counteract the escapist utopia or pseudo-utopia built up by that sector of Spanish society that cast its gaze back to the period of Emperor Charles V in search of dreams of glory. This longing for the medieval heroic ideal was still prevalent in the Spain of that time as a result of the Reformation and was reinforced by the myth of the Golden Age, sustained by the recent discovery of America. According to Maravall, the pastoral-heroic ideal so dear to Don Quixote underwent at Cervantes' hands an ironic examination precisely because it had no relation to reality and had become the receptacle of all the anachronistic beliefs of the backward-looking elements in Spanish society during that period. But at the same time, in the character of Don Quixote Maravall sees traits that reveal not only a nostalgia for the times of the empire and the heroic ideal but also an aversion to the emergence of modern methods of state organization that threatened to circumscribe individual free will.[4]

In Faulkner's fiction we see the same myth of the past as a time of heroism and unshifting values expressed through the backward-looking characters of Quentin Compson and Gail Hightower, and the same longing for a past Golden Age and rejection of the new order in the character of Isaac McCaslin. We also see characters such as Gavin Stevens who take it as a personal responsibility to try to halt the decline of the South. Faulkner's feelings about the sterile nature of escapist utopias were explicit and left no room for misunderstanding. For example, he has this to say about Ike McCaslin's attitude in "The Bear":

> There are some people in any time and age that cannot face and cope with the problems. There seem to be three stages: The first says, This is rotten, I'll have no part of it, I will take death first. The second says, This is rotten, I don't like it, I can't do anything about it, but at least I will not participate in it myself, I will go off into a cave or climb a pillar to sit on. The third says, This stinks and I'm going to do something about it. McCaslin is the second. He says, This is bad, and I will withdraw from it. What we need are people who will say, This is bad and I'm going to do something about it, I'm going to change it. (*FiU* 245–46)

4. José Antonio Maravall, *Utopia and Counterutopia in the "Quixote,"* trans. Robert W. Felkel (Detroit: Wayne State University Press, 1991); originally published as *Utopía y contrautopía en el "Quijote,"* (Santiago de Compostela: Pico Sacro, 1976).

However, as much as he criticizes Isaac McCaslin's conservative idealism, Faulkner also expresses through him a tribute to nature in its virgin state, a sort of eulogy to the splendors of a purer world that progress has damaged beyond repair. Faulkner's ambivalent respect for the past can also be seen in his response to a question about the Compsons and the Snopes representing two opposite stances in life, when he said, "I feel sorry for the Compsons. That was blood which was good and brave once, but has thinned and faded all the way out. Of the Snopes, I'm terrified" (*FiU* 197).

In Faulkner, the sense of decline and fall springs from an epic notion of former times that were simpler than the present in the sense that man was not plagued with doubts about his purpose and place in the world, about his identity. These were times in which heroic action was still possible and money was not yet the power nexus that determined social relations. Louis D. Rubin believes that the origin of this feeling of decline and fall that informs the history of Yoknapatawpha County is to be found in Faulkner's heroic conception of its early settlers as "dashing, reckless men of action, . . . gallant patricians who live perilously and die gloriously." Rubin also finds that "Faulkner's attitude toward [these men] is compounded both of admiration and a certain amount of skepticism." The myth woven around Yoknapatawpha's settlers comes from what W. J. Cash has called the "fiercely self-assertive" nature and "intense individualism" of the "basic Southerner," a frontiersman who was "an exceedingly simple fellow. . . . A man, indeed, who, because of one, two, or more generations in the backcountry was an even more uncomplex sort than had been the original immigrants from Europe." The most salient features of 'this rustic figure" are "great personal courage, unusual physical powers, the ability to drink a quart of whiskey or to lose the whole of one's capital on the turn of a card without the quiver of a muscle."[5]

According to Joseph Blotner, Colonel William Clark Falkner, Faulkner's great-grandfather and his model for Colonel Sartoris, was a self-made man who forged his personality in the arduous frontier way of life. He led a turbulent and eventful existence and was no stranger to violence, duels, and even charges of murder. Colonel Falkner's uncle, John Wesley Thompson, brought him up in accordance with the codes that prevailed in those unexplored territories of northern Mississippi, and he learned the lessons well.

5. Louis D. Rubin, Jr., "The Discovery of a Man's Vocation," in *A Gallery of Southerners* (Baton Rouge: Louisiana State University Press, 1982), 6; Cash, *Mind of the South*, 30–39.

"The governing code there was an uncomplicated one," Joseph Blotner remarks, transcribing the words of a chronicler of that period who said, "A man ought to fear God and mind his own business. He should be respectful and courteous to all women; he should love his friends and hate his enemies. He should eat when he was hungry, drink when he was thirsty, dance when he was merry, vote for the candidate he liked best, and knock down any man who questioned his right to these privileges."[6] William Faulkner's grandfather would tell his grandson stories about the "Old Colonel," who was not only a qualified lawyer, planter, writer, and leading figure behind the first Mississippi railroad but also a lieutenant at the siege of Monterey and a Confederate colonel in the Civil War. Matchless stories, one could say, such as might enthrall the imagination of a Quentin Compson. Faulkner draws upon the myth of those times in his depiction of a world idealized by those of his characters who seem to believe a past superior order can provide them with the spiritual recognition and gratification they lack in their present circumstances.

Marthe Robert's description of the romantic aspects of quixotism in her stimulating study of *Don Quixote* is clearly applicable to Faulkner's worshipers of the past: "The quixotic intelligence is enamoured of romanticism's respect for the past, its faith in the myths of childhood, its belief in an eternal recurrence—a consolation for the inability to live, for the fear of the present. The quixotic adventurer also believes in the ideal, in love and unity. . . . Always drawn backward, the quixotic character hopes for a return to a primal state that would destroy history and restore primitive purity and unity. . . . Indeed, Don Quixote might be taken for the brother, even for the true spiritual master, of all romantics." Many of Faulkner's characters commonly called "romantic" do share many traits with the romantic hero, but they also share with Don Quixote an awareness of the deceptive nature of their longings. It is in such self-awareness that Robert finds the distinction between romanticism and quixotism: while the romantic "makes a virtue of necessity and disguises as a choice his incurable inability to live, the quixotic figure feels it imperative to see himself as he really is: chimerical, irresponsible, dissatisfied."[7] Thus, in the same way that Don Quixote knows that Dulcinea is not really a lady, so Quentin knows

---

6. Joseph Blotner, *Faulkner: A Biography*, 2 vols. (New York: Random House, 1974), 1:12.

7. Robert, *The Old and the New*, 42–43.

that his sister Caddy is aware of what she is doing and the consequences her acts might have. He also knows that his obsession with defending her nonexistent honor is nothing more than a reflection of his own convulsed mind. Likewise, Ike McCaslin understands that the world of Sam Fathers, which he wishes to perpetuate at all costs, has finally come to an end, as must all things that have fulfilled their destiny.

The need felt by these last patricians of Yoknapatawpha County to make their lives conform to some ideal scheme can also be seen as a consequence of their belonging to a social class that has lost its function. Erich Auerbach remarks that Don Quixote's flight from reality is an effort "to enforce his claim to the function proper to the class to which he belongs."[8] Similarly, through Quentin Compson in *The Sound and the Fury* and Gavin Stevens in *The Town* and in *The Mansion* Faulkner depicts the decline of the knightly function and the attempt to play the knightly role when it has already become obsolete. As the plains of La Mancha are to Amadis' mythical land, so the new South is to the legendary South of former times in the county of Yoknapatawpha. So we see Gavin Stevens, in his desire to restore Yoknapatawpha's former honor and pride, striving hopelessly to prevent the Snopeses from taking over the county.

In Faulkner's portrait of the Snopeses it is easy to see what the new South represented for him: the arrival on the political and economic scene of a new self-seeking and rapacious class that replaces dignity and honor with ambition and that sees economic success as the fundamental value of social prestige. Faulkner is convinced that the South died in the Civil War: "There is a thing known whimsically as the New South to be sure, but it is not the south." He sees the rise of the Snopeses and their depredations in the town of Jefferson as something rotten and sickly and never refers to them without pointing out their brutish nature and degrading materialism. For example, he deplores their "shooting . . . does not only when law but the Master too said not, shooting them not even because the meat was needed but leaving the meat itself to be eaten by scavengers in the woods, shooting it simply because it was big and moving and alien, of an older time than the little grubby stores and the accumulating and compounding

---

8. Erich Auerbach, *Mimesis: The Representation of Reality in Western Literature*, trans. Willard R. Trask (Princeton: Princeton University Press, 1953), 137.

money."[9] And in an interview Faulkner remarked that the unscrupulous Snopes "creep over [the town of Jefferson] lahk mold over cheese and destroy its traditions and whatever lav'liness there was in the place" (*LiG* 39). We may also associate the new class with the ferocious capitalism prevailing in the North, which rapidly undermined the Jeffersonian dream of democracy and equality, the same dream that Faulkner cherished for America as a whole. The Snopeses represent what can happen to people when they forget what is vital to their fulfillment as human beings, the "absolutes" such as love, honor, mercy, pride and humility that Faulkner emphasized repeatedly—in short, the praiseworthy values of the chivalric spirit. The Snopeses "are men that can cope with the new industrial age," Faulkner acknowledges, "but there will be something left . . . of the old cavalier spirit that will appear, that does appear. By cavalier spirit, I mean people who believe in simple honor for the sake of honor, and honesty for the sake of honesty" (*FiU* 80).

But the complexity of Faulkner's world cannot be encapsulated in the facile dichotomy of patricians and plebeian upstarts, the former devoted to the chivalric ethic as an ideal of behavior, the latter a symbol of vulgarity and spiritual banality. Consider Faulkner's objections to the attitude of the last young descendants of the patrician families in the county: "There are too many Jasons in the South who can be successful, just as there are too many Quentins in the South who are too sensitive to face its reality" (*FiU* 17). Not only does Faulkner censure the attitude of Jason Compson, who in order to survive in a world dominated by the Snopeses becomes one of them, he also criticizes Quentin, whose inability to see anything positive in his present drives him deeper into an idealism that will eventually destroy him. Thus, from the perspective of the South at a historic crossroads, facing the contending forces of a declining rural order and the emerging industrial capitalism at the dawn of the twentieth century, Faulkner shares Cervantes' critical stance toward all those who seek to evade history by resorting to myth as a substitute for reality. There are elements of the chivalric ethic, however, for which Faulkner reserves a special esteem: courage,

---

9. William Faulkner, "An Introduction to *The Sound and the Fury*" (*Mississippi Quarterly* version), in *William Faulkner: "The Sound and the Fury,"* ed. David Minter (New York: Norton, 1987), 221; William Faulkner, "Mississippi," in *Essays, Speeches, and Public Letters,* ed. James B. Meriwether (New York: Random House, 1965), 12–13.

essential for any man of self-respect, and a sense of honor, which, according to Cleanth Brooks, in Faulkner means "something very close to self-respect—an unwillingness to stoop to certain actions that a man believes are degrading and contemptible." Gavin Stevens' words to his nephew Chick Mallison are a statement of Faulkner's ethics: "Some things you must always be unable to bear. Some things you must never stop refusing to bear. Injustice and outrage and dishonor and shame. . . . Not for kudos and not for cash: your picture in the paper nor money in the bank either. Just refuse to bear them."[10]

In many instances Faulkner's characters carry the defense of honor to quixotic lengths. For them honor is intrinsically associated with both self-respect and personal identity. The defense of honor in Faulkner is closely related to a moral force that makes these characters even more determined to follow a course of action even though they are aware of its ultimate futility. As a result of this moral attitude, their actions never appear grotesque and sometimes may even seem admirable, even when the author does not appear to share in their obsessions. Cleanth Brooks regards this close alliance between honor and moral strength (a courage that in turn gives rise to physical valor) as a salient feature in Faulkner's work, and he cites the example of Bayard Sartoris in *The Unvanquished* sallying forth unarmed to meet Redmond, the man who killed his father. His act may be considered quixotic folly, but Faulkner finds the defense of personal conviction praiseworthy even when it seems doomed to failure from the start, even when, as in Bayard's case, it redounds to his own disadvantage. In this episode Bayard shows that for him the notion of honor is no longer associated with outer displays of bravery but resides in an inner courage that springs from an awareness of what is right and needs no validation from the outside world. Redmond shows great courage and a highly developed sense of honor by sparing Bayard's life, walking away from the scene and leaving Jefferson and Mississippi never to return. And if both men make a great display of quixotic boldness, it is precisely to this valiant conduct that Faulkner refers when he insists on the human being's capacity to preserve a lofty moral bearing even in the most extreme situations. For both Bayard and Redmond, self-respect is as important as life itself. Bertram Wyatt-

10. Cleanth Brooks, *On the Prejudices, Predilections, and Firm Beliefs of William Faulkner* (Baton Rouge: Louisiana State University Press, 1987), 20; William Faulkner, *Intruder in the Dust* (New York: Random House, 1948), 206.

Brown has pointed out how "honor in both its heroic and inglorious aspects was the central theme of much of [Faulkner's] work."[11] The preceding example shows the heroic face of honor. In Faulkner's "champion of dames" we find the less brilliant side of honor. In both instances, however, and in equal measure, moral courage and a quest for goodness drive the characters and fuel their futile quixotic strivings.

When Faulkner claims for his denizens of Yoknapatawpha the undeniable right of every individual to dignity—the gentlemen, the blacks and poor whites alike—he has Don Quixote firmly in mind, not so much because of his swaggering and braggadocio but rather for his fragile obstinacy. For example we see Lucas Beauchamp in *Intruder in the Dust,* whose self-respect is virtually his sole possession in the world, clinging to his meager purse as if to self-esteem itself and scrupulously counting from it the coins until he has the two dollars he owes lawyer Stevens for "representing [his] case." For the last descendants of the Yoknapatawpha patricians, a sense of honor is the final glimmer cast by the code of their class. For the dispossessed it is a way of combating the degrading conditions of life and a means of clinging to some semblance of humanity. Both classes demonstrate, as in Alexander Welsh's assessment of Don Quixote's obstinance, "the quantity of self-assertion, the disproportion between personal commitment and rational motive, inherent in efforts to save individual integrity."[12]

Sense of honor and the quixotic quest are closely intertwined in the Bundren family in *As I Lay Dying*, as they stubbornly insist on taking Addie to the Jefferson cemetery to be buried in compliance with her last wishes. They withstand all the mishaps and calamities that befall them with a kind of blind resolution. The journey becomes an epic of pyrrhic dimensions as the imbalance between their fidelity to their promise and the huge effort required to keep it gives rise to scenes of burlesque heroism worthy of the Knight of La Mancha. The Bundrens' undertaking is accepted without demur by everyone in family except Darl, the only one who regards it as an act of madness. The fulfillment of their pledge appears to all who witness it

11. Cleanth Brooks, *On the Prejudices*, 19–23; Bertram Wyatt-Brown, *Southern Honor: Ethics and Behavior in the Old South* (New York: Oxford University Press, 1982), 21.

12. Faulkner, *Intruder in the Dust*, 244; Alexander Welsh, *Reflections on the Hero as Quixote* (Princeton: Princeton University Press, 1981), 27.

to have no connection with reality: "She's been dead long enough to get over that sort of foolishness," says Samson, one of the Bundren's neighbors. "I got just as much respect for the dead as ere a man, but you've got to respect the dead themselves, and a woman that's been dead in a box four days, the best way to respect her is to get her into the ground as quick as you can." Other characters, such as Tull, Armstid, and Dr. Peabody, all agree that the Bundrens' determination to comply with Addie's last wishes is madness. But her widowed husband, Anse, responds to all his neighbors' reproaches in the same blunt way: "It's Addie I give the promise to. Her mind is set on it."[13]

In spite of the grotesque nature of the characters and the setting of the story, in *As I Lay Dying* Faulkner stresses the family's firm resistance to misfortune. No matter how imbalanced their behavior may seem, it is never pathetic. When Cleanth Brooks defines the Bundrens' exploit as "a commentary upon man's power to act and endure, upon his apparently incorrigible idealism . . . appalling but not scathing or debunking,"[14] he is pointing out not only the quixotic nature of their eccentric undertaking but also a characteristic peculiar to some of Faulkner's poor whites: they may be preposterous in purpose without necessarily being moral or practical failures. The Bundrens' quixotism—their exaggerated defense of family honor and insistence on completing a journey against all considerations of common sense—is not necessarily fruitless or hopeless, nor does it lead to tragedy; on the contrary, it brings out the best in them and reveals their resourcefulness in the face of adversity.

If the Bundrens' venture is quixotic, that of the tall convict in "Old Man," a perilous odyssey which takes him through the great Mississippi floods of April 1927, is no less so. His wanderings take place over a month, beginning and ending in the Parchman Penitentiary, from which he is released with the express purpose of rescuing a man and a woman who are in danger of being swept away by the river's swollen current. The tall convict, a mental adolescent in Faulkner's own estimation of his character (*FiU* 174), ingenuously believes in the authenticity of the deeds reported in "the Diamond Dicks and Jesse Jameses and such," and like Cervantes' Sorrowful Knight he, too, is deceived by literature. He was imprisoned at

---

13. William Faulkner, *As I Lay Dying* (1930; reprint, New York: Vintage, 1987), 102, 101.

14. Cleanth Brooks, *William Faulkner: First Encounters* (New Haven: Yale University Press, 1983), 94.

nineteen for "attempted train robbery," because he wanted not "the crass loot" but the glory that came with the deed, "a badge to show that he too was the best at his chosen gambit in the living and fluid world of his time." The convict soon learned the difference between life and fiction, for after "he had followed his printed (and false) authority to the letter . . . the day came [when] he did not even have a chance to go through the coaches and collect the watches and the rings, the brooches and the hidden money-belts, because he had been captured as soon as he entered the express car where the safe and the gold would be." The convict pays dearly for trying to emulate his fictional heroes. Nevertheless, he achieves something akin to heroism because of his unshakable sense of honor. "They cling to it: to give it up means giving up their humanity," Cleanth Brooks remarks on this virtue of Faulkner's poor whites. Like the Bundrens, the convict's highly developed sense of honor launches him on an epic journey that brings out his innate heroism.[15]

The convict's extraordinary rescue mission is shot through with the spirit of the Knight of La Mancha. This is evident both in his tenacity in the face of the many ordeals that befall him and seem to mock his purpose and in his unbreakable sense of honor. Witness his will to protect his charge, the woman—even against his own sexual impulses—and her new-born child, both of whom he has rescued from the waters, and take them back to the penitentiary against all odds. Or see how stubbornly he refuses to board the steamboat carrying the flood victims or to leave the Cajun hut unless he is allowed to salvage the skiff he was entrusted with and is deter-mined at all costs to take back with him. Even the final "reward" he re-ceives as compensation for his loyalty—a further ten years added to his sentence—is yet another demonstration of the blundering that invariably accompanies both the prisoner's and Don Quixote's undertakings. On his return to the penitentiary, the convict hands over to the sheriff everything he had promised to bring back: "Yonder's your boat, and here's the woman. But I never did find that bastard on the cottonhouse."[16] With these blunt words, full of comic undertone, Faulkner sums up his charac-ter's venture, the significance of which might be expressed thus: the mix-ture of naïveté, obstinacy, and clumsiness by which some of Faulkner's

---

15. William Faulkner, *The Wild Palms* (New York: Random House, 1939), 20–24; Brooks, *First Encounters*, 22.

16. Faulkner, *Wild Palms*, 278.

poor whites withstand the buffetings of fate enable them to rise above their allotted station in life and aspire to the heroic at the same time that their almost preposterous steadfastness wins for them a higher degree of humanity.

The same mixture of unmindful daring and stubbornness can be found in Lena Grove of *Light in August*, for whom Faulkner felt a strong attachment. Such qualities enable her to bear the unenviable fate that life holds for her. In the opening pages of the novel, memorable for their placid beauty and the warm and simple portrait they draw of a very lovable character, we see Lena pregnant, trusting, and unsuspecting as she trudges along the road. Lena sets out on the journey from her native Alabama to Jefferson, Mississippi, in search of Lucas Burch, the man whose child she carries in her womb. She wants her unborn child to have a father, according to God's will as she understands it: "I reckon a family ought to all be together when a chap comes. Specially the first one. I reckon the Lord will see to that" (*LA* 18). Armstid and his wife, Cora, somewhat confounded by this mixture of confidence and helplessness, believe that Lena will certainly need that divine assistance. But Lena goes impassively on her way, hitching rides on one wagon after another with the steadfastness of a goddess, or perhaps with the unmindful courage of someone who has nothing to lose, "backrolling now behind her a long monotonous succession of peaceful and undeviating changes from day to dark and dark to day again, through which she advanced in identical and anonymous and deliberate wagons as though through a succession of creakwheeled and limpeared avatars, like something moving forever and without progress across an urn" (*LA* 6).

Lena's capacity for bending reality to fit the dictates of her desires leads her to dismiss any doubts that might endanger her purpose. "Like as not, he already sent me the word and it got lost on the way" (*LA* 17), says Lena of the man she is looking for, repeating this explanation every time she tries to persuade others to believe what she insists on believing. When she eventually reaches Jefferson and comes into contact with the circles frequented by Burch, she learns that a man named Joe Brown coincides with the description she gives of Lucas Burch. He lives in a cabin with another man, Joe Christmas, and rumors are circulating to the effect that both men are involved in the illicit production of whiskey and are suspected of involvement in a fire that has recently destroyed the big rambling house near their cabin, the property of a certain Miss Bundren. Lena learns all this from Byron Bunch, to whom she has erroneously gone in the course of her wandering search. She learns enough to know that Joe Brown and Lucas Burch are in fact the same person: "It has been three days. She must know, whether you told her or not. She must have heard by now," says the Reverend Gail Hightower to Byron, his friend and confidant (*LA* 263). Byron's reply, both shrewd and to the point, confirms what we have suspected from the start—that this young woman, absurdly convinced that a bright future awaits both her and her child, is not about to let go of her deeply held beliefs:

> I never even had any need to keep it from her, to lie it smooth. It was like she knew beforehand what I would say, that I was going to lie to her. Like she had already thought of that herself, and that she already didn't believe it before I even said it, and that was all right too. . . . It's like she was in two parts, and one of them knows that he is a scoundrel. But the other part believes that when a man and a woman are going to have a child, that the Lord will see that they are all together when the right time comes. Like it was God that looks after woman, to protect them from men. (*LA* 263–64)

Byron's reflections illustrate that Lena's story is a tale of resolve that knows how to wrest something for itself from inauspicious reality. Although things turn out very differently than she expected when she reaches Jefferson, at least she finds in Byron a father for her child and a more hopeful future. Asked about what he thought of Malcolm Cowley's view that most of his characters, including Lena Grove, were "hunted, obsessed, driven forward by some inner necessity,"[17] as if ruled by a feeling of submissiveness to their fate, Faulkner offered this corrective with regard to his spirited heroine: "I would say that Lena Grove in *Light in August* coped pretty well with hers. It didn't really matter to her in her destiny whether her man was Lucas Burch or not. It was her destiny to have a husband and children and she knew it, and so she went out and attended to it without asking help from anyone. She was the captain of her soul. . . . She was never for one moment confused, frightened, alarmed. She did not even know that she didn't need pity" (*LiG* 253).

The peaceful coexistence of these two sides of Lena's personality as

17. Malcolm Cowley, "Introduction" to *The Portable Faulkner*, rev. and enl., ed. Malcolm Cowley (New York: Viking Press, 1967), xxiii.

Byron Bunch has described them, one side with a firm grasp of reality, the other refusing to see it when it does not suit her, keeps Lena going, accompanied now by Byron himself, transformed into her gallant protector. And she carries on without dwelling much on the ruffian whom two months before she had set out to find. "Here comes Saulsbury," announces the furniture dealer in whose truck Byron, Lena, and her son are traveling, "Saulsbury, Tennessee." Lena, astonished at the distance they have covered, utters these subdued words of amazement as sole epitaph for her troubled journey: "My, my. A body does get around. Here we aint been coming from Alabama but two months, and now it's already Tennessee" (*LA* 444). Faulkner implicitly reaffirms Lena's ability to cope with her destiny in these final words.

In *The Reivers* Faulkner explores once more the possibilities of the quixotic journey, this time in its picaresque form. When he launches eleven-year-old Lucius Priest, Boon Hogganbeck, and Ned McCaslin on a journey from Jefferson to Memphis in Lucius' grandfather's automobile, it is not in quest of the heroic, as we have seen with the Bundrens or the tall convict, but in pursuit of high adventure. While at first glance each of their separate goals appears to be entirely unrelated to one another—Boon is after a sexual adventure, Ned after financial gain, and young Lucius hits the road to get away from daily routine at home—all three adventurers become entangled in the worthy defense of a prostitute's honor and in the valiant search for a golden tooth belonging to a black maid.

But unlike Don Quixote and his squire Sancho, these boys are not ill-equipped to face the ordeals they encounter along the way. For the trials of Hurricane Creek and the mudhole of Hell Creek they count on Boon's physical strength, with some assistance from a mudfarmer and his "color-blind mules." They rely on Ned's shrewdness, as shown in his scheme for the horse race, and Lucius is the moral guide for them all. Their zest in overcoming misfortune is quixotic, as Lucius observes after conquering Hell Creek: "It did seem as though we had won a reprieve as a reward for invincible determination, or refusal to recognize defeat when we faced it or it faced us" (*Rv* 93). And quixotic, too, are their blunders, as when Lucius, baffled at the inconsistencies of progress, charges the automobile, the "expensive useless mechanical toy rated in power and strength by the dozens of horses," with being "helpless and impotent in the almost infantile clutch of a few inches of the temporary confederation of two mild and pacific elements—earth and water" (*Rv* 87). But these Mississippian knights do not fail practically in the manner of the Don. On the contrary, they achieve a greater reward than they might have expected at the start of their journey. Lucius' moral stance causes Miss Corrie to regain her self-respect. Boon, by virtue of Lucius' act, also acquires some self-esteem when he chooses to respect and to love the reformed prostitute, now Everbe Corinthia. And Ned, "a Missippi [sic] swamp rat," can experience the glory and recognition he has always longed for. Once more the strong will and often preposterous determination of these characters yields practical results.

Of all the quixotic journeys discussed so far, that portrayed in *The Reivers* is the most faithful to the plot of the chivalric romance. There is the departure followed by the perilous journey and the return with a reward for the trials undergone. But the parody of the chivalric romance built upon the bizarre, mismatched trio of knights—a well-mannered young boy, a giant simpleton, and a shrewd black servant—and upon the imbalance between their identities and the roles they perform never loses its benevolent tone. As Olga W. Vickery has rightly observed, this parody "is not permitted to destroy the shining thread of idealism which is [the book's] very essence."[18] For example, when Lucius finds himself face to face with vice at Miss Reba's brothel, where he had "to learn too much too fast, unassisted" (*Rv* 155), this sordid reality is transformed by his idealism—his firm belief that disrespect, humiliation, and outrage are unacceptable even in that setting—and by his steadfast defense of his conviction. His presence alone turns a sordid brothel into an almost respectable place, where, as Boon puts it, grumbling at Miss Corrie's objection to his rough language, "we'll have to try to forget the whole English language before we can even pass the time of day" (*Rv* 138). Most importantly, awareness, hope, and self-respect are now possible there. In *The Reivers*, his last work, Faulkner draws once more upon his conviction that, however misguided or wicked people's actions may sometimes be, human beings are always capable of nobility if they respond with the best in themselves.

"Honor for the sake of honor" is best depicted in Faulkner's portrayal of his champions of dames, who attempt to uphold the knightly function when it has little bearing upon reality. Quentin Compson in *The Sound and*

---

18. Olga W. Vickery, *The Novels of William Faulkner: A Critical Interpretation,* rev. ed. (Baton Rouge: Louisiana State University Press, 1964), 228.

the Fury and Gavin Stevens in *The Town* and *The Mansion* are the two most outstanding examples. Quentin Compson III, one of the last descendants not only of the Compson family but also of that legendary generation of men who in the not too distant past had fought valiantly in the Civil War, has sometimes been viewed as a southern Hamlet.[19] His portrait as a troubled and sensitive young man at odds with his surroundings and plunged into introspection lends itself well to comparison with Shakespeare's Danish prince. However, there is a dimension to Quentin's personality that places him closer to Don Quixote than to Hamlet. Very much like the Knight of La Mancha, Quentin protects himself against his importunate confusion by seeking shelter in an abstract world of his own making, and also in the manner of Don Quixote he tries to bring these abstractions to bear upon the world of facts with totally ineffectual results. His unfruitful attempts to bring his sense of honor and virtue to bear upon the events taking place around him confirm him as a quixotic figure. Thus we see him in the mission he assigns himself as defender of his sister's and the Compson family's honor and in the way he seizes upon it as a prop for his own moral scheme.

Also like Don Quixote, Quentin seeks to restore an outmoded social function by becoming the sole custodian of a presumably higher moral order, which, in Faulkner's literary imagination, existed in the fairly recent past and was relinquished in as little as two generations. "Quentin inherited [a basic failure] through his father, or beyond his father," Faulkner says. "Something had happened somewhere between the first Compson and Quentin" (*FiU* 3) that caused the decay of the "princely line." Quentin harks back to the time before this failure in an attempt to grasp a world of immovable certainty and to evade all the moral infirmities underscored by change and the passing of time. His obsession with a code of honor that

19. For views on Quentin Compson as a southern Hamlet see William R. Taylor, *Cavalier and Yankee: The Old South and American National Character* (New York: Braziller, 1961; reprint, London: W. H. Allen, 1963), 159–60; Richard Chase, "Faulkner, The Great Years: *The Sound and the Fury*," in *William Faulkner: "The Sound and the Fury,"* ed. David Minter (New York: Norton, 1983), 313; and Timothy K. Conley, "Resounding Fury: Faulkner's Shakespeare, Shakespeare's Faulkner," in *Shakespeare and Southern Writers: A Study in Influence,* ed. Philip C. Kolin (Jackson: University Press of Mississippi, 1985). For objections to the view of Quentin as a Hamlet figure see Irving Howe, *William Faulkner: A Critical Study* (1952; reprint, Chicago: Ivan R. Dee, 1991), 169–70.

has lost all relevance, "abstract, rigidified, even literary," as Cleanth Brooks has defined it, is a result of such an attitude. In an appendix given over to the Compson's lineage, Faulkner pinpoints Quentin's case thus: "QUENTIN III. Who loved not his sister's body but some concept of Compson honor precariously and (he knew well) only temporarily supported by a minute fragile membrane of her maidenhead as a miniature replica of all the whole vast globy earth may be poised on the nose of a trained seal."[20] Quentin's fragile world rests on obsolete and inflexible principles. It is tangled up with his father's bitter philosophy and deprived of affection by an unfeeling mother. It is "precariously" sustained by his sister's fragile chastity and collapses completely when Caddy flings herself into promiscuity in an attempt to make up for a loveless childhood. Thus Quentin's confrontation with Dalton Ames over a question of honor is really the outcome of his overriding need to cling to the rigid principles of his moral world even though such principles no longer have any relation to reality.

The duel between Quentin and Ames resembles Don Quixote's challenge to the Knight of the White Moon insofar as Quentin's fragility and naïveté stand out sharply against the arrogance of Ames, who is masterful and at ease in his own world. Faulkner casts a tender and compassionate gaze upon Quentin's shortsighted defense of his sister's chastity, to which she ascribes little or no importance. Faulkner's compassion for his character is manifest in the picture of Quentin defeated but not ridiculous. By providing him with insight into his real condition, Faulkner spares him from sheer ridicule. The exchange between the Quentin and Ames on the bridge illustrates this quite precisely. Although at first we see Quentin trying very hard to comply with what is required of a man of honor—he utters such resounding phrases as "I came to tell you to leave town" and "Ill give you until tonight" (*SF* 159–60)—we are left in no doubt that he is not up to the role he intends to perform. He is shaking, his mouth says things he doesn't want to say, and, quite unlike someone who dares to stage a showdown, he is incapable of fighting. His opponent is not in the least impressed with Quentin's bravado. "Listen no good taking it so hard its not your fault kid it would have been some other fellow," he tells Quentin in-

20. Cleanth Brooks, *William Faulkner: The Yoknapatawpha Country* (New Haven: Yale University Press, 1963), 337; William Faulkner, "Appendix: The Compsons (1699–1945)," in *The Portable Faulkner*, rev. and enl., ed. Malcolm Cowley (New York: Viking Press, 1967), 709–10.

decorously, to which Quentin replies: "Did you ever have a sister did you." Ames answers, "No, but theyre all bitches" (*SF* 160), reaffirming his modern crassness. Quentin then rushes at him and tries unsuccessfully to hit him: "I hit him I was still trying to hit him long after he was holding my wrists but I still tried then it was like I was looking at him through a piece of colored glass I could hear my blood and then I could see the sky again and branches against it and the sun slanting through them and he holding me on my feet" (*SF* 161). Ames does no more than restrain his attacker until he calms down, and when Quentin shows no sign of relenting, Ames decides to stand aside, leaving Caddy without offering any explanation. But here Quentin does not mistake reality. He knows he has been no match for Ames. "I knew that he hadnt hit me that he had lied about that for her sake too and that I had just passed out like a girl," he says and adds, "but even that didnt matter anymore" (*SF* 162), as if to imply that no victory over his adversary would free him from his anguish at his sister's shameless sexuality and Dalton Ames's overt masculinity.

Two more instances from *The Sound and the Fury* show Quentin trying to bring his code to bear upon the world of facts with the same unsuccessful results. His confrontation with Herbert Head, his sister's fiancé, is another quixotic rendezvous, and once more he makes a display of unrealistic behavior. Although we may sympathize with Quentin's efforts to keep his sister from marrying "a liar and a scoundrel," we are wholly aware that his endeavor is quite beside the point, especially considering the actual facts he overtly chooses to ignore—that Caddy finds herself pushed into this quick marriage of convenience because of her erratic conduct and that in her condition she has little choice. Herbert, unaware of Caddy's pregnancy, hopes that his marriage into the Compson family will redeem his reputation. So Quentin is quite right when he accuses him of being hypocritical and lacking any decent principles, although he fails to acknowledge that Herbert is also being cheated in this tragedy of interests. Disregarding all the evidence, Quentin assumes the role of the man of honor who has caught the villain red-handed. "I dont know but one way to consider cheating I dont think I'm likely to learn different at Harvard" (*SF* 108), he says, resuming his moral stance at Herbert's suggestion that life will eventually teach him how to compromise. Quentin threatens to expose Herbert's cheating at cards and midterm exams and rejects all of Herbert's offers to buy his silence out of hand. ("To hell with your money" [*SF* 110], he says.) Quentin's words acquire an even more pathetic ring when we learn that Herbert has already "bought" the Bascomb side of the family. He has offered Jason a job and provided Mrs. Compson with a way out of family disgrace, which is her only worry. Thus Herbert's description of Quentin as a "half-baked Galahad," takes on deeper resonance. It is left to Caddy, however, to disclose the futile nature of Quentin's quest: "You're meddling in my business again didn't you get enough of that last summer" (*SF* 111), she reprimands him. But Quentin is too immersed in his own fixations to make any sense of her words.

Quentin's retreat from reality proves to be even greater at Harvard when he encounters the Kentuckian Gerald Bland, a bully who enjoys bragging about his virility and his sexual conquests. Bland makes an improper remark in Quentin's presence about the easy virtue of certain women. Quentin, fired by the memory of his promiscuous sister, instantly springs at Bland. Later, unable to account for his own behavior, he listens to Spoade's description of the incident: "The first I knew was when you jumped up all of a sudden and said, 'Did you ever have a sister? did you' and when he said No, you hit him. I noticed you kept on looking at him, but you didn't seem to be paying any attention to what anybody was saying until you jumped up and asked him if he had any sisters"(*SF* 166). Shreve and Spoade, Quentin's classmates at Harvard, see their friend as an unusual case, a species on the road to extinction: "the champion of dames," Spoade exclaims mockingly. "Bud, you excite not only admiration, but horror" (*SF* 167). When Quentin announces that he intends to apologize to Gerald, Spoade further mocks his code of honor and the inflexibility of his principles: "He ought to go back so they'll know he fights like a gentleman. . . . Gets licked like one, I mean" (*SF* 167). Then, when Quentin is accused of kidnapping Julio's sister, Shreve says, "Well, bud . . . I'll be damned if you dont go to a lot of trouble to have your fun. Kidnapping, then fighting. What do you do on your holidays? burn houses?" (*SF* 165). Shreve's remark is prompted by the same kind of inopportune blundering on Quentin's part that characterizes so many of Don Quixote's deeds.

However much Quentin's last-ditch attempts to defend his sister's virtue are justified by a question of honor, his obsessive and tormented behavior suggests that he is more afraid of not conforming to the male standards of the society he lives in with regard to sexual matters. Acceptance of his sister's sexual conduct would be tantamount to throwing all the known and trusted tenets of his own world overboard. In this regard Louis D. Rubin observes, "What has motivated Quentin's quixotic assault upon the much more powerful Gerald is less [the defense of female honor] than fear that Gerald's view of the world is right and that sexual promiscuity is inescapable." It is not family honor or his sister's virginity that Quentin defends with such vehemence but rather a system of values that are comprehensible to him. As a new ethic collides with the old values of a society in decline, when the Compsons are no longer among the elect but are tarnished and in decay, and when Caddy, the putative inheritor of the role of lady, places on her virginity "no value whatever"—since "the frail physical stricture" is to her "no more than a hangnail would have been," Quentin still persists in trying to uphold that which no one calls him to uphold.[21]

Quentin's virginal quality contrasts sharply with the profile Faulkner draws of his opponents, who are portrayed as having an uncomplicated way of dealing with reality, from which, in turn, they try to derive as much satisfaction as they can. On the other hand, they lack what Quentin has too much of—manners, principles. Doubtless they all "missed gentility," as Quentin puts it, referring to Dalton Ames, whom he accuses of being a "theatrical fixture. Just papier-mache" (*SF* 92). Likewise, Gerald Bland, pretentious and despotic, comes across as a sorry parody of the dashing southerner, and Herbert Head seems to lack any decency or self-esteem. Quentin is certainly no exemplar of good sense, but neither does Faulkner endow his opponents with any outstanding virtues. And to the extent to which they show no understanding of Quentin's profound distress, we are faced with a disparity of sensibilities. Faulkner frequently expresses admiration for those of his characters who know how to make the best of their circumstances, but here he reveals his sympathy for Quentin's predicament. Thus Quentin, agent and victim of ineffectual action, and without any rewarding relation with the world around him, appears as the epitome of "all that is ingenuous and afflicted in the world,"[22] to borrow Fernando Saveter's description of Don Quixote.

The most salient of Quentin's quixotic traits is that he stands completely alone with his own contrivances. Out of this solitude he struggles against windmills of his own making, leaving him, in the words of his creator, "about halfway between madness and sanity" (*FiU* 95–96). A brief consideration of the other characters of Quentin's generation is enough to

21. Rubin, "A Man's Vocation," 12; Faulkner, "Appendix," 710.
22. Savater, *Instrucciones*, 14–15.

demonstrate that none of them share the obsessions of the hopeless protagonist. Shreve McCannon, the most sound-minded among them, cannot comprehend Quentin's ancestral reversions to the South. "Listen, I'm not trying to be funny, smart. I just want to understand it if I can," he says in *Absalom, Absalom!*, trying to explain how alien Quentin's attachment to the past seems to him. The moral scheme and the code of honor that Quentin seeks so jealously to preserve seem equally remote to the southerners Gerald Bland and Spoade. The former keeps himself busy with his "horses," his "niggers," and his "women." Of Spoade, Quentin observes— not without humor—that he is "the world's champion sitter-around" (*SF* 92); he is the prototype of the placid and indolent southerner, virtually untroubled by life. Finally there is Quentin's brother, Jason, whom Faulkner ironically calls "the first sane Compson since before Culloden." Jason is the exact opposite of Quentin. He is rational and practical, able to make of necessity a virtue and firmly rooted in the material world, after the manner of Sancho Panza, when it comes to making the most of circumstances.[23]

But is Quentin's solitude the solitude of the tragic hero or the solitude of Don Quixote? Fernando Savater makes a distinction between the two types of hero that sheds some light on Quentin Compson's case. Savater finds similarities between the two, insofar as "the tragic figure," like Don Quixote, "neither compromises nor yields to persuasion" but "persists in his springs of action, redoubles his obsession and goes unswervingly on his way until his final undoing; he is both possessed and fastidious." Thus far they are the same, but herein lies the difference: the tragic hero is defined by insurmountable contradictions and impossibilities, yet we understand that "had the world been otherwise, he might have triumphed, or by his actions made the world a better place." Don Quixote, on the other hand, could never have "triumphed" or improved the world around him. Savater explains that this is because his actions arise from "purely private choice, unshared by anyone in the social context of his adventures," and thus he is "defeated at the very outset. He is out of tune with both the possibilities and the difficulties of his age. He is absurdly alone."[24]

23. William Faulkner, *Absalom, Absalom!* (New York: Random House, 1964), 361; Faulkner, "Appendix," 715. Olga W. Vickery has said of Jason Compson that he "sees himself as a modern Sancho Panza who could never mistake a windmill for an army, but who has no objections to others doing so, especially if he can turn it to his own advantage." See her *"The Sound and the Fury: A Study in Perspective,"* in *William Faulkner: "The Sound and the Fury,"* ed. David Minter (New York: Norton, 1983), 305.

24. Savater, *Instrucciones*, 14–15.

Viewed in the light of Savater's distinctions, Quentin indeed possesses some of the traits of the tragic hero. We are aware of the reasons that compel him, and we may conceive that his life might have unfolded differently if his world had been other than it was, if his family environment had been more propitious, if his mother had been more capable of love and affection, or if his father had not been such a broken reed. Quentin is driven to suicide by problems he cannot resolve, which eventually become unbearable obsessions. They are problems typical of an adolescent, but in him they grow out of proportion. It is reasonable to suppose that under different, more supportive family conditions, Quentin might have found a way through his anguish and so avoided a tragic end. But if these considerations place him among the descendants of "the race of Ajax and Antigone," there are others by which he might be more properly compared with Don Quixote. These concern his vain and lonely determination to seek solutions to the problems that plague him by enclosing himself within a world of his own making that allows no encroachment from without. Quentin is "absurdly" alone in his insistence on being the self-appointed defender of his family's and his sister's honor. The values of his private world are forever being refuted by reality until they become grotesque and anachronistic, and his efforts to maintain them are futile and misguided. He is fighting a battle that is lost before it is begun.

In Quentin Compson, Faulkner depicts the conflicts of an individual who cannot find his niche in history. Faulkner presents Quentin's drama as the shadowy side of the denial of reality with the fateful consequences attendant upon a life ruled by abstract values and transformed into the only view of reality possible. Quentin's unresolved problems with virginity and his pitiable way of holding onto abstract values in order to avoid confronting reality account for his emotional disturbances. Idea and matter, spirit and flesh, vice and virtue remain hostile, irreconcilable pairs to him. However, between Quentin's benighted obsessions and his father's nihilism, summed up in the lapidary phrase "nothing is even worth the changing of it" (*SF* 78), Faulkner inclines toward the former, examining Quentin's futile, desperate, stumbling quest and treating with dignity his agonizing way of dealing with the world.

The epithet "champion of dames" applies equally well to Gavin Stevens, without doubt the most notable representative of chivalric love in Faulkner's work. Gavin Stevens closely resembles Cervantes' prodigious knight, as much for the misfortune heaped on his head because of his lady as for the crusade he carries on against the Snopeses. Once again Faulkner explores the theme of the incorrigible idealism that strives to prevent reality from ruining its dreams. He achieves this, in great measure, by means of a dialogue between the straightforward, astute, and humane sewing-machine salesman V. K. Ratliff and Gavin Stevens, the cultured, highly sensitive lawyer. Ratliff is akin to Sancho Panza, in his shrewd observation of reality and his ability to express his premonitions bluntly and clearly. Gavin Stevens is a born idealist who tries to impose his heart's desire on reality. Once more we witness a questing knight seeking to defend what he believes must be defended even though no one has asked him to do so.

Faulkner tells us that Gavin is "a good man" even though he suffers from an overdose of idealism, for which reason "he didn't succeed in living up to his ideal" (*LiG* 225). Excess, as J. R. Longley, Jr., has so rightly observed, is Stevens' most salient feature.[25] It is manifest in the degree to which he devotes himself to his cause, in his tendency to magnify the object of his love, and even in his honesty, since, as Ratliff puts it, Gavin is "a feller that even his in-growed toenails was on the outside of his shoes" (*Twn* 342). In *The Town* and *The Mansion* Gavin Stevens evinces enough quixotic attributes to establish himself as the most distinctly quixotic character in Yoknapatawpha County. He is portrayed as a cultured man of some sensibility with a sound university education, all of which provides him with an intellect unusual among those of his social acquaintance. He is so well read that he seems almost comical and eccentric when set against the kind of society he moves among in Jefferson. V. K. Ratliff, who provides the most conspicuous authorial voice in these novels, particularly in diagnosing the paradoxes that bedevil Gavin's life, describes him as "a town-raised bachelor that was going to need a Master of Arts from Harvard and a Doctor of Philosophy from Heidelberg just to stiffen him up to where he could cope with the natural normal Yoknapatawpha County folks that never wanted nothing except jest to break a few aggravating laws that was in their way or get a little free money outen the county treasury" (*TM* 116).

One might add that for all his potential, Gavin Stevens is unable to achieve success in his greatest undertaking, namely, to rid Yoknapatawpha

---

25. John Lewis Longley, Jr., *The Tragic Mask: A Study of Faulkner's Heroes* (Chapel Hill: University of North Carolina Press, 1963), 38. Longley sees Gavin Stevens' problems as "a matter of degree of excess," and not derived from being "self-deceived or a fool."

County of the Snopeses. A further discrepancy between the ideal and reality in Gavin Stevens' life is his proclivity to romantic idealization, which prevents him from achieving tangible fulfillment in love. Ratliff has something to say about this, too: "It wasn't that he was born too soon or too late or even in the wrong place. He was born at exactly the right time, only in the wrong envelope. It was his fate and doom not to been born into one of them McCarron separate covers too instead of into that fragile and what you might call gossamer-sinewed envelope of boundless and hopeless aspiration Old Monster give him" (*TM* 128). McCarron is the young man who won Eula Varner's favor when she lived with her parents in Frenchman's Bend and who was forced to run away when she became pregnant. McCarron is the exact opposite of Gavin; he knows what he wants, and he knows how to get it when the right opportunity presents itself. By means of this contrast, Faulkner brings up again the dichotomy we have already remarked upon in *The Sound and the Fury* between the man who accepts things for what they are and the man who is a prey to idealization. Eula Varner's first flame, McCarron, and Manfred de Spain, her long-time lover, are instances of the first type. Gavin is a clear example of the second.

V. K. Ratliff explains how Eula Varner becomes involved in Gavin's life in *The Mansion*. Eula, recently settled in Jefferson with Flem Snopes, makes her first appearance in public in the main square, "where not jest Lawyer but all Jefferson too would have to see her" (*TM* 115). Ratliff tells us that Gavin is captivated the first time he lays eyes on her, mesmerized by a spiritual ideal in which he hopes to find justification for an impossible love: "There Lawyer was, rushing headlong into that engagement that not only the best he could expect and hope for but the best he could want would be to lose it, since losing it wouldn't do nothing but jest knock off some of his hide here and there. Rushing in with nothing in his hand to fight with but that capacity to stay nineteen years old the rest of his life" (*TM* 116). Ratliff thinks Eula is too much of a woman for Gavin. He also believes that Gavin knows it, too, "being nineteen years old and already one year at Harvard. Though even without Harvard," he is quick to add, "a boy nineteen years old ought to know that much about women jest by instinct, like a child or a animal knows fire is hot without having to actively put his hand or his foot in it" (*TM* 116). Nevertheless, ignoring instinct, Gavin Stevens chooses Eula as his object of ideal love, even though her affair with Manfred de Spain is common knowledge in Jefferson. Indeed, Gavin does his best to ignore this fact, too. "Just what is it about this that you cant stand?

That Mrs. Snopes may not be chaste, or that it looks like she picked Manfred de Spain out to be unchaste with?" Gavin's sister, Maggie, asks him, to which he replies: "Yes! . . . I mean no! It's all lies—gossip" (*Twn* 49). But the moment arrives when Gavin can no longer go on deceiving himself. He wages all-out war on Manfred de Spain. It is an unequal fight, however, in which Gavin stretches himself to the limit of his capabilities only to fall flat on his face most of the time, thwarted by de Spain's arrogance and mockery.

The rivalry acquires all the characteristics of a duel in burlesque. Gavin and de Spain decide to send corsages to all the women in the city, for instance; de Spain races by Gavin's house in his cut-out and, to compound his mockery, sends Gavin a bouquet with a used condom in it. Their rivalry culminates in a fistfight at the Christmas cotillion. The irony with which Gavin's brother-in-law, Charley, refers to the expectation surrounding the encounter is in itself an indication of what the outcome will be. Charley calls the antagonists "two red-combed roosters strutting at one another" and adds that expectations for a good fight will not be fulfilled because "Gavin don't know how to make trouble," to which Maggie objects protectively, "Gavin's a gentleman." "Sure," replies her husband. "[T]hat's what I said: it aint that he dont want to make trouble: he just dont know how. Oh, I dont mean he wont try. He'll do the best he knows. But he just dont know how to make the kind of trouble that a man like Manfred de Spain will take seriously" (*Twn* 58). That Gavin himself is aware of the improvidence of his act is made clear when he dismisses his sister's advice to stop at the barbershop: "If I'm to go on this crusade with any hope of success, the least I can do is look wild and shaggy enough to be believed" (*Twn* 49). Yet he insists on going through with his feeble role to the end. Faulkner restages the duel between Quentin Compson and Dalton Ames in the persons of Gavin Stevens and Manfred de Spain, Gavin's "mortal victorious rival and conqueror" (*TM* 129) in Ratliff's words. Gavin's idealistic and ingenuous nature bears the loser's brand and is thrown into highest relief against the brazen self-assuredness of his rival.

Chick provides a shrewd analysis of the events at the cotillion, accurately describing every paladin of chivalrous love: "Uncle Gavin wasn't trying any more to destroy or even hurt Mr de Spain because he had already found out by that time that he couldn't. . . . What he was doing was simply defending forever with his blood the principle that chastity and virtue in women shall be defended whether they exist or not" (*Twn* 76). This concurs precisely with Faulkner's own estimation of his derided knights-errant: "A constant sad and funny picture . . . the knight that goes out to defend somebody who don't want to be defended and don't need it. But it's a very fine quality in human nature. I hope it will always endure. It is comical and a little sad. And Quentin and Stevens were that much alike" (*FiU* 141).

Like Quentin, Gavin knows that an impossible love both enshrines and vindicates ideal love, safeguarding it from the touchstone of reality. It is a sophistry concealing a deeper feeling that Quentin is unable to express, but not Gavin Stevens, who, although similar in many ways to Quentin, is able to understand this deeper feeling as well as to voice it. Nothing illustrates this better than Gavin's first meeting with Eula, which takes place after the unpleasant events at the ball. (Eula, who has sent Gavin a note asking him to meet her one night at his office, hopes to get Gavin to drop the suit against de Spain over the brass stolen from the city powerhouse.) Gavin approaches the meeting with uncertainty and expectation. He is disturbed by the encounter, which he fears more than he desires. The reason for his fear comes to the surface as soon as he is face to face with the woman who has captivated him, "too small to have displaced enough of my peace to contain this much unsleep, to have disarranged this much of what I had at least thought was peace" (*Twn* 90). This moment of recognition coming at the moment when the object of Gavin's adoration is within his grasp parallels that which Maria Zambrano has described in Don Quixote. She asks whether Don Quixote really believes in Dulcinea as a creature of flesh and blood. "Does he not deliberately avoid meeting her face to face?" she asks. "Does not her absence constitute an imposed condition that is platonic in the extreme?" Torrente Ballester remarks, too, that Dulcinea is the pretext that allows Don Quixote to reject all other possible inamoratas. He thus avoids all temptations of the flesh, which, had he yielded to them, would have quickly demolished all his illusions.[26]

Eula symbolizes sensual pleasure and unhindered sexuality, and as such she is the exact opposite of Gavin, who seeks transcendence through love.

---

26. Maria Zambrano, *España, sueño y verdad* (Spain, dream and reality) (Barcelona: Edhasa, 1982), 27 (my translation); Gonzalo Torrente Ballester, *El "Quijote" como juego* (*Don Quixote* as a game) (Madrid: Guadarrama, 1985), 71–72. In a section entitled "Dulcinea as a Complicated Invention" the author argues that the knight rejects both sex and money in order to avoid any reality that might compromise his own fiction.

"You spend too much time expecting," she says. "Dont expect. You just are, and you need, and you must, and so you do. That's all. Dont waste time expecting" (*Twn* 94). The ease and directness of Eula's relations with the world contrast sharply with the difficulties that hinder Gavin. His vigorous rejection of Eula is his way of preventing the object of his idealization from taking human form. If the ideal becomes tangible and accessible, it becomes altogether too worldly. Gavin is well aware of his own romantic nature. He tries to explain to Eula why he could never bring himself to go through with the relationship: "So if I had only had sense enough to have stopped expecting, or better still, never expected at all, never hoped at all, dreamed at all; if I had just had sense enough to say *I am, I want, I will and so here goes*—If I had just done that, it might have been me instead of Manfred? But dont you see? Cant you see? I wouldn't have been me then?" (*Twn* 94).

With his customary shrewdness, V. K. Ratliff pinpoints the nature of Gavin's fate in love. It is hopeless to try to be other than what one is, he says. It was never a matter of lawyer Stevens being unable to win Eula Varner, because Manfred de Spain had beaten him to it; rather it is that Gavin "was faced with a simple natural force repeating itself under the name of De Spain or McCarron or whatever into ever gap or vacancy in her breathing as long as she breathed; and that wouldn't never none of them be him" (*Twn* 101). For Gavin, love is a "supposition," but never a real "possibility." He is the knight who worships his lady without ever possessing her. Ratliff's wisdom accounts for the most recondite wiles of every champion of courtly love when he says: "Not ever body had Helen, but then not ever body lost her neither" (*Twn* 101). Like Don Quixote, who, objecting to the discrepancy between the real and the imagined Dulcinea, turns a deaf ear to the news Sancho brings from Aldonza,[27] Gavin Stevens shies away from the real, bodily Eula in order to preserve her ideal image. Some years after their abortive meeting, Ratliff recalls how Gavin deceived himself once more by believing that his experience with Eula had finally cured him of his romanticism: "That's what he thought then: that he was

27. "I imagine all I say to be true," says Don Quixote to Sancho, "neither more or less, and in my imagination I draw her as I would have her be, both as to her beauty and her rank; unequalled by Helen, unrivalled by Lucretia, or any other famous woman of antiquity, Greek, Barbarian or Roman. Let anyone say what he likes, for though the ignorant may reproach me for it, men of judgment will not condemn me." See Cervantes, *Don Quixote,* 210–11.

all right now; he had done been disenchanted for good at last of Helen, and so now all he had to worry about was what them Menelaus-Snopeses might be up to in the Yoknapatawpha-Argive community while he had his back turned. Which was all right; it would ease his mind. He would have plenty of time after he come back to find out that aint nobody yet ever lost Helen" (*TM* 130). Ratliff is right: Gavin finds his "Helen" again in the person of Linda, Eula's daughter, whom he intends to save from the influence of her adoptive father, Flem Snopes. With a mixture of paternalism and sublimated love, Gavin tries to defend his liaison with Linda against gossip and insinuation, convinced that "to save Jefferson from Snopeses is a crisis, an emergency, a duty. To save a Snopes from Snopeses is a privilege, an honor, a pride" (*Twn* 182).

With Gavin's newly embraced crusade, Faulkner carries his character's chivalric penchant through to the end. This time his rival is Linda's boyfriend, Matt Levitt, and as with Major de Spain he is kicked and ridiculed when he tries to defend her from what he sees as Matt's indecorous conduct. "By Cicero, Gavin, . . . You're losing ground," Gavin's brother-in-law remarks burlesquely. "Last time you at least picked out a Spanish-American War hero with an E. M. F. sportster. Now the best you can do is a Golden Gloves amateur with a homemade racer. Watch yourself, bud, or next time you'll have a boy scout defying you to mortal combat with a bicycle" (*Twn* 187). Here Faulkner cannot refrain from mocking his hero, whose chivalrous penchant is now lost on a youngster who, in Ratliff's words, has "the merry look of a fellow that hadn't heard yet that they had invented doubt" (*Twn* 189).

If with the passage of time Gavin's romantic leanings yield to an apparent compromise with life as it is (as seen in his tardy marriage to Melisandre Backus), the same cannot be said of the heroic component of his quixotism. To a certain extent, he is capable of accepting that his dreams of idealized love may never come true, but he cannot afford to give up his lifelong aspiration to transcend himself by commitment to a cause outside himself, one that might warrant all his vigor and passion. This is a trait that lies too close to the core of his identity—hence his commitment to form Linda's mind, as he likes to call his devotion to her. But in this he is every bit as unsuccessful as in all his other endeavors. True, he helps her cultivate her sensibility, and he gets her away from Jefferson, but insofar as she does not, after all, live up to his expectations, he fails completely. After Eula's suicide, Linda's marriage, and her return to Jefferson, and after his own marriage to Melisandre Backus, Gavin proves to be just as vulnerable to his illusions as in the past. He agrees, at Linda's request, to sign a petition of bail for Mick, unaware that she is using him as just another pawn in her maneuver to get her accomplice out of jail. When Gavin eventually discovers Mick's true identity, he realizes that once again he has been the victim of his own credulous nature. Gavin Stevens, champion of the fight against the Snopes, has given his support to one of them. With a mixture of sarcasm and compassion, and not without his inimitable touch of humor, Ratliff comments thus on Gavin's latest blunder: "I don't know if she's already got a daughter stashed out somewhere, or if she jest aint got around to one yet. But when she does I jest hope for Old Lang Zyne's sake she dont never bring it back to Jefferson. You done already been through two Eula Varners and I dont think you can stand another one" (*TM* 434). Ratliff's remark, prompted by his friend Stevens' chronic romanticism, draws to a close the story of the last quixote of Yoknapatawpha County at the age of sixty and deluded once more by the last flickering visions of Helen. We know that Faulkner, speaking of Charles Mallison, remarked, "The boy, I think he may grow up to be a better man than his uncle. I think he may succeed as a human being" (*LiG* 225). We may suppose that Faulkner is alluding here to the boy's overcoming the moral idealism that so afflicted his uncle and consequently to the end of the line of quixotic patricians in the county.

Among the poor whites of Yoknapatawpha County, however, Faulkner casts a further representative of chivalric zeal. Byron Bunch, the man determined to put an end to Lena Groves's senseless wanderings in *Light in August*, proves to be a true peer to the genteel champions of dames in the county. Byron is a gentleman, not by breeding but in spirit. He possesses a refinement and a sensibility unusual among the poor whites. His determination to protect Lena against gossip and suspicion, his attempts to convince his friend Hightower that her odyssey has dignity and meaning, and finally his fight with Lucas Burch over Lena's honor confirm him as a champion of chivalric love. Here is Faulkner's ironic portrait of this self-deluded knight:

Byron Bunch, that weeded another man's laidby crop, without any halvers. The fellow that took care of another man's whore while the other fellow was busy making a thousand dollars. And got nothing for it. Byron Bunch that protected her good name when the woman that owned the good name and the man she had given it to had both thrown it away, that got the other fellow's bastard born in peace and quiet and at Byron Bunch's expense, and heard a baby cry once for his pay. Got nothing for it except permission to fetch the other fellow back to her soon as he got done collecting the thousand dollars and Byron wasn't needed anymore. Byron Bunch. (LA 365)

The desire of Byron's heart stands in stark defiance of the facts: Lena is a luckless girl, abandoned to her fate, who travels the roads of strange places with a child in her womb and the absurd conviction that the man who has forsaken her is building a life for her somewhere. Byron's only friend and confidant in Jefferson, the Reverend Gail Hightower, knows that, being a sensitive, respectful, puritanical, and compassionate man, Byron is likely to mistake love for his heart's desire and fall into a trap of his own making. That is why he urges him to leave Jefferson and forget all about Lena since she has already had her chance to choose and has passed it over. "Give yourself at least the one chance in ten, Byron," he advises him. "If you must marry, there are single women, girls, virgins. It's not fair that you should sacrifice yourself to a woman who has chosen once and now wishes to renege that choice." Then Hightower gives his friend his own interpretation of Byron's quixotic stance: "For the Lena Groves there are always two men in the world and their number is legion: Lucas Burches and Byron Bunches. But no Lena, no woman, deserves more than one of them. No woman" (*LA* 276).

But it is precisely because he belongs to the second class of men in Hightower's classification that Byron refuses to give up Lena. On the contrary, he takes no notice of his friend's advice and follows the dictates of his own impulses. He takes Lena to the cabin Christmas and Brown shared, far away from the town and all its gossip, and looks after her until she gives birth (for which event he relies on Hightower's help). He then pressures the sheriff to force Brown into a meeting with Lena as soon as the child is born. When he confronts Brown, Byron Bunch considers his new position: " 'You are bigger than me,' Byron thought, 'But I dont care. You've had every other advantage of me. And I dont care about that neither. You've done throwed away twice inside of nine months what I ain't had in thirty-five years. And now I'm going to get the hell beat out of me and I dont care about that, neither' " (*LA* 384).

As the only "champion of dames" among the Yoknapatawpha poor whites, Byron defends Lena's honor against Lucas Burch just as Quentin defended Caddy's against Dalton Ames and Gavin Stevens defended Eula's against Manfred de Spain. And also like them, Byron takes a stand by confronting the rogue, well aware of his inferiority and in spite of the fact that he knows beforehand he will be beaten. Yet his attitude seems praiseworthy, and the character maintains dignity in defeat. In Faulkner's estimation it is irrelevant whether Lena holds her self-esteem highly or not or whether she is in the least aware of even having been wronged. What matters is the dignity of the human being, which is sacred and cannot be forsworn. For the rest, despite his tendency to idealization, Byron is capable of making something out of what life holds in store for him. Eventually he will win the woman he desires and live with her in the flesh, even though their idyll is somewhat less romantic than his friend Hightower would have wished.

With Lucius Priest in *The Reivers*, Faulkner forges his final tribute to the chivalric virtues so pervasively present in his fiction. But this time the young knight succeeds where his predecessors failed, when his lofty action has an impact upon reality. In his last novel and through his youngest champion of dames Faulkner achieves the almost unbelievable by making an eleven-year-old boy's visit to a Memphis brothel an edifying experience and, inversely, by making a prostitute's honor worth his pains and even his loss of innocence. The result is a tour de force of self-respect, a moral tale of love and pain, a salutation to the loftiness of men, shot through with irony and humor and treated with great compassion.

Even before Lucius finds himself fighting Otis over Everbe's virtue, he already knows that certain things must never be accepted. Hearing Mr. Binford say to one of the prostitutes at the supper table, "the trouble with you ladies is, you dont know how to quit acting like bitches" (*Rv* 110), Lucius feels the humiliation of the victim in himself: "She was alone. It was just that she shouldn't have had to be here, alone, to have to go through this. No, that's wrong too. It's that nobody should ever have to be that alone, nobody, not ever" (*Rv* 110). Lucius Priest defends Everbe's honor every bit as vehemently as Quentin Compson defends Caddy's, and his experience with vice is also excruciating. When Lucius hears Otis's account of how Everbe was abused and exploited in Arkansas and of the peephole by means of which the hateful boy procured money, Lucius jumps at him: "I knew nothing about boxing and not too much about fighting. But I knew exactly what I wanted to do: not just hurt him but destroy him" (*Rv* 157). Immediately after his almost instinctive response, he tells us the source of his rage while disclosing his ethical principles: "I was hitting, clawing, kicking not at one wizened ten-year-old boy, but at Otis and the procuress both: the demon child who debased her privacy and the witch who debauched her innocence . . . more: not just those two, but all who had participated in her debasement: not only the two panders but the insensitive blackguard children and the brutal and shameless men who paid their pennies to watch her defenceless and undefended and unavenged degradation" (*Rv* 157). But contrary to Quentin's experience, Lucius' act does not fall on stony ground. "You fought because of me," Everbe tells Lucius. "I've had people—drunks—fighting over me, but you're the first one ever fought for me" (*Rv* 159). With these words Faulkner endows his heroine with an insight into her own plight and a potential to react to the moral quality of her defender's act. And in so doing, he pays his last homage to his admired Don Quixote.

4

FAULKNER AND
THE QUIXOTIC UTOPIA

Sancho my friend, you must know that, by the will of Heaven, I was born in
this iron age of ours to revive the age of gold or, as it is generally called, the
golden age.

—Miguel de Cervantes Saavedra, *The Adventures of Don Quixote*

"Three different paths, at all times," observes Johan Huizinga in *The Waning of the Middle Ages*, "have seemed to lead to the ideal life" or, we might say, to utopia. The first of these is "forsaking the world. (The more beautiful life seems attainable only in the beyond.)" The second is the poetic solution, "to escape from the gloomy actual" and reach "a world more beautiful" through the dream of "the heroism, the virtue or the happiness of an ideal past." This is the path "trodden in all ages and civilizations, the easiest and also the most fallacious of all." The third is "amelioration of the world itself, by consciously improving political, social and moral institutions and conditions."[1] Clearly, Don Quixote follows the second of these paths, and so, we shall see, do many of William Faulkner's protagonists.

J. A. Maravall has outlined three elements of the quixotic utopia that were expressed in Castilian society during Cervantes' time: the attempt to perpetuate the traditional heroic ideal, embodied in the seigniorial society;

---

1. Johan Huizinga, *The Waning of the Middle Ages: A Study of the Forms of Life, Thought, and Art in France and the Netherlands in the Fourteenth and Fifteenth Centuries*, trans. F. Hopman (London: E. Arnold, 1924), 28–29.

the desire to restore the Golden Age by means of "the sublimation of a traditional agrarian economy with a broadly rural basis"; and the rejection of the modern state in an effort "to halt the advance of modernity." These three elements are also present in Faulkner's portrait of his Yoknapatawpha County. Maravall further contends that Cervantes "articulates perfectly the two sides of the utopian coin, the pastoral and the chivalric, in order to turn them inside out by reflecting them in the mirror of irony."[2] Faulkner's outlook on his characters' utopian dreams of evasion is also tinted with such Cervantesque irony.

Isaac McCaslin in "The Bear" and "Delta Autumn" and Reverend Gail Hightower in *Light in August* represent, respectively, nostalgia for the pastoral and the chivalric elements of the quixotic utopia in the decades following the South's defeat in the Civil War. On one hand, the lost war provided quixotic southerners a backdrop to their longing for heroic gesture. On the other, the waning of the South's traditional ways of life in the aftermath of the war left southerners with a sense of loss that in some cases, developed into a feeling of unjust dispossession and forced struggle in a harsh and inglorious age. In Faulkner's life these legacies were felt in a special sensitivity toward a recent past when men like Colonel William Clark Falkner enjoyed their hour of glory and when untamed nature still provided those men who had left behind "the old world's corrupt and worthless twilight" (*GDM* 259) with the chance of experiencing the fruits of Eden.

When William Faulkner was growing up, some parts of northern Mississippi still seemed virtually unexplored. In "Mississippi," Faulkner says of his home state during his own boyhood that "some of the land was still virgin in the early nineteen hundreds when [he] himself began to hunt." All around him, sections abounded where "there were deer to drift in herds as alarmless as smoke . . . and bear and panther and wolves in the brakes and bottoms, and the lesser beasts—coon and possum and beaver and mink and muskrat."[3] The fascination that this world held for Faulkner as a boy left its imprint particularly on "The Bear," a tale whose protagonist is the wilderness itself in communion with young Isaac McCaslin—"the wilderness the old bear ran," which was Ike's "college," where "the old male bear itself" became "his alma mater" (*GDM* 210).

2. Maravall, *Utopia and Counterutopia*, 134.

3. Faulkner, "Mississippi," 12.

This pastoral account contrasts vividly with the time of disgrace for the South that followed the war as it appears in Faulkner's narrative. It was a time when a class of men without principle and without honor left little but ignominy in their wake. In a long and detailed account he mercilessly criticizes this new usurping race, "threefold in one and alien even among themselves save for a single fierce will for rapine and pillage . . . who followed the battles they themselves had not fought and inherited the conquest they themselves had not helped to gain " (*GDM* 290). Yet as much as he repudiates the lack of moral principles of the carpetbagger and "all that other nameless horde of speculators in human misery, manipulators of money and politics and land" (*GDM* 290–91) that came on the southern political scene during Reconstruction, he is also very severe with the nostalgic, backward-looking attitude represented by Isaac McCaslin and Reverend Gail Hightower. These idealists themselves bring about their own banishment from paradise by repudiating and shrinking from the life that stands before them. The courageous stance, Faulkner maintains repeatedly, is to strive for the improvement and perfection of the world as it stands.

However, one also finds the antithesis of this critical attitude in Faulkner's nostalgic evocations of values that were lost during Reconstruction. Seen in this light, J. A. Maravall's view of Cervantes' melancholy perception of his own time could apply equally well to Faulkner. "It was believed by some" in Cervantes' time, Maravall observes, "that the course of the society of that period would abandon the path of heroism formerly esteemed as lasting and brilliant. . . . Among people of this mind, such a perception produced a bittersweet melancholy which accompanied their acceptance of the unavoidable failure of the heroic ideal."[4] Faulkner's defense of the values concomitant to the rural way of life in the South—that is, the values of a society not yet merged with entrepreneurial capitalism—turns both melancholic and bitter when he is faced with the unchecked development in the region following Reconstruction. Through Isaac MacCaslin, Faulkner voices an energetic protest against "the machine in the garden," an implacable criticism of the unbridled wave of land speculation wrongly understood as progress that was about to engulf the fine endowments of his native soil.

The myth of the Golden Age in Yoknapatawpha County is most force-

---

4. Maravall, *Utopia and Counterutopia*, 24. Maravall specifies that the word *heroism* in his book is meant to identify the morals of traditional society.

fully embodied in the character of Isaac (Ike) McCaslin in the story "The Bear" and its sequel, "Delta Autumn." As a boy, Ike grows up surrounded by quasi mythical characters in the unspoiled region of northern Mississippi: the venerated and fearsome Old Ben, the great bear who for years was the undisputed master of that territory; Boon Hogganbeck, the woodsman who eventually slays the bear; Lion, the crossbred wolfhound and Old Ben's only rival; and Sam Fathers, son of a quadroon slave woman and a Chickasaw chief, "the wild man not even one generation from the woods, childless, kinless, peopleless" (*GDM* 240). From Sam, Ike learns the code of his forefathers, the code of nature in its pure state, founded on courage, humility, and pride. "Be scared," Sam tells him. "You can't help that. But don't be afraid. Ain't nothing in the woods going to hurt you if you don't corner it or it don't smell that you are afraid. A bear or a deer has got to be scared of a coward the same as a brave man has got to be" (*GDM* 207).

Ike is initiated into the life of nature by Sam Fathers and in the hunting parties in the woods every November. So closely does he identify with this world that when Lion, who prompts Old Ben's eventual slaying, appears on the scene, Ike sees the dog as the harbinger of the decline of a whole order—a premonition that the subsequent death of Sam Fathers, high priest of the woods, will only serve to confirm: "So he should have hated and feared Lion. Yet he did not. It seemed to him that there was a fatality in it. It seemed to him that something, he didn't know what, was beginning; had already begun. It was like the last act on a set stage. It was the beginning of the end of something, he didn't know what except that he would not grieve. He would be humble and proud that he had been found worthy to be a part of it too or even just to see it too" (*GDM* 226).

And the premonition comes true. After Old Ben and Sam have died and Major de Spain, the owner of the hunting camp, has sold the timber rights to a lumber company in Memphis, Ike returns to the woods just before the company begins to cut the timber. But this time at the annual hunt meeting he will witness the beginning of the end. Nostalgically he recalls the log train with its little locomotive disappearing into the woods, whence it emerges again innocent and harmless as a toy, "empty and noisy and puerile, carrying to no destination or purpose sticks which left nowhere any scar or stump" (*GDM* 320). It is the same train that only ten years after this idyllic vision has lost its innocence in Ike's eyes. It then appears to him as the harbinger of the forest's destruction: "This time it was as though the train . . . had brought with it into the doomed wilderness, even before the actual axe, the shadow and portent of the new mill not even finished yet and the rails and ties which were not even laid; and he knew now what he had known as soon as he saw Hoke's this morning but had not yet thought into words: why Major de Spain had not come back, and that after this time he himself, who had had to see it one time other, would return no more" (*GDM* 321). However, we learn in "Delta Autumn" that Ike continues going back to the camp every November, and we see him as an old man after a lifetime devoted to the vain task of trying to restore Old Ben and Sam Father's mythical legacy. He has spent his life yearning for those meetings at Hoke's, and every year on entering the delta he evokes his recollections of some sixty years ago when the Big Bottom, a virgin territory in his boyhood, was only thirty miles from Jefferson and to him seemed like a corner of paradise. Ike mourns the fact that the land that was once an Arcadia[5] is now stripped and despoiled: "Now a man drove two hundred miles from Jefferson before he found wilderness to hunt in. Now the land lay open from the cradling hills on the east to the rampart of levee on the west, standing horseman-tall with cotton for the world's looms . . . the land across which there came no scream of panther but instead the long hooting of the locomotives" (*GDM* 340–41).

Isaac McCaslin, more than any other character in Faulkner's work, brings to mind Don Quixote's famous words to Sancho Panza describing his own view of his destiny: "Sancho, my friend, you must know that, by the will of Heaven, I was born in this iron age of ours to revive the age of gold or, as it is generally called, the golden age." For both Don Quixote and Isaac McCaslin the Golden Age was a time when personal property was unknown: "Happy the age and happy the times on which the ancients bestowed the name of golden," says the Don, "not because gold, which in this iron age of ours is rated so highly, was attainable without labour in those fortunate times, but rather because the people of those days did not know those two words *thine* and *mine*."[6] Similarly, Ike "owned no property and never desired to since the earth was no man's but all men's as light and air and weather were" (*GDM* 3). Arguing with his cousin Cass Edmonds about the property rights the McCaslins have inherited from Lucius

5. For an analysis of the dream of Arcadia in *Go Down, Moses*, particularly that of Ike McCaslin, see Lucinda MacKethan, *The Dream of Arcady: Place and Time in Southern Literature* (Baton Rouge: Louisiana State University Press, 1980).

6. Cervantes, *Don Quixote*, 149, 85.

Quintus Carothers McCaslin, who in turn bought the land from the Chickasaw chief Ikkemotubbe, Ike says that God "made the earth first and peopled it with dumb creatures, and then He created man to be His overseer on the earth and to hold suzerainty over the earth and the animals on it in His name, not to hold for himself and his descendants inviolable title forever, generation after generation, to the oblongs and squares of the earth, but to hold the earth mutual and intact in the communal anonymity of brotherhood" (*GDM* 257).

But Faulkner's regret for the passing of this Golden Age has no Rousseaunean connotations, since he makes no protest on behalf of the "noble savage." The society of the American Indian was no paradise; the land the white man found was not unspoiled, but "already accursed . . . already tainted even before any white man owned it" (*GDM* 258–59). And this white man, whom God saved from the darkness of the Old World to carry out the conquest of a better life in the New, sinned most directly against God and against himself by spurning piety, humility, and endurance, virtues on which God had based His plan for man to achieve full humanity. In this way the white man, whose mission it was to be the exemplar of the New World, turned away from God's design and made the earth a mere material means for the fulfillment of his own ambitions, using his absolute power over other men and women—as did Ike's grandfather—to satisfy his own rapacious desires.

Ike leafs through the yellowing pages of the old ledgers that since the days of old Carothers have been gathering dust on the shelves of the commissary store, ledgers in which the most important events of the lives of the slaves are recorded—their purchase, their offspring, their death. Here Ike discovers his family's murky past, "that chronicle which was a whole land in miniature, which multiplied and compounded was the entire South, twenty-three years after surrender and twenty-four from emancipation" (*GDM* 293). This discovery is a crucial moment in Ike's life. From now on he must face up to the enormous difference between the code taught him by Sam Fathers, of the mythical world of undefiled nature into which he had the privilege of being introduced as an adolescent, and the reality of a past sullied by the greatest indignity a man can commit, the enslavement of other human beings, the destruction of self-respect through years of humiliation, abuse, and subjection, even to the point of incest. This is the transgression committed by his grandfather, Lucius Quintus Carothers McCaslin, who begot a child to his own daughter, Tomasina, after which the mother, Eunice—herself bought in New Orleans and brought to the plantation to be his mistress—drowned herself out of desperation. These facts were clumsily concealed in the ledgers and in old Carother's will, in which a provision of one thousand dollars is made for the offspring of an unmarried slave woman. And it is a transgression for which Ike fully intends to atone.

Ike's efforts to atone for his family's infamy are twofold. First, he renounces his inheritance in order to uphold the very values that are being trampled all around him. Second, he launches himself on a quest to make amends for the damage inflicted upon the blacks by his ancestors. Ike can be included among the ranks of the southerners in Faulkner's fiction who disapproved of slavery, like Uncle Buck and Uncle Buddy, who, according to Cleanth Brooks, were a great influence on Ike.[7] Such an attitude in itself does not make quixotic figures of these characters, but it certainly evokes certain traits that suggest a lack of adjustment to their social milieu and an inability to perform their presumed social function. In that respect, Ike and Uncles Buck and Buddy are very much alike. Uncle Buck comes across as a caricature of the southern planter. His unsuccessful attempts in "Was" to stop Tomey's Turl's calls on his beloved Tennie at the slaves quarters of Mr. Hubert Beauchamp's plantation and the pitfalls Buck endures in pursuit of the slave (such hilarious episodes as the hunt in which the hounds befriend the slave they are supposed to chase and Uncle Buck's ending up in the most undesired of places, Miss Sophonsiba's bed) are good examples of Buck's inadequacy to the planter stereotype and in many ways are reminiscent of Don Quixote's blunders.

Ike's personal decision to give up an inheritance that he believes has been acquired from the rape of the land and consolidated by the fruits of slavery can be seen as quixotic inasmuch as he attempts to transform this renunciation into the emblem of an impossible ideal, the illusion that modern man can conform to the absence of private ownership inherent in nature. Ike's talks with his cousin McCaslin (Cass) Edmonds about the inheritance can be seen in the light of the moral idealism so dear to Don Quixote. Cass understands the legacy of the past as a legitimate right to be passed down through the generations: " 'Relinquish,' McCaslin said. 'Relinquish. You, the direct male descendant of him who saw the opportunity and took it, bought the land, took the land, got the land no matter how,

---

7. Brooks, *First Encounters*, 146.

held it to bequeath, no matter how, out of the old grant, the first patent, when it was a wilderness of wild beasts and wilder men, and cleared it, translated it into something to bequeath to his children, worthy of bequeathment for his descendants' ease and security and pride, and to perpetuate his name and accomplishments' " (*GDM* 256). But Ike does not share his cousin's vision. His position is diametrically opposed to Cass's:

> I can't repudiate it. It was never mine to repudiate. It was never Father's and Uncle Buddy's to bequeath to me to repudiate, because it was never Grandfather's to bequeath them to bequeath me to repudiate, because it was never old Ikkemotubbe's to sell to Grandfather for bequeathment and repudiation. Because it was never Ikkemotubbe's fathers' fathers' to bequeath Ikkemotubbe to sell to Grandfather or any man because on the instant when Ikkemotubbe discovered, realized, that he could sell it for money, on that instant it ceased ever to have been his forever, father to father to father, and the man who bought it bought nothing. (*GDM* 256–57)

Ike has been molded by a code of conduct that prevents him from accepting Cass's argument. Ever since the day Sam Fathers marked Ike's young face with the blood of the buck that he himself had killed, Ike understood, without being aware of it then, what his fate would be. As an old man, childless but dubiously honored as "uncle to half a county and father to no one" (*GDM* 3), Ike recalls the instant he killed his first animal, which was to prove so crucial in his future life: "*I slew you; my bearing must not shame your quitting life. My conduct forever onward must become your death*" (*GDM* 351). This solemn promise prefigures Ike fully grown, who will devote his life to righting the wrongs of his predecessors. If in the end he is unable to repair all the damage that has been done, and all his efforts are in vain, nevertheless he will have made his rejection plain: "Himself and McCaslin juxtaposed, not against the wilderness but against the tamed land, the old wrong and shame itself, in repudiation and denial at least of the land and the wrong and shame, even if he couldn't cure the wrong and eradicate the shame, who at fourteen when he learned of it had believed he could do both when he became competent, and when at twenty-one he became competent he knew that he could do neither but at least he could repudiate the wrong and shame" (*GDM* 351).

Ike McCaslin suffers many setbacks and pitfalls in his attempts at restitution and atonement. He wishes to leave a guilt-free inheritance for future generations and thus refuses any connection with his family's legacy. He lives with his wife in a small rented room and works as a carpenter, leading an ascetic life, attempting to follow Christ's example. But his own stubbornness prevents attainment of his goal. "When he was going to throw the plantation away for idealistic folly," Faulkner remarks, referring to Ike's wife's reaction to her husband's drastic decisions, "the only revenge she had was that. At least he would have no children from her. He'd have no wife from her" (*FiU* 276). His wife refuses to give him the child he desires unless he changes his mind about the inheritance. Ironically, the act of renunciation by means of which he seeks to release his unborn child from the disgraceful burden of the past will deprive him of that child forever. This twofold renunciation, sensual and material, conforms to Don Quixote's code of behavior. Don Quixote molds his life to the conventions of the chivalric ideal, which in turn springs directly from the Christian ethic of spurning worldly things for the sake of supreme good. Cervantes observes with irony the sterility inherent in such a quest in the person of his self-deceiving knight. Faulkner, who observes Isaac McCaslin from a similar viewpoint, gives us the picture of a good man who is equally self-deluding in his pursuit of an unattainable ideal. Lewis P. Simpson has defined Ike's quixotic stance as a confrontation between pastoral myth and historical reality, observing that "there can be no return from the self-consciousness of history to the mythic existence, not even for [Ike] who, as a boy has been privileged to enter at least into the margins of the mythic."[8]

Ike's idealistic stance is also manifest in the responsibility he feels toward the black descendants of his family, and here, too, his failure is complete. He tries to trace James Beauchamp (Tennie's Jim), his half cousin, with the intention of protecting him and handing over part of the money that old Carothers had bequeathed to his black offspring. Ike records his fruitless search in the old ledgers: "*Vanished sometime on night of his twenty-first birthday Dec 29 1885. Traced by Isaac McCaslin to Jackson Tenn. and there lost. His third of legacy $1000.00 returned to McCaslin Edmonds Trustee this day Jan 12 1886*" (*GDM* 273). Twenty years later, Ike learns that Tennie's Jim is the owner of a prosperous New Orleans brothel. Fonsiba, Tennie's Jim's sister, had gone to Arkansas to rejoin her husband, a haughty, circumspect black man who is obstinately convinced that the

---

8. Lewis P. Simpson, *The Brazen Face of History: Studies in the Literary Consciousness in America* (Baton Rouge: Louisiana State University Press, 1980), 222.

promised land of Canaan has finally come to the men and women of his race. For years Ike knows nothing of her whereabouts; he then sets out on an agonizing pilgrimage to find her. With the money that rightly belongs to her, Ike tirelessly searches for Fonsiba, "as the slow interminable empty muddy December miles crawled and crawled and night followed night in hotels, in roadside taverns of rough logs and containing little else but a bar, and in the cabins of strangers, and the hay of lonely barns, in none of which he dared undress because of his secret golden girdle" (*GDM* 277).

As in his search for Tennie's Jim, the purpose of Ike's search for Fonsiba is to find out what has happened to her and to deliver her part of the legacy. "*I will have to find her*," he repeats over and over to himself. "*I will have to. We have already lost one of them. I will have to find her this time*" (*GDM* 277). When he finally does find her, she is living in a shack, in the midst of misery and desolation, and she seems remote, lost in her own muted drama. Her husband, who gives off "that rank stink of baseless and imbecile delusion, that boundless rapacity and folly, of the carpet-bagger followers of victorious armies" (*GDM* 278), is impervious to Ike's entreaties that he desist from his absurd belief that freedom in and of itself is enough. Ironically, it is Ike who here plays the realist as he tries to make the black man aware of his blinkered perception of reality: " 'Don't you see? . . . Don't you see? This whole land, the whole South, is cursed, and all of us who derive from it, whom it ever suckled, white and black both, lie under the curse? Granted that my people brought the curse onto the land: maybe for that reason their descendants alone can—not resist it, not combat it—maybe just endure and outlast it until the curse is lifted. Then your people's turn will come because we have forfeited ours. But not now. Not yet. Don't you see?' " (*GDM* 278). But all Ike's arguments are rebutted both by the man's absurd and blind faith and by his submissive wife. He is forced to give up, losing yet another battle. The one thousand dollars he has so carefully carried during his search he now deposits in a Jefferson bank, the three dollars per month interest ensuring that for twenty-eight years at least Fonsiba will not have to face hunger.

All Ike's efforts are frustrated. His motives are misunderstood. His advice falls on deaf ears. Everything combines to turn his crusade into a sterile act. His repudiation of the legacy becomes quixotic folly. This appears to be Faulkner's view, as we see when, at the end of his days, Ike has to confront the fact that he has wasted his life in pursuit of a chimera. The meeting between Ike, now an old man, and the young woman in "Delta

Autumn" constitutes a clear indication of the futility of his renunciation. History repeats itself; old Carothers' sin reemerges in the person of Roth Edmonds, third cousin to Ike and now the head of the McCaslin plantation, who has begotten a child to the last descendant of the black slave Eunice, the granddaughter of Tennie's Jim, although Roth is unaware of the blood tie between himself and the woman. Roth, like old Carothers, will not take responsibility for his child. The woman, who accepts her fate (she and Roth had mutually agreed to have no entangling alliances), refuses to take the money Roth had left for her, just as Thucydus, Eunice's husband, had rejected old Carothers' cash and ten acres of land with which the McCaslins had hoped to wash their guilt away and repair the slave's humiliation. Then old Ike advises her to forget all about Roth, go north and marry a man of her own race to raise the child with. To this proposal, which comes full circle back to the original sin (as old Carothers married off Eunice after getting her pregnant), the woman reacts with these words: " 'Old man . . . have you lived so long and forgotten so much that you don't remember anything you ever knew or felt or even heard about love?' "(*GDM* 363). Her words highlight Ike's vain quest. His rejection has served no purpose. His supposedly exemplary life has amended no wrongs and brought no restitution. His foolish stance is incomprehensible even to those for whom it was intended. Ultimately, as the woman's words attest, the curse set on the land proves as indomitable as love's curse.

Faulkner was unequivocal about the absurdity of his character's act of repudiation. On one occasion an interviewer voiced admiration for Ike McCaslin precisely because of his rejection of the inheritance. Faulkner countered with the question: "Do you think it's a good thing for a man to reject an inheritance?" To which the interviewer replied, "Yes, in McCaslin's case. He wanted to reject a tainted inheritance. You don't think it's a good thing for him to have done so?" Faulkner's answer was blunt and to the point: "Well, I think a man ought to do more than just repudiate. He should have been more affirmative instead of shunning people" (*LiG* 225). Here we see Faulkner reaffirming his belief in the sterility of repudiating life in the present for irrelevant ideals of the past. Nevertheless, the critical, ironic perspective through which Faulkner presents Ike's attempts to make amends for his tainted inheritance does not exclude a salute of admiration. Although the path that Ike's life takes proves fruitless, the same cannot be said of his moral code, for he still preserves the values he learned from Sam Fathers. These values, Faulkner reminds us, "didn't give him success but they gave him something a lot more important, even in this country. They gave him serenity, they gave him what would pass for wisdom" (*FiU* 54).

Through Isaac McCaslin, Faulkner condemns the destruction of wilderness and the greed that accompanied it. In this respect Ike does not represent the hope for a restoration of the old ways, the ethic of the past, so much as he stands for a rejection of the ways of incipient industrial capitalism. Ike mourns a world that is fast disappearing and expresses pessimism about the future of the country:

> This Delta, he thought: This Delta. *This land which man has deswamped and denuded and derivered in two generations so that white men can own plantations and commute every night to Memphis and black men own plantations and ride in Jim Crow cars to Chicago to live in millionaires' mansions on Lake Shore Drive; where white men rent farms and live like niggers and niggers crop on shares and live like animals; where cotton is planted and grows man-tall in the very cracks of the sidewalks, and usury and mortgage and bankruptcy and measureless wealth, Chinese and African and Aryan and Jew, all breed and spawn together until no man has time to say which one is which nor cares.* (*GDM* 364)

Faulkner's pessimism resembles Twain's in *A Connecticut Yankee*: America has no chance of becoming what it originally set out to be, nor will progress redeem its inhabitants. Those who, like Hank Morgan, cherish the dream of progress and liberty and those who, like Isaac McCaslin, believe in the dream of the promised land will find themselves face-to-face with the same absurd and unworkable situation. What, then, is the road that the sensitive man must take when the America of the Jeffersonian dream seems to have vanished? Time and again Faulkner makes it clear that the only choice remaining is to face up to life as it stands: "It's foolish to be against progress because everyone is a part of progress and he'll have no other chance except this one, so . . . it's silly not to cope with it, to compromise with it" (*FiU* 98). This of course is not the choice that Ike makes; rather, his identity is defined by his refusal to accept this consummated fact.

Just as unspoiled nature has been curtailed and encroached upon, "since its purpose was served now and its time an outmoded time" (*GDM* 343), so Ike knows that his time has come and gone. The legacy handed down to him by Major de Spain and Sam Fathers, which he accepted "gladly, humbly, with joy and pride," will find in him its last defender: "He seemed to see the two of them—himself and the wilderness—as coevals . . .

the two spans running out together, not toward oblivion, nothingness, but into a dimension free of both time and space, where once more the untreed land warped and wrung to mathematical squares of rank cotton for the frantic old-world people to turn into shells to shoot at one another, would find ample room for both" (*GDM* 354). This mixture of disillusion and nostalgic farewell to the more beautiful life he knew in his youth is Ike's way, in final communion with declining nature, of accepting his fate.

If the pastoral ideal constitutes one of the aspects of the quixotic utopia, the other aspect revolves around the heroic ideal, which in the South fed on the legend surrounding the Civil War and magnifies a period of its history in which gallant men heroically defended a cause in which they fervently believed. Both as a young boy and as an adolescent, William Faulkner himself grew up immersed in a family environment in which the Civil War was regarded as a heroic exploit but where none of war's cruelty and poignancy arose to counteract the myth. Blotner describes the regular meetings of W. C. Falkner's Partisan Rangers, organized by John Wesley Thomson Falkner, William Faulkner's grandfather, during which young "Billy" and his brother Jack listened to first-hand accounts of the dangers the "Old Colonel" (Faulkner's great-grandfather) and the men of his regiment faced. High-flown language accentuated the belief that "this service and sacrifice was a privilege of the highest order."[9] This oral legacy of the Civil War, idealized with the passing of time and with all horror suitably removed, would emerge as a significant part of the author's own life.

In his fiction dealing with the Civil War, Faulkner at times counteracts the romantic outlook by means of burlesque inflections. Such is the case of Bayard Sartoris, who loses his life in a rash act while trying to steal anchovies from a Federal camp. Bayard dies not in an attempt to strike at enemy forces but at the hands of a scared cook who happens to notice his presence. What is one to make, then, of a war hero of the stripe of Bayard Sartoris, or of General Joe Stuart, for that matter, who volunteers to enter the enemy camp in order to capture a saddle for his prisoner? Gallantry and heroism take on quixotic connotations and revert to unheroic and swaggering gestures. When an astonished Yankee officer asks Stuart if he would really be capable of risking his own life and that of all his men "in order to provide for the temporary comfort of a minor prisoner of his sword," Stu-

9. Blotner, *Faulkner: A Biography*, 1:103.

art replies without hesitation, "Not for the prisoner, Sir . . . but for the officer suffering the fortune of war. No gentleman would do less." The Yankee mayor replies as if speaking for the author himself, "No gentleman has any business in this war. There is no place for him here. He is an anachronism, like anchovies." Cleanth Brooks points out Faulkner's irony when he says that although "in some sense, the American Civil War was the first modern war . . . some of the soldiers, particularly cavalry officers, insisted on fighting it as if they were paladins of romance," yet "the old heroics were—though those bent on heroism were unwilling to admit the fact—passé."[10]

An even more significant example of Faulkner's deflating view of the romanticism of the war is to be found in the passage of *Light in August* where Reverend Hightower gives Cinthy a grandiose account of his grand-father's regiment riding into Jefferson and "the shouts, the shots, the shouting of triumph and terror, the drumming hooves, the trees uprearing against that red glare as though fixed too in terror." Suddenly Cinthy inter-rupts. "And of course he would be right in de way of hit," she says, refer-ring to the way her master died, and then goes on to say, "Stealin' chickens. A man growed, wid a married son, gone to a war whar his business was killin' Yankees, killed in somebody else's henhouse wid a han'ful of feath-ers. Stealing chickens" (*LA* 424–25). Hightower's inflated rhetoric is starkly contrasted with the mundane, deflating tone of Cinthy's words, telling him how her master really died during a cavalry raid on Grant's stores in Jeffer-son. The effect is a burlesque counterpoint full of quixotic resonance.

William Faulkner is "no Mississippi Cervantes," Daniel Aaron remarks in an attempt to pin down Faulkner's mock depictions of southerners' deeds and attitudes in the Civil War, for his humor, "so often based (like Mark Twain's) upon the disproportion between illusion and reality, is shot through with pain." In fact, when Faulkner seeks to deflate the legend of war heroics, he is trying to come to terms with his own attraction for this legend, which Aaron calls "the pull of what he disbelieved"; however, at the same time he aims at debunking bravado and exposing the fateful con-sequences of fanaticism, just as Cervantes does with Don Quixote. In Faulkner's scorn toward the inflated legend, in his compassion for the self-deluded, and in his veiled nostalgia for the heroic deed—in sum, in his

10. William Faulkner, *Flags in the Dust* (New York: Random House, 1973), 18; Cleanth Brooks, *Toward Yoknapatawpha and Beyond* (New Haven: Yale University Press, 1978), 171.

"admiring disapproval" of the war, in Aaron's words—we recognize his lifelong admiration for the derided Don Quixote. From this perspective one can see Faulkner and Cervantes in the same light.[11]

John Sartoris, his brother Bayard Sartoris III, Quentin Compson, and the Reverend Gail Hightower exemplify to a high degree the quest for oblivion in the delusion of a heroic, more fully meaningful past—a delusion nurtured by the legends surrounding the war—that develops into an insoluble inner conflict. These descendants of the war's heroes remain trapped in a conception of heroism that proves irrelevant to their own lives and that they themselves are unable to decipher. Quentin Compson, crushed by obsessions with honor and virtue from which he can find no outlet, throws himself into the Charles River. John Sartoris dies in World War I, the victim of a completely unnecessary act of valor curiously similar to that which brought about the death of his great uncle in the American Civil War. And "young Bayard," twin of John, lives self-destructively until he eventually crashes a plane he is test-piloting at an airfield in Ohio.

But without doubt the greatest mythomaniac of the Civil War and its legend is the Reverend Gail Hightower in *Light in August*. Around Gail Hightower, Faulkner weaves a grotesque and tragic tale with the Civil War as a backdrop and the South as its setting, a familiar mise-en-scène entirely appropriate for demonstrating the consequences of the romantic conception of the past. Rollin G. Osterweis argues that "Faulkner perceptively senses the anachronistic qualities in the Lost Cause legend by depicting the tragedies of those of his characters who fail to come to terms with it." They are "trapped by the myth," and although they are aware of the "futility of it as a faith in the modern society," they hold fast to it, for it offers "a more appealing value system than that of the amoral new day."[12] Accordingly, life for Gail Hightower makes sense only when seen through the memory of his grandfather's regiment's glorious entry into the town of Jefferson. It is enough for him simply to recall this phantasmagoric fresco or to spout an exalted vindication of war heroes from his church pulpit, the only occasion on which he himself can experience feelings of grandeur, albeit vicariously. But for Hightower, as for Don Quixote, the time of heroism has passed. His fantasy world will end by closing him off from life, alienating

11. Aaron, *The Unwritten War*, 322–23, 315, 119.

12. Rollin G. Osterweis, *The Myth of the Lost Cause, 1865–1900* (Hamden, Conn.: Archon Books, 1973), 148.

him from his surroundings and preventing him from having any positive relation with them. Faulkner confirms this when he says, "Hightower was a man who wanted to be better than he was afraid he would. He had failed his wife. Here was another chance he had, and he failed his Christian oath as a man of God, and he escaped into his past where some member of his family was brave enough to match the moment" (*FiU* 45).

In Gail Hightower, Faulkner gives us the portrait of a character seemingly fated to failure, marked by an unhappy childhood during which he became habituated to wrapping himself up in an idealized world overshadowed by the Civil War. Hightower's obsession with the heroics of the war were a way of escaping the grim reality of his childhood home, with his father's increasing aloofness and his mother's lack of health and vitality. Both parents are referred to as "phantoms," implying their scant emotional presence in their son's life. The black slave woman, Cinthy, a third phantom in Hightower's life, imbues him with her own obsessions about the war, to which both her husband and her master departed never to return. Through Cinthy's tales, the figure of Hightower's grandfather, who died in Jefferson during Van Dorn's cavalry raid on General Grant's stores, becomes a "ghost," gradually taking on the substance of a real entity. These early fantasies so marked Hightower as a child that he would never be able to break free of them.

Part obsessive preacher, part ascetic sage, Hightower does not know how to apply his wisdom to his own life. His monomania becomes the only conceivable truth. Swayed by flights of epic romanticism, he eschews all living choices and turns away from any situation that might involve him with the present. Faulkner describes him at eight years of age as already steeped in the mysticism of the war, examining with a mixture of awe and barely contained delight the heavy military cape his father wore through four years of service in the Confederate army. The contemplation of this object awakens within him a fantasy world that consumes his whole being: "To him, the child, it seemed unbelievably huge, as though made for a giant; as though merely from having been worn by one of them, the cloth itself had assumed the properties of those phantoms who loomed heroic and tremendous against a background of thunder and smoke and torn flags which now filled his waking and sleeping life" (*LA* 410).

This secret childlike veneration for the epic of the war in time becomes idolatry. Later, grown up and an ordained minister of the church, his sole obsession is to make a living in Jefferson so that he can relive for himself the images that have captivated him in the very town where they took place: his grandfather, the cavalry officer, struck down by a stray bullet while General Grant's stores were consumed in a blaze after having been boldly set alight by an intrepid group of young Confederates. "I know the very street that they rode into town upon and then out again. I have never seen it, but I know exactly how it will look. I know exactly how the house that we will someday own and live in upon the street will look," Hightower tells his wife on the train ride that is taking them to his longed-for post in Jefferson, "where we can look out the window and see the street, maybe even the hoofmarks or their shapes in the air, because the same air will be there even if the dust, the mud, is gone" (*LA* 423).

Hightower will spend the rest of his days in Jefferson, pursuing the funereal, creaking apparition of deeds performed by men in the war, deeds that can be glorified only because they have been stripped of all human vestige, "just ghosts, never seen in the flesh, heroic, simple, warm" (*LA* 419). Gradually, this eccentric preacher will go more and more into his shell, isolating himself from everybody and everything. First he loses his wife. Forced to live a life not of her own choosing and driven to desperation, she puts an end to her life in an obscure Memphis brothel. Then he loses his parishioners, driven away by his long-winded sermons. Finally he loses his own self-respect, accepting all manner of humiliation as long as he can remain in Jefferson. He endures all this for the few moments that can still afford him any pleasure, those few moments every day when he sits at his study window at twilight to watch for his grandfather entering the streets of Jefferson, until the lifeless, repetitive vigil finally brings him to an awareness of his own unreality: "I know that for fifty years I have not even been clay: I have not even been a single instant of darkness in which a horse galloped and a gun crashed" (*LA* 430).

Just as Don Quixote, preparing to imitate the desperately rejected Amadis and do penance in the Sierra Morena, tells Sancho not to waste his time trying to persuade him to give up "so rare, so happy, and so unprecedented an imitation,"[13] so Hightower in his moment of lucidity recognizes his overriding need to believe in a romantic past. He describes to his wife his need to believe implicitly in old Cinthy's tales: "This is what Cinthy told me. And I believe. I know," he tells her. "It's too fine to doubt. It's too fine, too simple, ever to have been invented by white thinking. A negro

13. Cervantes, *Don Quixote*, 203.

might have invented it. And if Cinthy did, I still believe. Because even fact cannot stand with it" (*LA* 424). What Hightower wants to hear in Cinthy's stories is a portrayal of war as a fantastic exploit of "a handful of men . . . performing with the grim levity of schoolboys a prank so foolhardy that the troops who had opposed them for four years did not believe that even they would have attempted it." These young men, enveloped in their halo of heroic splendor, "were not men after spoils and glory; they were boys riding the sheer tremendous tidal wave of desperate living" (*LA* 423). The war came to signify for him "that fine shape of eternal youth and virginal desire which makes heroes" (*LA* 424) and not the defense of a cause. The longing for that unattainable quality is what shuts Hightower off from contact with the real world—as his very name implies. Only on the few occasions when reality does impinge upon his consciousness do we see his humanity emerge from his confused and contradictory feelings toward his fellow human beings. We witness this in his acts of solidarity with other people, when, in spite of himself, he briefly forgets the argument ("I have bought immunity. I have paid. I have paid" [*LA* 270]) he has used for years to justify his isolation from the rest. The help he gives to the pregnant black woman, his assistance to Lena in childbirth, and finally, after moments of agonizing indecision, his tardy, fruitless, but sincere attempt to protect Joe Christmas are examples of his desire to make up for long years of wasted life.

Through the character of Hightower, Faulkner focuses on the immoderate worship of the past so deeply rooted in the southern mind, which stems from an illusion of a time when men were equal to the demands of circumstance, and which rests on an idealized notion of courage, gallantry, and daring that can only find an outlet in action. This explains why Hightower is drawn more to the figure of his grandfather than to the example of his father, whose life he would undoubtedly dismiss as dull and obscure. (On the front his father never came across splendid young heroes, but wounded, suffering people from both sides, whom he tried to help with no medical training and with no means.) For Robert Penn Warren, Gail Hightower represents Faulkner's conscience about his own romantic feelings toward the war. Warren sees in Faulkner "some deep personal bias toward violence, some admiration of the crazy personal gesture," and "an idealized vision of the South's old war," all of which, Warren contends, were processed through Faulkner's imagination and subjected to his keen awareness "of the depth of the human soul." The result, therefore, is an insightful view of "projections—and purgations of potentials in Faulkner himself."[14]

In light of Warren's cogent observations, and taking into account Faulkner's sensibility as reflected in characters such as Quentin Compson and Ike McCaslin, the literary visions of Cervantes and Faulkner begin to converge. Faulkner and Cervantes coincide not only in their similar ironic examinations of human beings' proclivity to devise quixotic utopias but also in their similar insights into their own enthusiasms and disillusionments. Faulkner, with an unusual combination of heartfelt knowledge of his locale and historical circumstances and acute awareness of his own delusions, wrote about the propensity of human beings to mythmaking and their ordeals in the pursuit of excellence with the same sympathetic irony, love, and compassion for their plight as did Cervantes. And like Cervantes, Faulkner is exceptional because he portrayed with an uncommon poetic vision the seemingly simple fact that our greatness as human beings is best found in our most unpretentious acts and in our courage in defeat.

14. Warren, "Past and Future," 3.

5

BECAUSE A FIRE WAS IN MY HEAD
Eudora Welty on the Nobility of Failure

As I looked longer and longer for the origins of this passionate and strange character, at last I realized that Miss Eckhart came from me.
—Eudora Welty, *One Writer's Beginnings*

Is not Don Quixote the prototype of the hero who cannot triumph, the prototype of the hero who can never be defeated?
—Maria Zambrano, *España, sueño y verdad*

"As a failure, Don Quixote of La Mancha is, and will always be, upright, unassailable and without blemish," contends Fernando Savater. He then goes on to say, "In this world of prefabricated successes, every triumph seems somehow hollow. Defeat, however, is agreeably redolent of sincerity."[1] The various epithets by which Savater defines Don Quixote's dignity in defeat—such as "The Incorruptible Prince of the Fallen" and "The angel who betrays himself and is expelled from the paradise of dreams"—are precisely the reflections of the Knight of the Sorrowful Countenance that one may find in the works of Eudora Welty.

Failure, without doubt, is the perennial bedfellow of all those in the history of literature who in one way or another, have emulated Don Quixote. But characters like Miss Eckhart in "The Golden Apples" or Miss Julia Mortimer in *Losing Battles* seem especially relevant to the Quixote motif as

---

1. Savater, *Instrucciones*, 23.

Torrente Ballester describes it: "Don Quixote fulfills himself equally as much in adventure as in defeat. He does not pursue success; neither does he require it in order to be what he is. Don Quixote is the embodiment of 'courage' and 'endeavor,' but not necessarily victory."[2] Courage, endeavor, and passion, an extreme passion for fulfillment, are what drive Welty's two heroines to spurn the hostile and intransigent aspects of the society that bears down upon them. They battle against the windmills of ignorance and spiritual vulgarity, against the ennui and alienation to which the individual spirit is subjected by a closed, inward-looking society vigilantly and jealously guarding its established codes and norms of behavior. Just such societies are found in Morgana, Mississippi, provincial and self-satisfied, and in the small community of Banner in the hills of northern Mississippi, where the Beechams and the Renfros, after surrendering their individual identities to the confining family nucleus, are entrenched against the threat of the outside world, protecting themselves, also with quixotic resolve, against the passage of time and the awareness of their own uniqueness.

Curiously, a woman who has led a quiet life in Jackson, Mississippi, has been able to convey to us with the greatest insight the servitude of a life lived within the narrow confines of a closed community. A high price must be paid by anyone who dares to step out of line or fails to abide by or adapt to the prevailing rules and customs or simply ignores them or pretends they do not exist. Eudora Welty shines a penetrating light on the dimly lit terrain where dreams interact with reality and on the region of despair, where the ideal of what human beings would like to be comes up against the crushing pressures of actuality. One has to be a Quixote to challenge the accepted rules and values of the group or to exceed the established boundaries within which its members may realize their identities. One, indeed, has to feel the urgent need, as Eudora Welty's heroines do, to bring about some change in the world, even though they know they are all too likely to fail in the attempt. The writer herself is explicit in this regard: "Even though you are losing the battle, it doesn't mean that you aren't eternally fighting them and brave in yourself."[3]

The efforts of these characters reflect the effects of modernity as it seeks

2. Torrente Ballester, *El "Quijote" como juego* (*Don Quixote* as a game), 23. My translation.

3. Charles T. Bunting, " 'The Interior World': An Interview with Eudora Welty," *Southern Review* 3 (1972): 720.

to find a way through the atavism of tradition, which stubbornly resists the transforming force of time. *Modernity* should be understood here to mean the assertion of individual consciousness against collective consciousness, the increasing hopes of individual choice vis-à-vis the collective straitjacket that threatens to bind and cripple the personal dream. In short, Miss Julia Mortimer's and Miss Lotte Elizabeth Eckhart's fights represent the struggle of the modern man or woman, specifically situated in the rural American South during the first half of the twentieth century. This struggle takes place at a crossroads in time where everything that may readily be associated with change or progress—culture, education, rationality, and personal achievement—is regarded not only with distrust and suspicion but even as a harbinger of chaos and disintegration.

"Places like Morgana—human communities," Louis D. Rubin observes, "exist to ward off and mask, through ritual and social complexity, an awareness of the finally unanswerable and inexplicable nature of existence in time and eternity."[4] Thus art, taken as the highest expression of the individual consciousness and revealing to us first and last truths about the human condition, must necessarily be suspect in such communities because it disturbs the drift toward dullness, opacity, reserve, and narrowness in man. Art may not be a palpable reality for Miss Julia Mortimer as it is for Miss Eckhart in "The Golden Apples." Nevertheless, it is present in a profound sense, insofar as she strives to illuminate the dark zones of consciousness where habit and fear numb and immobilize the spirit.

The dream of these women, a dream turned crusade, monomania, or passion (this latter a term much preferred by their creator), is to take their stand wherever ignorance, inertia, and the submissive acceptance of fate make of the individual an alienated and fearful creature, a soul without passion. In light of this passion these characters are descendants of Don Quixote. Miss Mortimer's attempts to imbue the hill dwellers of rural Mississippi, whites disinherited from the America of progress, with a thirst for knowledge and Miss Eckhart's efforts to inspire an appreciation of art in the provincials of Morgana find their most eminent precursor in the figure of Don Quixote, the self-appointed righter of wrongs and injustices as he journeys across the arid plains of La Mancha.

A most salient feature in Don Quixote's personality is his improbability.

---

4. Louis D. Rubin, Jr., "Art and Artistry in Morgana, Mississippi," in *A Gallery of Southerners* (Baton Rouge: Louisiana State University Press, 1982), 62.

P. E. Russell calls it "inauthenticity," and defines it as "the fact that [Don Quixote] is, physically as well as socially, lacking in the essential qualities of the literary heroes whose company he sets out to join."[5] We have come across this feature before in some of Faulkner's characters, such as Quentin Compson and Gavin Stevens, with their chivalrous-heroic pretensions. Welty's heroines, however, do not evince these characteristics. They are teachers, and their identities are in accord with the task they wish to carry out, namely, the opening up of new approaches to the worlds of culture, progress, reason, and art by the very means and in the very places where they practice their profession. The essential contradiction in their personalities is to be found in the imbalance between intention and reality, namely, in the discrepancy between their purpose on the one hand and on the other those for whom it is conceived, those who regard it as nothing less than a threat to their routine and ritualistic ways of life, a threat, indeed, to their very identities.

Miss Mortimer's and Miss Eckhart's quixotic qualities lie in their unwillingness to accept the communities' limitations on their tasks and their inability to reconcile themselves to the impossibility of ever opening up Morgana or Banner to the world. In vain, also, are their attempts to convince their fellow citizens of the unique and precious personal gains to be derived from the struggle to wrest one's own identity from the collective morass. Here indeed resides their failure, as well as their pathos, as we shall have occasion to observe.

The ability of Welty's obstinate teachers to imagine themselves beyond the boundaries of pressing actuality speaks uniquely of one of the author's more heartfelt concerns: the disparity between what life is and what one wishes it to be. The passion for art as a means of confronting contingency has been the permanent obsession of a writer with an outstanding capacity for sounding the most recondite and subtle recesses of the human heart. In "Finding a Voice," one part of her autobiographical work, *One Writer's Beginnings*, the author describes her defense of the imagination as a means of discovering the world, as a way of entering into more intimate contact with it. She claims for the artist the same dynamics of fantasy that children use to explore the world without and within themselves. She describes the landscape as she observed it at the age of ten through the window of a moving train: "I saw it going by, the outside world, in a flash," she recalls.

---

5. Peter E. Russell, *Cervantes* (Oxford: Oxford University Press, 1985), 34.

"I dreamed over what I could see as it passed, as well as over what I couldn't. Part of the dream was what lay beyond, where the path wandered off through the pasture. . . . A house back at its distance at night showing a light from an open doorway, the morning faces of the children who stopped still in what they were doing. . . . I never saw with the thought of their continuing to be there just the same after we were out of sight. For now, and for a long while to come, I was proceeding in fantasy." Once in an interview she mentioned *Don Quixote* as one of her favorite books and described its appeal glowingly: "That feeling of discovery you get with such a novel is the most marvelous thing. A door has been opened."[6]

This passion for knowledge—for the revelation of the truth underlying visible reality—which becomes a compulsive drive in the adult Eudora Welty, is the same motivating force we find in the characters of Miss Julia Mortimer and Miss Elizabeth Eckhart. In a hostile environment, they struggle constantly against the windmills of ignorance, suspicion, and incomprehension. Similarly Eudora Welty refers to incidents in the life of her mother, Chestina Andrews Welty, during her experience teaching school in the mountains of West Virginia as a veritable heroic quest. Chessie was fifteen years old when her father died, and Eudora tells us how, immediately afterward, she "piled up her hair and went out to teach in a one-room school, mountain children little and big alike. . . . She left home every day on her horse; since she had the river to cross, a little brother rode on her horse behind her, to ride him home, while she rowed the river in a boat. And he would be there to meet her with her horse again at evening." That period of her mother's life holds for Eudora Welty the powerful fascination of a woman of unshakable fortitude bravely facing up to adversity, traits which would later be reflected in the lives of her fictitious heroines. "The first day, some fathers came along," she writes of her mother's experience, "to see if she could whip their children, some who were older than she. She told the children that she did intend to whip them if they became unruly and refused to learn, and invited the fathers to stay if they liked and she'd be able to whip them too. Having been thus tried out, she was a great success with them after that." On another occasion, when someone remarked that schoolteachers figured largely in her work, Welty acknowledged the

6. Eudora Welty, *One Writer's Beginnings* (Cambridge, Mass.: Harvard University Press, 1984), 74–75; Eudora Welty, interview by John Griffin Jones, in *Conversations with Eudora Welty*, ed. Peggy Whitman Prenshaw (Jackson: University Press of Mississippi, 1984), 324.

influence that such women had exercised in her own life: "My mother was such a teacher, although she didn't teach me, but I heard her tales of school teaching in the mountains of West Virginia," later adding, in reference to her fictional characters: "She was the same kind of soul that these other teachers were."[7]

Teachers became increasingly important in southern communities during the 1930s. As M. E. Bradford notes, "by 1941 the presiding figures of the region were less and less certainly the heads of landed families, political spokesman, lawyers and clergy. Teachers—with the support of business and professional men whom they have helped to train, plus a new breed of journalist, and the ubiquitous helpful outside visitors—rose to be the figures of reference and instruments of alteration."[8] But in Eudora Welty's fictional universe the teachers representing the thirst for knowledge and the zeal to fulfill one's own identity are doomed to ostracism and solitude. They are ardent beings whose unveiled passion is a threat to the other members of the group, stirring in them unwanted emotions. The others may be often wracked with passion, too, but they keep it private and hidden from the community instead of expressing it openly as was Julia Mortimer's cherished wish. So their wrath against the Miss Eckharts and Miss Mortimers is in part an effort to deny the existence of the same emotion in themselves. But Welty's heroines are clear examples of the type of beings who have learned to live with failure, and therefore they are able to run the risks involved with living out their passion in all its consequences.

As quixotic behavior is fundamentally characterized by the implausible nature of the protagonists' actions as well as by their stubborn resistance to all reverses in fortune, Eudora Welty appropriately places her characters in situations similar to that of the eternal idealist, Don Quixote. However, in a South at the crossroads between a traditional society and the America of progress, this Mississippi writer does not charge her own Quixotes with recreating a heroic-legendary past by means of some futile and anachronis-

---

7. Welty, *One Writer's Beginnings*, 51–52; Eudora Welty, Shelby Foote, and Louis D. Rubin, Jr., "Growing Up in the Deep South—A Conversation" in *The American South: Portrait of a Culture*, ed. Louis D. Rubin, Jr., Forum series (Washington, D.C.: United States Information Agency, 1991), 66.

8. M. E. Bradford, "Looking Down from a High Place: The Serenity of Miss Welty's *Losing Battles*," in *A Still Moment: Essays on the Art of Eudora Welty*, ed. John F. Desmond (Metuchen, N.J.: Scarecrow Press, 1978), 105.

tic gesture, such as we have seen fellow Mississippian William Faulkner do. Rather, she places them squarely before the challenge of the future, as Mark Twain does his Connecticut Yankee. But while Twain's character possesses a blind faith in the achievements of an industrial and capitalist America, Welty's heroines champion a more private cause: the cause of culture and knowledge as sources of personal liberation. Furthermore, unlike Hank Morgan, whose adventures are stained by his bitter disillusionment with the cause he had so enthusiastically defended, Miss Julia Mortimer and Miss Eckhart never renounce their own causes. On the contrary, they remain convinced that both their causes and the passion with which they uphold them are right and just. Armed with pride and even arrogance, they persevere in spite of the scorn to which they are subjected, clinging firmly to the sole dignity remaining to them in their condition—the nobility of failure.

One of Eudora Welty's most exemplary quixotic characters is Miss Lotte Elizabeth Eckhart, a lady of German extraction who made her appearance one fine day alongside her mother in the little town of Morgana in the Mississippi delta region just a few years before the outbreak of World War I. There she rents the ground floor of a house belonging to the MacLain family and proceeds to set up what she called her piano "studio." For a while the daughters of the middle-class families of Morgana come to the studio to receive lessons. But by the end of the story Morgana banishes both Miss Eckhart and her music, abandoning her to her tragic fate.

Key witnesses to the tragic final unfolding of Miss Eckhart's downfall are the two Morrison children, whose parents live next door to the MacLains: Cassie Morrison, their teenage daughter, and her little brother, Loch, confined to his room with an attack of malaria. Cassie, busy at home dyeing some scarves, hears the notes of a familiar melody that remind her of the time when she used to go to the studio to take piano lessons from Miss Eckhart. She recalls another student, Virgie Rainey, Miss Eckhart's favorite pupil and the only one truly blessed with a natural gift for music. *Für Elise* is the melody that reaches her ears from the now empty MacLain house: "*Für Elise* was always Virgie Rainey's piece. For years Cassie thought Virgie wrote it, and Virgie never did deny it. It was a kind of signal that Virgie had burst in; she would strike that little opening phrase off the keys as she passed anybody's piano—even the one in the café. She never abandoned *Für Elise*; long after she went on to the hard pieces, she still played that" (GA 292). Such is the evocative power of these strains that Beethoven's melody becomes the symbol of Miss Eckhart's fate in Morgana. Every note of this magical melody is resonant with illusions and defeats: with the dreams and hopes deposited not only in an exceptional musical talent but also in Virgie Rainey's future in the wide world beyond; resonant also with a natural gift that might have become a true vocation, but instead is irrevocably wasted and lost. Miss Eckhart says "over and over" that "Virgie Rainey . . . had a gift . . . and must go away from Morgana. From them all. . . . In the world, she must study and practice her music for the rest of her life" (GA 303).

This is Miss Eckhart's quixotic undertaking, in pursuit of which she will meet with her most resounding defeat. Although the Raineys have rented an old piano for their daughter to practice on—which had been "butted and half-eaten by the goats one summer day," we are told—they know from the start that "Virgie would never go, or study, or practice anywhere, never would even have her own piano, because it wouldn't be like her" (GA 303). And not only the Raineys but the whole of Morgana have different plans for teacher and pupil: "Perhaps nobody wanted Virgie Rainey to be anything in Morgana any more than they had wanted Miss Eckhart to be" (GA 306). In truth, Morgana's relations with Miss Eckhart are never friendly. The woman is a foreigner and an eccentric, and no one knows anything about her past. She is never well received in the town: "Missie Spights said that if Miss Eckhart had allowed herself to be called by her first name, then she would have been like other ladies. Or if Miss Eckhart had belonged to a church that had ever been heard of, and the ladies would have had something to invite her to belong to. . . . Or if she had been married to anybody at all, just the awfullest man—like Miss Snowdie MacLain, that everybody could feel sorry for" (GA 308). Never for a moment averting her implacably critical gaze, Eudora Welty ironically points out that if Miss Eckhart had compromised in these matters perhaps her life in Morgana would have been more bearable, and perhaps she would not have been so cruelly mocked and shunned.

Even so, neither her eccentricity nor her stubbornness is the kernel of her conflict with Morgana. There is something much stranger about Miss Eckhart, much more bizarre and disturbing to the town than her behavior or her way of life. It is her passion—personal, individual, completely at odds with Morgana's criteria for its citizens' aspirations. Her passion for music and her deep need to communicate it give her a mistaken idea of her own potential, finally rendering her vulnerable to her surroundings.

For we are told that "the very place to prove Miss Eckhart crazy was on her own subject, piano playing: she didn't know what she was talking about" (GA 308).

One day after a lesson, a violent summer storm breaks over the town. Cassie, Virgie Rainey, and little Jinny Love Stark are unable to leave the studio. At once Miss Eckhart sits down at the piano and begins playing "as if it were Beethoven," revealing to the children the depths of her soul: "In playing it Miss Eckhart assumed an entirely different face. Her skin flattened and drew across her cheeks, her lips changed. The face could have belonged to someone else—not even to a woman, necessarily. It was the face a mountain could have, or what might be seen behind the veil of a waterfall. There in the rainy light it was a sightless face, one for music only." At the sight of Miss Eckhart playing the piano, lost as if in some rapture, the children feel frightened and embarrassed, for "something had burst out, unwanted, exciting, from the wrong person's life." From behind the piano teacher's strict, fussy, and distant demeanor there emerges quite unexpectedly this music which, for Cassie Morrison, has an almost scandalous resonance: "It lay in the very heart of the stormy morning—there was something almost too violent about a storm in the morning" (GA 301–2).

The abyss separating Miss Eckhart's dreams from the realities of Morgana is most graphically illustrated in the event that takes place at her studio every June, when school is out for summer, and a noisy, childlike sense of freedom is in the air. It is then that Miss Eckhart's pupils give their recital: "The recital was, after all, a ceremony. Better than school's being let out—for that presupposed examinations—or the opening political fireworks—the recital celebrated June" (GA 311). Weeks in advance, Miss Eckhart meticulously sets the stage, "like a military operation," says Cassie's father sarcastically. She asks her pupils to keep a most rigorous secret of the program contents: "You're not to tell anyone what the program is to be, Miss Eckhart warned at every lesson and rehearsal, as if there were other music teachers, other classes, rivaling, and as if every year the program didn't begin with 'The Stubborn Rocking Horse' by the one boy and end with '*Marche Militaire*' for eight hands" (GA 309). Everything is ready and everybody is looking forward to the evening of the recital, the one time in the year when for a few hours Miss Eckhart is allowed to occupy the limelight in Morgana: "And Miss Eckhart pushed herself to quite another level of life for it. A blushing sensitivity sprang up in her every year at the proper time like a flower of the season, like the Surprise Lilies that came up with no leaves and overnight in Miss Nell's yard" (GA 311).

The highlight of the evening is Virgie Rainey's performance, for undoubtedly "recital night was Virgie's night, whatever else it was." Virgie is to play *Fantasia on Beethoven's Ruins of Athens*, and of course she is determined to shine. So euphoric and agitated is Miss Eckhart on this June evening that her students, highly nervous because of the occasion, are readily forgiven for their mistakes and even have reassuring smiles bestowed upon them by their teacher. For, as Cassie puts it, "It was as though Miss Eckhart, at the last, were grateful to you for *anything*" (GA 313). As the evening draws to a close and the assembled mothers congratulate her, Miss Eckhart is moved to joke good humoredly with her students and even speaks to them in German. It is then that the deep satisfaction she feels is revealed in all its magnitude: "In the still night air her dress felt damp and spotted, as though she had run a long way" (GA 315).

Nevertheless, the June recital is no more than a brief flickering in Miss Eckhart's darkening life in Morgana. Her cherished dream, which these summer evenings manage to illuminate with a fleeting spark of reality, appears even more wild and futile against the community's dim attitude toward her. For the inhabitants of Morgana the recital is little more than a social gathering. They are oblivious to the hopes of this foreign lady whose only pretension is to live her life according to her own lights and give something of herself to others. Her most fervent desire—that of realizing her artistic vocation, of living it out to the full—is something to which Morgana will never consent. As Louis D. Rubin observes, "The role Morgana plays for its inhabitants can only be effective if they act in concert to exclude from their lives any kind of stark, wholly passionate experience that would remind them of the world outside. This had doomed Miss Eckhart, for she had not been willing to subordinate her Beethoven to the everyday proportions of the town's social needs."[9]

Little by little, without noise or fuss, as though following a preordained course, Morgana turns its back on Miss Eckhart and her piano lessons. This rejection may be a result of her refusal to leave town after being attacked and raped by a black man. Miss Eckhart's attitude is largely uncomprehended in Morgana except by Miss Perdita Mayo, the only one who

---

9. Louis D. Rubin, Jr., "The Golden Apples of the Sun," in *The Faraway Country: Writers of the Modern South* (Seattle: University of Washington Press, 1963), 148.

dares to venture an explanation: "Miss Perdita Mayo, who took in sewing and made everybody's trousseaux, said Miss Eckhart's *differences* were why shame alone had not killed her, and killed her mother too; that differences were reasons" (GA 302). Or perhaps the reason for the community's refusal can be found in her strange behavior in the cemetery at the burial of Mr. Sissum, with whom it is rumored she had been in love: "Miss Eckhart, a stranger to their cemetery, where none of her people lay, pushed forward with her unstylish, winter purse swinging on her arm, and began to nod her head—sharply, to one side and then the other" (GA 299). Whatever the motives, Miss Eckhart is gradually left without any pupils and therefore without any means of livelihood in Morgana. Her dreams remain forever locked away in the studio of the ground floor of the MacLain house, next to the old piano, the metronome, and the fragile gold chairs that so often formed part of the audience at the evening recitals, as if in mockery of the spirit and the ingenuousness of the tenant. The illusory nature of Miss Eckhart's aspirations take on a bitter shade of irony in Cassie's eyes when they are reflected in the mirror of harsh reality: "How much later had it occurred to Cassie that 'the studio' itself, the only one ever heard of in Morgana, was nothing more than a room that was rented? Rented because poor Miss Snowdie MacLain needed the money?" (GA 288).

But Miss Lotte Elisabeth Eckhart's final defeat is crystallized most starkly in the person of Virgie Rainey, in whom she places her greatest hopes, which soon come crashing to earth. When the Raineys are faced with serious economic difficulties after their stable is destroyed in a storm, Miss Eckhart offers to give Virgie piano lessons free of charge in exchange for a little help picking figs and pecans in her yard. But after her brother dies in France, Virgie stops attending lessons altogether and accepts a job at the Bijou, Morgana's local movie theater: "She belonged now with the Gish and the Talmadge sisters. With her yellow pencil she hit the tin plate when the tent opened where Valentino lived." Virgie would never again play *Für Elise,* or rather, she would play it only as an accompaniment to the advertisements at the Bijou, "moodily while the slide of the big white chicken on the watermelon-pink sky came on for the Bowles' [Grocery]. . . . *Für Elise* never got finished any more; it began, went a little way, and was interrupted by Virgie's own clamorous hand" (GA 303).

The unfortunate Miss Eckhart can do nothing to prevent her prize pupil from slipping from her grasp. As if destiny were laughing at her vain illusions, her attempts to rescue Virgie for music now appear foolish, even grotesque, as when she makes her a present of "an armful of books that were written in German about the lives of the masters, and Virgie couldn't read a word; and Mr. Fate Rainey tore out the Venusberg pictures and fed them to the pigs." All her efforts prove hopeless, even though she perseveres with uncommon fortitude and integrity to the end: "Miss Eckhart tried all those things and was strict to the last in the way she gave all her love to Virgie Rainey and none to anybody else, the way she was strict in music; and for Miss Eckhart love was just as arbitrary and one-sided as music teaching" (GA 307). Miss Eckhart's ventures into the world represented by Morgana and her search for a way of transmitting her artistic vision and showing how art can be a way of life seem blighted by error and invariably meet with ridicule and defeat. Eudora Welty is explicit about how her heroine's intentions collided with reality: "Her love never did anybody any good" (GA 307), she informs us. From the very beginning we are in no doubt that Miss Eckhart's seeds of culture will fall on stony ground.

It seems that "it might have been Virgie's stopping that took away Miss Eckhart's luck for good," and after Cassie, the last student to desert Miss Eckhart, takes her leave, "to make up for her mother's abhorrence, to keep her mother as kind as she really was" (GA 306), Miss Eckhart's fate is sealed. Eventually she is forced to vacate her studio by Mrs. Vince Murphy, who has bought the house from Miss Snowdie MacLain, and all the furniture remains in Mrs. Murphy's possession, too, including the piano. Abandoned and alone, Miss Eckhart wanders over the fields, a distressing figure, victim of the fate that Morgana always held in store for her: "Where did Miss Eckhart come from, and where in the end did she go? In Morgana most destinies were known to everybody and seemed to go without saying. It was unlikely that anybody except Miss Perdita Mayo has asked Miss Eckhart where the Eckharts came from, where exactly in the world, and so received the answer. And Miss Perdita was so undependable: she couldn't tell you now, to save her life. And Miss Eckhart had gone down out of sight" (GA 308).

Solitary in a room in Old Man Holifield's house on Morgan's Wood Road, Miss Eckhart grows old. "People said you could look at her and see she had broken," though she still retains something of her former bearing and disposition: "she could still stop young, unknowing children like Loch on the street and ask them imperative questions, 'Where were you throwing that ball? Are you trying to break that tree?' " But "of course, her only associates from first to last were children; not counting Miss Snowdie" (GA

307). The novel's climactic conclusion, in which Cassie and Loch look on from a window in their house as Miss Eckhart tries to set fire to her old piano and studio while Virgie is dallying with a sailor on an old mattress in an upstairs room, puts the final touch of bitter irony and pathos to Miss Eckhart's quixotic quest in Morgana. But with the flames consuming her piano and metronome on that summer afternoon in the MacLains' empty house Miss Eckhart goes down fighting in a final settling of accounts with the reality that has always borne down implacably upon her. Like Don Quixote, who, when defeated by the Knight of the White Moon on the beach at Barcelona requests that his rival take his life rather than renounce his ideal, Miss Eckhart also refuses to forswear her ideal, preferring to bring about her own demise. When finally Miss Eckhart is dragged from the house by Old Man Moody and Mr. Bowles, she comes face to face for the last time with Virgie Rainey, who, alarmed by the fire, has just rushed into the street. Cassie expects a visible reaction from Virgie, but that is not the case: "the meeting amounted only to Virgie Rainey's passing by, in plain fact" (GA 325).

In a further ironic twist of fate, it is not Miss Eckhart's favorite pupil, Virgie Rainey, who is able to understand the significance of her teacher's life and accept her own involvement in the drama. This is left to Cassie, the only person capable of feeling sympathy for the teacher's plight, and upon whom Miss Eckhart has never bestowed any special attention. Cassie thinks that "somewhere, even up to the last, there could have been for Miss Eckhart a little opening wedge—a crack in the door. . . . But if [she] had been the one to see it open . . . [she] might have slammed it tight for ever. [She] might" (GA 308). Louis D. Rubin maintains that even though Miss Eckhart fails with Virgie Rainey, the lesson is not lost upon Cassie Morrison. He points out that Cassie does not quit Morgana but stays there until she manages to perceive the truth underlying the surface reality, and therefore, "the old German teacher had, after all, found her apprentice."[10]

The lesson that Cassie learns from Miss Eckhart is that "there [is] more than the ear could bear to hear or the eye to see" (GA 301), that the passion which compels certain spirits towards the achievement of their ideal is stronger than the bare fact of their failure, and the need to communicate this ideal becomes the fulcrum of their lives. Eudora Welty is little given to talking about herself in relation to her characters, convinced as she is that

10. Rubin, "Art and Artistry," 66.

they must live independently of their author. She has, however, made an exception in the case of Miss Eckhart:

> As I looked longer and longer for the origins of this passionate and strange character, at last I realized that Miss Eckhart came from me. There wasn't any resemblance in her outward identity: I am not musical, not a teacher, nor foreign in birth; not humorless or ridiculed or missing out in love; nor have I yet let the world around me slip from my recognition. But none of that counts. What counts is only what lies at the solitary core. She derived from what I already knew for myself, even felt I had always known. What I have put into her is my passion for my own life work, my own art. Exposing yourself to risk is a truth Miss Eckhart and I had in common. What animates and possesses me is what drives Miss Eckhart, the love of her art and the love of giving it, the desire to give until there is no more left.[11]

Cassie, the conscientiously developing artist, will also learn through Miss Eckhart that this same passion is the stuff on which dreams are made, and that nobody, least her, should try to pin them down. The hummingbird that visits Cassie every year, hovering outside her window, is an apt, living metaphor for the ever-elusive dream in the girl's mind: "Metallic and misty together, tangible and intangible, splendid and fairy-like, the haze of his invisible wings mysterious, like the ring around the moon—had anyone ever tried to catch him? Not she. Let him be suspended there for a moment each year for a hundred years—incredibly thirsty, greedy for every drop in every four-o'clock trumpet in the yard, as though he had them numbered—then dart" (GA 308).

Holding on to one's dreams in the face of reality is also the motif of *Losing Battles*, the novel in which Eudora Welty most definitively deals with defeat and quixotic resolve. "I don't feel it's a novel of despair at all," she says of this novel. "I feel it's more a novel of admiration for the human being who can cope with any condition, even ignorance, and keep a courage, a joy of life, even, that's unquenchable." As for the time and place in which she chooses to set her story, she explains:

> I wanted to get a year in which I could show people at the rock bottom of their whole lives, which meant the Depression. I wanted the poorest part of the state,

---

11. Welty, *One Writer's Beginnings*, 110.

which meant the northeast corner, where people had the least, the least of all. I wanted a clear stage to bring on this family, to show them when they had really no props to their lives, had only themselves, plus an indomitable will to live even with losing battles . . . the losing battles of poverty, of any other kind of troubles, family troubles and disasters. I wanted to take away everything and show them naked as human beings.[12]

In the nature of this work, in the unswerving determination of the novel's characters to face up to a reality that offers few rewards, and little prospect for substantial change, there is an unmistakable quixotic element. It is to be found in the characters' mistaken apprehension of reality and the possibilities it offers them, in the causes lost beforehand, causes that they nevertheless embark upon with tenacity and an absurd and blind faith in their ability to change the future.

The novel is set in the little community of Barner, in Boone County, a depressed area in northeast Mississippi where, according to Uncle Dolphus, "there ain't nothing running no more but snakes on the ground and candidates for office" (*LB* 194). The Beecham-Renfro families are convinced that Jack, eldest son of Beulah Beecham and Ralph Renfro, who has recently been discharged from the Parchman Penitentiary, is going to save them from ruin and penury. "We're relying on Jack now. He'll haul us out of our misery" (*LB* 194), says Uncle Curtis, voicing the opinion of the entire family, who have entrusted all their hopes of prosperity to Jack. Aunt Birdie is even more emphatic about the providential powers of her nephew: "When Jack jumps out in those fields tomorrow, he'll resurrect something out of nothing" (*LB* 326). These are forceful opinions, which elevate Jack to the status of a quasi hero. Jack, with his all-purpose truck, his enormous energy and optimism, will put an end to all the ills besetting the large family presided over by the centenarian Granny Jordan Vaughn. As for himself, Jack Renfro, in addition to sharing with his relations all of the unfounded optimism in his own capabilities, possesses all the courage and foolhardiness characteristic of quixotic heroes. "I still believe I can handle trouble just taking it as it comes," he remarks with conviction when the incidents at Banner Top are turning ugly and Judge Moody's Buick is in serious danger of hurdling down a precipice. "It takes thinking! We've got to think," urges the judge (*LB* 390). But foresight is not one of Jack's

12. Bunting, "The Interior World," 720–21.

strong points, something he amply demonstrates by escaping from the penitentiary just one day before he was due to be released, in order to attend the family gathering for Grandma's birthday party: "Our reunion is one that don't wait, sir," Jack explains to Judge Moody, the very man who sentenced him. "Nobody, not even my wife, would have forgiven me for the rest of my life if I hadn't showed up today" (*LB* 195).

But if Jack is naive and incapable of foreseeing the consequences of his actions, his wife, Gloria Renfro, who seems to be more realistic than her husband, is nevertheless equally prone to overlook the many impediments that will prevent her from fulfilling her aspirations. What Gloria Renfro desires is to get Jack away from the family influence and help him build a life for them both, far removed from the Renfro clan. She dreams of having her own house and her own life: "I'm keeping on trying! I'll save him yet! . . . I don't give up easy!" (*LB* 198), she cries right in the middle of Granny's birthday party, when the family's impregnable solidity is ritually confirmed at this annual celebration. However, Gloria has already been warned about what sort of family she is dealing with, even before she married Jack. This warning has been given by Miss Julia Mortimer, Gloria's mentor and one-time schoolteacher in Banner. Gloria turns a deaf ear to her advice, the same response that most of Banner's inhabitants give to Miss Julia's counsel during the many years she spends among them.

Of all the struggles unleashed in Banner during the hard times of the Depression, perhaps the most vain and unfruitful is that of Miss Julia Mortimer, who for years, and with the same stubbornness and perseverance we have observed in Miss Eckhart, clings firmly to her own convictions and refuses to yield before a hostile reality. A woman of iron will and quixotic tenacity even in such an inauspicious and inhospitable part of the world, she has managed to educate and launch on their careers "a Superior Court judge, the best eye, ear, nose, and throat specialist in Kansas City, and a history professor somewhere" (*LB* 305). Miss Mortimer had taken up the most difficult challenge of her life by moving from Ludlow, where she was born and had lived all her life, to the little town of Banner, "the very pocket of ignorance" in Judge Moody's words, to take charge of the newly erected schoolhouse that Grandfather Renfro had been instrumental in building on Banner's side of the river. Before the schoolhouse was built, the Renfro sons, if they wanted schooling, had been obliged to make the arduous journey upriver on horseback until they could find a place to cross, thereafter to continue along the trail on foot until they reached the nearest school, in

Alliance. Soon after Banner gets its schoolhouse, Ralph Renfro is heard to remark ironically that "there was a little breathing space while they could hope the teacher they prayed for'd never come" (*LB* 273). But the inhabitants of Banner were soon to get their schoolteacher, or rather, as Miss Lexie expresses it, "they didn't have to find her. She'd found them. Banner school was ready for a teacher, and that was all she needed" (*LB* 273).

Miss Julia is a female character not unusual in the South during the early decades of the twentieth century. Although Welty may ascribe excessive, even obsessive traits to this tenacious schoolmistress, such traits existed in a real-life character, Miss Lorena Duling, to whom Eudora Welty refers on several occasions and who bears some resemblance to her fictional creation in *Losing Battles*. The parallelism between Miss Duling and the character of Miss Julia Mortimer is obvious in the following passage, where Welty describes her former schoolteacher in her hometown of Jackson:

> Miss Duling, a lifelong subscriber to perfection, was a figure of authority, the most whole-souled I have ever come to know. She was a dedicated schoolteacher who denied herself all she might have done or whatever other way she might have lived. . . . I believe she came of well-off people, well-educated, in Kentucky, and certainly old photographs show she was a beautiful, high-spirited-looking young lady—and came down to Jackson to its new grammar school that was going begging for a principal. She must have earned next to nothing; Mississippi then as now was the nation's lowest-ranking state economically, and our legislature has always shown a painfully loud reluctance to give money to public education. That challenge *brought* her.[13]

Disproportion is a fitting term to describe an undertaking such as Miss Julia Mortimer's, so radically opposed as it was to the wishes of the inhabitants of Banner, for as Lewis P. Simpson points out, "She would bring them under the imperatives of ambition and progress, so that they 'can change the future.' In other words, though she is not capable of thinking in such terms, she would bring a world based on family tribalism into the modern American bourgeois commercial and industrial society."[14]

Remarks made by Uncle Percy and Uncle Noah Webster illustrate the

---

13. Welty, *One Writer's Beginnings*, 24–25.
14. Lewis P. Simpson, "The Chosen People," *Southern Review* 6 (1970): xxii.

attitude of members of the Beechman, Renfro, and Vaughn families toward Miss Julia's crusade. The family group, serving as a microcosm for the entire region, firmly believes that she wants nothing less than to meddle in and shape their whole lives: "She had designs on everybody. She wanted a doctor and a lawyer and all else we might have to holler for some day, to come right out of Banner. So she'd get behind some barefooted boy and push. . . . She put an end to good fishing. . . . She thought if she mortified you long enough, you might have hope of turning out something you wasn't" (*LB* 235–36). Miss Julia's fight against ignorance in all its many manifestations is a fight without quarter, driving her, in the eyes of the people of Banner, to increasingly outlandish, eccentric, and extremely fastidious behavior. They fail to understand why she becomes indignant over the fact that many of their children have no birth certificates or are underfed. To cap it all, she takes her job far too seriously. Five months of schooling a year are not nearly enough for her, and when a cyclone blows the roof off the schoolhouse she urges everybody to rebuild it at once with whatever materials are at hand. As Uncle Curtis remarks with a mixture of perplexity and resentment, "She never quit holding school while they was overhead pounding. Rain or shine, she didn't let father or son miss a day. 'Every single day or your life counts,' she told 'em all alike. 'As long as I'm here, you aren't getting the chance to be cheated out of a one of 'em' " (*LB* 239). But of all the things Miss Julia is determined to put right in Banner, the one that is both her prime target and the rock on which she founders is the self-satisfaction of these people, who take pride in their precarious condition. Beulah expresses it clearly when she says: "She told us a time or two what her aim was! She wanted us to quit worshipping ourselves quite so wholehearted !" (*LB* 236).

In the Beechams' and Renfros' world there is no room for self-criticism or introspection. Quite the contrary, it is precisely their complacency that keeps them united and closed to anything disturbing or to anyone from without, who, like Miss Julia, might bring them to an awareness of their true situation. After Miss Julia has finally been driven to defeat and her name has become a legend in Banner, an exchange among Aunt Birdie, Miss Beulah, and Uncle Curtis attests to her resounding failure in this regard:

> "I wish she'd minded her own business and not ours," said Aunt Birdie.
> "She never did that in her life. And so brag on her, brag on her all you want!

But I'll tell you this when you've finished," Miss Beulah warned them all. "She never did learn how to please."

"No," said Uncle Curtis, "she never. You're right Beulah, and you nearly always are. . . . Knowing the way to please and pacify the public and pour oil on the waters was entirely left out when they was making her pattern."

. . . .

"Didn't even know how to please when she picked a day to die, to my notion!" cried Aunt Birdie loyally. "But she didn't damage our spirits much—howsoever she might have liked to. Not ours!" (*LB* 293)

Aunt Birdie's last comment laconically summarizes the futility of Miss Julia's attempts to infuse these men and women with what, according to Captain Billy Bangs, she once said to him, " 'We ain't standing still, Captain Billy,' she says, 'No, sir, the world's round and goes spinning' " (*LB* 424). The pages of *Losing Battles* leave us in no doubt about the outcome of this struggle against the windmills of backwardness and ignorance in Banner. When asked if Miss Julia had met with utter defeat, the author herself is quite unequivocal: "Well, look at the people around her. All her class, all the people she'd taught, they didn't know a thing, except the thing that mattered most to them, which I think is most valuable—that is, their love for one another and dependence upon one another, and their family, and their pride, and all that. But nothing Miss Julia had tried to teach them had ever taken root. Nothing."[15]

The most painful aspect of Miss Julia's defeat revolves around the person of Gloria Short (later Renfro, wife of Jack), the orphan whom she has encouraged and helped to study for her diploma at the grade school in Ludlow. There are notable parallels here to Virgie Rainey and Miss Eckhart in "The Golden Apples," a situation that also ends in failure. Miss Mortimer likewise pins all her hopes on Gloria. "Her dearest wish was to pass on the torch to me" (*LB* 244), Gloria explains to her new in-laws on the day of the family gathering. Although Gloria becomes a teacher at Banner summer school, she is not destined to fulfill the hopes that Miss Julia has placed in her. "When the torch was about to be handed on to me for good," she says, "I didn't want to take it after all" (*LB* 245). Gloria falls in love with Jack Renfro, one of her students, and informs her mentor of her

15. Jo Brans, "Struggling Against the Plaid: An Interview with Eudora Welty" (interview, November 1980), in *Conversations with Eudora Welty*, 303.

intention to marry him. Miss Julia counsels prudence and advises her to think carefully about her own background before hastily making such an important decision. Gloria has been reared in an orphan asylum, and nobody in Banner seems to have certain proof of her parents' identity. But the two letters that Miss Julia later sends her, urging her to come and see her in Alliance and warning her about the possible fateful consequences of the marriage, lead one to believe that Miss Julia might have known that Gloria was about to marry someone of her own blood. But these letters go unanswered. Gloria marries Jack Renfro and never goes to Alliance before or after her marriage, not even when her baby daughter is born and she suffers no stigma or ill-repute, not even to see her old teacher one last time when, sick and alone, Miss Julia fervently expects her to come. "Gloria Short will be here soon now. She knows it's for her own good to get here on time," Miss Julia says to Miss Lexie, who looks after her in the last days of her life. "Even in bed," Miss Lexie says, "she'd lean close to her window, press her face to the glass even on rainy mornings, not to miss the first sight of Gloria coming" (*LB* 279).

But as in the case of Virgie Rainey and Miss Eckhart, Gloria not only rejects Miss Julia's plans for her, she also refuses her any semblance of gratitude, sympathy, or even compassion. When Miss Lexie tells the family reunion of Miss Julia's low spirits and physical infirmity, her isolation and neglect, Gloria shows no reaction, not even when Miss Lexie says that she told Miss Julia, "Oh, she's just forgotten you, Julia, like everybody else has" (*LB* 279). Yet in spite of being abandoned and forgotten by all those whom she encouraged and tried to help, in spite of her loneliness and the ill-treatment to which Miss Lexie subjects her (on one occasion Miss Lexie snatches a pen from Miss Julia's hand, unable to contain her annoyance at her charge constant scribbling in the margins of the Bible, the only paper she has to write on), in spite of all this Miss Julia does leave one legacy to Banner: a letter to Judge Moody that she manages to slip into the mail without Miss Lexie's knowledge. On receiving the letter, Judge Moody, one of her former pupils, sets out to visit Miss Julia, only to run his Buick off the road on Banner Top to avoid running over Jack and Gloria Renfro's little daughter Lady May.

It is in this letter that Miss Julia Mortimer's voice is lifted to its most heartbreaking pitch but also in its most forceful and lucid cadences. It constitutes the sole personal and intimate testimony of her spirit in the novel, consistent to the point of extravagance. A testimony to her inner drama, it is also emblematic of her unshakable moral and human qualities. Julia speaks of the nature of the struggle she has been waging all her life, the necessary and inevitable struggle to survive, the same one the Renfros have been waging in the opposite camp, a struggle she plunged eagerly into because of her refusal to acquiesce in things as they are. It has been an arduous encounter, in which the odds have been stacked against her and in which her only weapons against the ranks of ignorance have been her courage and her perseverance. But whereas Don Quixote, at whose flank we have placed her, has a distorted vision of reality and imagines giants where there are only windmills, this obstinate school teacher suffers from no such hallucinations. She says in this letter: "All my life I've fought a hard war with ignorance. Except in those cases that you can count off on your fingers, I lost every battle. Year in, year out, my children at Banner School took up the cause of the other side and held the fort against me. We both fought faithfully and single-mindedly, bravely, maybe even fairly. Mostly I lost, they won. But as long as I was still young, I always thought if I could marshal strength enough of body and spirit and push with it, every ounce, I could change the future" (*LB* 298). This is the strength of which those at the family reunion who knew her have had ample proof; the same strength, as they have often repeated, they have had to put up with; the strength that has been put to the test and that still remains intact in the final moments of Miss Julia's life, as these further lines from the letter reveal: "Now that the effort it took has been put a stop to, and I can survey the years, I can see it all needs doing over, starting from the beginning. But even if Providence allowed us the second chance, doubling back on my tracks has never been my principle" (*LB* 299).

Julia Mortimer's indomitable fortitude and resolve testify to the dignity and strength of character that she manages to retain even in decline, when nothing but failure seems to result from all her efforts. Miss Julia rises above her senile obstinacy, opening up her heart and disclosing to us the most bitter aspect of her quixotic spirit in a passage replete with wisdom, revealing as it does with admirable sincerity the source of her ardent passion:

I'm alive as ever, on the brink of oblivion, and I caught myself once on the verge of disgrace. Things like this are put in your path to teach you. You can make use of them, they'll bring you one stage, one milestone, further along your road. You can go crawling next along the edge of madness, if that's where you've come to. There's a lesson in it. You can profit from knowing that you needn't be ashamed to crawl—to keep on crawling, to be proud to crawl to where you can't crawl any further. Then you can find yourself lying flat on your back—look what's carried you another mile. From flat on your back you may not be able to lick the world, but at least you can keep the world from licking you. I haven't spent a lifetime fighting my battle to give up now. I'm ready for all they send me. There's a measure of enjoyment in it. (*LB* 299)

An unbreakable will is at the bottom of this woman who has spent her life working to convince all those she knew to try to shape their destinies with their own hands, choosing the most difficult road as a means of reaching the highest rewards of self-esteem for themselves, an arduous struggle that is waged in solitude, requiring great inner strength, systematically excluding the dictates of the outside world. This is the strength that Miss Julia calls inspiration. "What I live by is inspiration," she states in her letter. "I always did—I started out on nothing else but naked inspiration," but, she is careful to add with great lucidity, "of course, I had sense enough to know that that doesn't get you anywhere all by itself" (*LB* 298).

It is equally true that Miss Julia has lived long enough to see some of her aspirations come to fruition. Oscar Moody and Gerald Caruthers were two of her protégés. The former has become a judge in Boone County "because she talked me into staying, doing what I could here at home" (*LB* 305), as he says himself. The latter has graduated from Pennsylvania University in medicine and returned home to set himself up in practice as a country doctor. Both have honored her ideas, and both have remained her friends. Moreover, some of her pupils who pursue their future beyond the confines of the inhospitable region where they were raised return to visit their old teacher and pay their last respects. As Uncle Homer remarks, "It ain't just Boone County that's over there. I saw tags tonight on cars from three or four different counties, and that ain't all—they're here from Alabama, Georgia, Carolina, and even places up North!" (*LB* 337). Banner and its townsfolk, however, have been her greatest challenge, and the hope of communicating the passion that had dominated her own life to Gloria Short has been her most cherished dream. In both these endeavors she has failed irremediably.

With a kind of eloquent sarcasm, Miss Julia retains her assertiveness to the last. Flatly refusing to allow her funeral to be clumsily orchestrated by the community, she dictates to them one by one the arrangements she wants for the ceremony down to the last detail, and when she is done she concludes with this parting shot: "And then, you fools—mourn me." Astute and perceptive, Beulah understands the message unerringly: "She may be dead and waiting in her coffin, but she hasn't given up yet. I see that. Trying to regiment the reunion into being part of her funeral!" (*LB* 292). Gloria Short, now Gloria Renfro, is equally unable to resist the influence of Miss Julia's personality. In spite of her reluctance she finally attends the funeral, prevailed upon to do so by her husband.

Ironically enough, Jack Renfro, who never meets Miss Mortimer but whose heart is big enough to allow for absurdity and to feel compassion, is the only person capable of experiencing empathy for the dilemma of this singular woman. "I heard that teacher's life," he tells Gloria. "That sounds about like the equal of getting put in the Hole! Kept in the dark, on bread and water, and nobody coming to get you out!" (*LB* 312). Then, with sincere compassion for the unfortunate Miss Julia, he adds, "I'm thankful I come along in time to save my wife from a life like hers" (*LB* 313) though Miss Julia herself would certainly not have shared in his sentiment. Even so, Gloria, in spite of herself Miss Julia's most gifted pupil, is the one who has best understood the obsession that has dominated the life of this exceptional woman. When the coffin containing Miss Julia's body and draped in the Mississippi state flag is lying in the ground in the Banner cemetery, she speaks of her former mentor for the first time in a way that is sincere and not merely an exculpation. Her words constitute an epitaph to the arduous life of a woman who conceived of human existence as a ceaseless striving toward ever greater domains of freedom: "Miss Julia Mortimer didn't want anybody left in the dark, not about anything. She wanted everything brought out in the wide open, to see and be known. She wanted people to spread out their minds and their hearts to other people, so they could be read like books." It is also left to Gloria to deliver the final judgment on the impractical nature of such a chimerical ideal: "People don't want to be read like books" (*LB* 432), she states emphatically. But Miss Julia Mortimer's indomitable spirit and passion were stronger than the ravages of solitude, neglect, isolation, and even death. Thus the little community of Banner, drowsing in the atavism of a world without contradictions, finally got its teacher, the one they asked for but definitely did not want. And to Banner Miss Julia journeyed one day, proud and unsubmissive, believing she could change the future.

6

WALKER PERCY AND THE LAST
GENTLEMAN OF SOUTHERN LITERATURE

My name is Williston Bibb Barrett, he said aloud, consulting his wallet to make sure, and I am returning to the South to seek my fortune and restore the good name of my family, perhaps even recover Hampton plantation from the canebrakes and live out my days as a just man and little father to the faithful Negroes working in the fields. Moreover, I am in love with a certain someone. Or I shall marry me a wife and live me a life in the lovely green environs of Atlanta or Memphis or even Birmingham, which, despite its bad name, is known to have lovely people.

　　　　　—Walker Percy, *The Last Gentleman*

Nothing is so sad as defeat, except victory.

　　　　　—William Alexander Percy, *Lanterns on the Levee*

It has been suggested that the person to whom the title of *The Last Gentleman* refers is not its protagonist, Williston Bibb Barrett, but rather his father, Ed Barrett. This line of argument has it that it is Ed Barrett more than his son who lives in accordance with the ethical values of his declining social class throughout his life: "In a sense the last gentleman of the novel is not Bibb Barrett, it's his father, because his father tried, however imperfectly, to live by the code. But Barrett [the son] can't understand the code. He can't even begin to live it, because he doesn't understand it."[1] Certainly,

---

1. Louis D. Rubin, Jr., et al., "Twentieth-Century Southern Literature," in *Southern Literature Study: Problems and Possibilities,* ed. Louis D. Rubin, Jr., and C. Hugh Holman (Chapel Hill: University of North Carolina Press, 1975), 139. In this panel discussion, Norman Brown made the statement cited here.

for Will's father the concepts of honor and noblesse oblige are the hallowed values on which his entire identity depends, the very foundations on which his world rests, so much so that when he sees his sense of honor and duty giving way to prejudice, unscrupulousness, and racial hatred, he feels unable to go on living with his own notion of dignity in the new order. He believes that the South, formerly so proud of its moral code, is slipping away fast and there is nothing he can do but stand by helplessly and watch its final collapse. Thus when the police tell him that the Klan has left town and his life is no longer under threat, he tells his son that this is not a victory but a defeat: "Once they were the fornicators and the bribers and the takers of bribes and we were not and that was why they hated us. Now we are like them, so why should they stay? They know they don't have to kill me." When all seems lost, he still retains his moral integrity, and nobody can take that away from him. "They may have won, but I don't have to choose that" (*LG* 330), he tells his son, presaging his suicidal end.

The term *noblesse oblige*, which had meant so much to Ed Barrett, takes on the decidedly negative connotation of *paternalism* in his son's time, and the notion of honor has become a relic of the past. In the new emerging South, these concepts have given way to new values such as racial equality grounded in the social philosophy and reassessment of the democratic culture of the sixties. Williston Bibb Barrett was born into a society undergoing great ethical and social transformations. Unfortunately, there are still staunch upholders of the old values, for whom these radical changes imply an insurmountable feeling of defeat. His father's suicide is one result of this attitude. As the years go by, Ed Barrett's tragic end comes more and more to resemble a singularly sterile act in the eyes of his son, whose overwhelming problems with personal identity have their origin in this early loss.

Walker Percy makes the generation gap between Will Barrett and his father the fulcrum of his story. He establishes a dialogue between past and present in which Will's romantic illusions and his conflicts and doubts about his place in the world are thrown into relief. One must consider here the importance of William Alexander Percy, a first cousin to Walker Percy's father in the molding of the character of Ed Barrett and in the conception of the novel as a whole. Ed Barrett's philosophy on the fate of the South and its finest men is taken from William Alexander Percy's *Lanterns on the Levee.* For such men as William Alexander Percy's father, Leroy Percy—planter, lawyer, United States senator, and one of the most influential Mississippi Delta figures of the early twentieth century—

membership in the ruling class meant above all the duty of serving the community. But those of William Percy's (and Ed Barrett's) generation saw their political power lost to demagogues and others that they considered to be riffraff. "The years Father served in the Senate were not dramatic or crucial years in the history of our country," wrote William Percy of his father's tenure in the Senate, "but they were the end of a period in which great men represented our people." Percy was forced to admit that "the bottom rail was on top" and that there was no hope of stemming the tide: "We of my generation have lost one line of fortifications after another, the old South, the old ideals, the old strengths." Deeply disillusioned, William Percy fell back on stoicism. Will Percy's bearing as a rightful man confronting in solitude the indignities of an age of vulgarity and corruption has indeed a quixotic aspect. As Fred Hobson states, "Will Percy was nearly an anachronism in 1940"; he certainly was when Walker Percy wrote *The Last Gentleman*.[2]

The quixotic aspect of southern stoicism as reflected in *Lanterns on the Levee* and in the reverberations of this philosophy found in Walker Percy's novels can hardly escape the attentive reader. The view of *Don Quixote* prevalent among the members of the generation of 1898 in Spain parallels this phenomenon. When the writers and intellectuals of this generation found themselves facing the crucial hour of disaster in the aftermath of the Spanish-American War, they turned to the character of Don Quixote as a remedy to their pessimistic vision of the country's fate. As a work expressive of their yearnings for reform, *Don Quixote* figured prominently in their attempts to bring about the spiritual regeneration of their nation. The generation of 1898 deemed Cervantes' sad knight a symbol of the tragic destiny of their country—"the irridescent gemlike Spain that could have been"—always on the verge of possibility, yet never reaching the desired harbor. José Ortega y Gasset exhorted Spaniards to "free [themselves] from the superstition of the past, lest [they] be seduced by it as if Spain were confined to the past." Cervantes' masterpiece offered that generation the key to the elusive, contradictory, problematic Spanish reality. Such men as José Ortega y Gasset and Miguel de Unamuno found the spiritual meaning

---

2. William A. Percy, *Lanterns on the Levee: Recollections of a Planter's Son* (1941; reprint with an introduction by Walker Percy, Baton Rouge: Louisiana State University Press, 1973), xvi–xvii, 146, 212–13; Fred Hobson, *Tell About the South: The Southern Rage to Explain* (Baton Rouge: Louisiana State University Press, 1983), 290.

of Spanish cultural history by "sublimating [Don Quixote's virtues] while repudiating the pejorative connotations of such terms as *quijote, quijotadas,* and their derivatives," thus transforming Cervantes' knight "into a paradigm of dignity and a symbol of revitalization."[3]

Such a transcendent view of Don Quixote, "the lanky figure [that] bends like an interrogation mark, like a guardian of the Spanish secrets, of the ambiguity of the Spanish culture," resembles closely the transcendent stance of the southern stoic facing his own cultural estrangement. The stoic's ideals having been unsettled by historical reality, he contemplates, stubborn and solitary, the fate of the South in modern times, vindicating the superiority of his ideals over the malaise of the modern age. The tenets of his philosophy are no longer in accord with the reality of southern life; he is like the Spanish hidalgos in Cervantes' time who, idle and purposeless, roamed the meager fields of Castile with sober demeanor, as living relics, real-life counterparts of the burlesqued knight. "Neither the ethos nor the traditional world view of the upper-class white Southerner," Walker Percy writes in 1956, "is any longer adequate to the situation." And he is aware of the appeal that such a stance once held. The "poetic pessimism" of the stoic attitude, he states, "took a grim satisfaction in the dissolution of its values—because social decay confirmed one in his original choice of the wintry kingdom of self. . . . [The southern stoic] was never more himself than when in a twilight victory of evil."[4]

According to Ortega and Unamuno, Spain repeatedly lost its grip on history; its progress toward modernity was always erratic and elusive, much like Don Quixote's grasp of reality. And there is a poetic pessimism in such a realization, since Don Quixote, in spite of his madness, upheld for that generation of writers the virtues of good will and relentless striving. The Knight of the Sad Countenance, "the gloomiest and most melancholy expression that sadness itself could assume," suffers "a discomfort from existing in his own unchivalric age, the Iron Age." Expressed in Kierke-

---

3. José Ortega y Gasset, *Meditations on "Quixote"*, trans. Evelyn Rugg and Diego Marín (New York: Norton, 1961), 106–07; Eric J. Ziolkowski, *The Sanctification of Don Quixote: From Hidalgo to Priest* (University Park: Pennsylvania State University Press, 1991), 172. *Quijote* and *quijotadas* are the Spanish terms for *impractical* and *absurdities*, respectively.

4. Ortega, *Meditations*, 101; Walker Percy, "Stoicism in the South," *Commonweal* 64 (1956): 343.

gaardian terms this idea could be referred to as *Angst*. Unamuno called it *congoja*, implying a view of the suffering knight "as a man led by his longings for immortality to a devastating sense of his own mortality."[5]

When William Alexander Percy considers the paradoxical challenge of rearing the Percy children in a world where his own values are no longer adequate, he uses the image of Don Quixote as a metaphor to express his dilemma, but he also finds his solution in the doomed knight's virtues:

> I had no desire to send these youngsters of mine into a life as defenseless as if they wore knights' armor and had memorized the code of chivalry. But what could I teach them other than what I myself learned? . . .
>
> Should I therefore teach deceit, dishonor, ruthlessness, bestial force to the children in order that they survive? Better that they perish. It is sophistry to speak of two sets of virtues, there is but one: virtue is an end in itself; the survival virtues are means, not ends. Honor and honesty, compassion and truth are good even if they kill you, for they alone give life its dignity and worth.[6]

Ortega's assessment of Don Quixote as a symbol of Spain's despair is not dissimilar to the stance held by the southern stoic: "Whenever a few Spaniards who have been sensitized by the idealized poverty of their past, the sordidness of their present, and the bitter hostility of their future gather together, Don Quixote descends among them and the burning ardor of his crazed countenance harmonizes those discordant hearts, strings them together like a spiritual thread, nationalizes them, putting a common racial sorrow above their personal bitterness." In the same way, the words uttered by Don Quixote as he opposes the shortsighted priest of Argamasilla may pinpoint the philosophy nurturing the stoic vision in *Lanterns on the Levee*: "It is, perchance, idleness and waste of time to wander through the world, seeking no pleasures but the austerities by which the virtuous ascend to the seat of immortality?" Alonso Quijano's austerities are not those of Christian withdrawal from the world for the compensation of the life beyond but those of chivalry in support of the ideals and values embodied in Arthurian romance. King Arthur's duty, as portrayed in the romances of Chrétien de Troyes, was not to "permit any baseness, falsity or arro-

5. Cervantes, *Don Quixote*, 857; Ziolkowski, *Sanctification of Don Quixote*, 261, 174.
6. William A. Percy, *Lanterns*, 312–13.

gance" but to "maintain truth and righteousness" and "support the law, truth, faith and justice."[7]

Walker Percy states his debt to his cousin William Alexander Percy thus: "Even when I did not follow him, it was usually in relation to him, whether with him or against him, that I defined myself and my own direction."[8] Walker Percy abandons the self-righteous attitude of the southern stoic and seeks an understanding of the world that is more adequate to his ethical principles and his contemporary existence. In *Lancelot* the redeeming heroic social order of southern stoicism is portrayed as a frantic quixotic attempt to repudiate history in a final assault on contemporary values. Lancelot Lamar's project of establishing utopia in Virginia draws heavily on southern stoicism. Lance Lamar is portrayed as an enraged Quixote determined to fight single-handedly against the contemporary malaise by forcing his apocalyptic views on an unheroic present. His stoicism conveys an intransigent religious view, a fanatic fundamentalism that enslaves him rather than freeing him. In Percy's assessment of his character's moralism, rage has displaced irony and rigidity human sympathy. Although Lance Lamar's plan for utopia is quixotically impractical, the character himself is no quixotic hero. Lancelot lacks compassion and empathy with the human condition, and his madness is rooted in revenge, not delusion. Nevertheless he exemplifies the individualistic "heroism" that Cervantes puts to a burlesque test in the character of Don Quixote. Don Quixote's words, "I know who I am," implying both his awareness of the role he is playing and his unwillingness to give it up, find an echo in Lance Lamar's "We know who we are and where we stand," words that demonstrate both Lamar's arrogant pride in his class and its tenets and his adamant refusal to accept alternative views.

In *The Last Gentleman* Walker Percy approaches his stoic heritage from a more temperate, sympathetic viewpoint. In this novel his conflicts with that heritage find full literary expression in the troubled, vulnerable character of Will Barrett. This character retains no vestige of the grave and melancholy stoic observer of the contemporary scene we see in William

---

7. Ortega, *Meditations*, 51; Cervantes, *Don Quixote*, 674; Edwin Williamson, *Half-Way House*, 7, quoting *Erec et Enide*, 24:1749–55. Williamson notes that for Arthurian references Cervantes relied more on the romances of Chrétien de Troyes than on the more nonsensical chivalric books produced in Spain during Cervantes' own time.

8. Walker Percy, Introduction to *Lanterns*, xi.

Alexander Percy's *Lanterns on the Levee*, but he is faithful to William Percy's commitment to old-time values and shares his sense of asynchrony with his own time. He becomes a bemused wayfarer, a candid seeker, quixotically searching for the truth in the puzzling scene of contemporary America. Will Barrett's sensibility in *The Last Gentleman* bears a closer resemblance to Walker Percy's own view of his southern heritage than any other character in his fiction. He endows this character with the virtues of the stoic tradition without allowing him to lapse into its sterility as Lance Lamar does in *Lancelot*. "At its best it enshrined the humane aspects of living for rich and poor, black and white," Walker Percy writes of the southern conservative tradition. "It gave first place to a stable family life, sensitivity and good manners between men, chivalry toward women, an honor code, and individual integrity." In his introduction to *Lanterns on the Levee* Walker Percy refers to "trying to 'understand the South' " as a "perennial American avocation." This, along with the elusive, problematic task of trying to understand himself, becomes Will Barrett's avocation as well.[9]

In *The Last Gentleman* the young Will Barrett is swept along on a delirious pilgrimage in search of a peaceful harbor where past and present might finally be reconciled. But in his attempts to free himself, Will is also a survivor of the outmoded principles so dear to his father, as he is often left bewildered by a reality he fails to comprehend. His inability to come to terms with himself, coupled with his clumsiness in practical matters, renders him ill-suited for life in the rapidly changing, pragmatic society of modern America. He is a misfit, a true descendant of the definitive last gentleman of Western literature, the Knight of the Sorrowful Countenance, a comic and ridiculous figure, the parody of the hero prototype. If we now reconsider our opening remarks in this light, we may well affirm that the eponymous hero of Walker Percy's *Last Gentleman* is indeed the young Will, a gentleman in spite of himself, as he comes to life under the author's ironic vision.

"The book is nothing but a journey," Walker Percy said of his novel. William R. Allen has defined it as an epic journey across the country that "takes place beside Augie's and Huck's adventures as a paradigm of the

9. Walker Percy, "A Southern View," *America* 97 (July 20, 1957): 428; Introduction to *Lanterns*, ix.

American picaresque form."[10] But if the plot of the novel is episodic and the protagonist has to discover values anew—two distinct traits of the picaresque mode—the sort of voyage Will Barrett undertakes also has all the constituents of a quixotic journey. There is a basic difference between the quixotic journey and the original version of the Spanish picaresque. *Don Quixote* stemmed from the picaresque but evolved into a different literary form as it raised questions about the substance and perception of reality, incorporating an unprecedented type of experience: the spiritual or inner journey. The picaresque and the quixotic protagonists are both unheroic. But a significant difference between them is that the picaro deals with tangible reality; that is, he takes to the road literally: his journey takes place in history, and he strives to see his travails compensated at the material level of existence. His quest is one of survival and self-betterment. Conversely, the quixotic hero travels in the realm of the imagination: his journey takes place outside history, and his labors are aimed at keeping the labeling hand of history off of his epic reading of the world. His quest is a figuration of his mind and is enmeshed with personal identity. Accordingly, Percy's protagonist is in flight from himself; his is a spiritual journey, and his misadventures follow from the twisted turnings of his mind; identity is precisely what he ceaselessly pursues in his tortuous journey from New York back to his native South, where his youth was suddenly truncated by the tragic event of his father's suicide. "When he was a youth," we are told of Will Barrett in the first pages of the novel, "he had lived his life in a state of the liveliest expectation, thinking to himself: what a fine thing it will be to become a man and to know what to do—like an Apache youth who at the right time goes out into the plains alone, dreams dreams, sees visions, returns and knows he is a man. But no such time had come and he still didn't know how to live" (*LG* 11).

Heir to a generation that witnessed the rapid downfall of its own codes and ideals, while at the same time a child of a new era, Will Barrett struggles without success to find a niche for himself and forge a personality. The last in the line of "an honorable and violent family" that "over the years . . . had turned ironical and lost its gift for action," Will sees only one course of

10. John C. Carr, "An Interview with Walker Percy" (1971), in *Conversations with Walker Percy*, ed. Louis A. Lawson and Victor A. Kramer (Jackson: University Press of Mississippi, 1985), 67; William R. Allen, *Walker Percy: A Southern Wayfarer* (Jackson: University Press of Mississippi, 1986), 46.

action open to him, to become "a watcher and a listener and a wanderer" (*LG* 9–10). The account that follows—eloquent of Will's confusion—of the decline and fall of the Barretts' boldness and readiness is reminiscent of the Percys'[11] in the same way that the Sartorises' decline is reminiscent of the Faulkners':

> The great grandfather knew what was what and said so and acted accordingly and did not care what anyone thought. He even wore a pistol in a holster like a Western hero and once met the Grand Wizard of the Ku Klux Klan in a barbershop and invited him then and there to shoot it out in the street. The next generation, the grandfather, seemed to know what was what but he was not really so sure. He was brave but he gave much thought to the business of being brave. He too would have shot it out with the Grand Wizard if only he could have made certain it was the thing to do. The father was a brave man too and he said he didn't care what others thought, but he did care. More than anything else, he wished to act with honor and to be thought well of by other men. So living for him was a strain. He became ironical. For him it was not a small thing to walk down the street on an ordinary September morning. In the end he was killed by his own irony and sadness and by the strain of living out an ordinary day in a perfect dance of honor. (*LG* 9–10)

The demise of southern heroics is at the center of William Faulkner's tragic vision, and some years later Walker Percy takes up this theme again from an ironic standpoint in the comic, troubled character of Will Barrett, who the author says "was trying to 'engineer' his own life, an impossible task."[12] Against this quixotic backdrop of dwindling heroics the troubled figure of Will Barrett is launched on a search for meaning in a postmodern world. With this purpose in mind, Will sets out on a sinuous quest for truth, which for him means simplicity, the privilege of those for whom action and conviction form a unified whole. This is the type of conviction

11. See Bertram Wyatt-Brown, *The House of Percy: Honor, Melancholy, and Imagination in a Southern Family* (New York: Oxford University Press, 1994), for an account of the Percys' sense of decline and fall from the family's early status "at the top of the social and political elite of the South in the nineteenth century" (10) into the democratic culture of mid-twentieth-century America with a strong sense of identity lost.

12. Zoltán Abádi-Nagy, "A Talk with Walker Percy" (1973), in Lawson and Kramer, *Conversations with Walker Percy*, 83.

summed up in the words of Senator Oscar Underwood, ostensibly to Will Barrett, that exemplify Will's quest and come to haunt him: "When you grow up, decide what you want to do according to your lights. Then do it. That's all there is to it" (*LG* 348).

As Will expects to find this truth somewhere outside of himself, he listens, observes, and time after time comes up against a hostile reality in his attempts to relate to the external world. His way of thinking is repeatedly shown to be obsolete and his behavior out of place. His ideals, illusions, naïveté, and compassion continually bring him into conflict with society, and he is thwarted by his own honesty and sensitivity. He has been compared to Prince Myshkin, whose extreme kindliness earned him the nickname the Idiot. Walker Percy himself has said that Will Barrett "bears a conscious kinship to Prince Myshkin," and that he used Will's psychological problems for dramatic ends: "I wanted a young man who could see things afresh, both the Northern and Southern culture. A slightly addled young man. His amnesia allows him to be a blank tablet, and that is what I mean by putting it to dramatic use."[13] A comparison has also been drawn between Percy's protagonist and Candide, another character with a pronounced philanthropic bent. But Will Barrett can be better compared with Don Quixote for one significant reason: his desire to transcend his distressing condition by holding fast to the idea that there is a definitive way of comprehending the world, a final understanding that will provide him with the key to his own existence. Sutter, the mouthpiece for Kierkegaardian existentialism in *The Last Gentleman*, sums up the futility of Will's quest when he says, "He wishes to cling to his transcendence and to locate a fellow transcender (e.g., me) who will tell him how to traffic with immanence (e.g., 'environment,' 'groups,' 'experience,' etc.) in such a way that he will be happy. Therefore I will tell him nothing. For even if I were 'right,' his posture is self-defeating" (*LG* 353). Sutter's words point out Will's inability to find a social role that he can identify himself with since the one passed onto him by his forebears has already been discarded from the social fabric of his time.

Walker Percy describes his protagonist as "a voracious and enraged pil-

13. Ashley Brown, "An Interview with Walker Percy," 1967, in *Conversations with Walker Percy*, 12–13. Prince Myshkin has often been compared with Don Quixote. Dostoevski himself acknowledges his debt to *Don Quixote* when preparing his piece about "a positively good man." See Introduction, note 2.

grim"; he is "an absolute seeker—a seeker and a demander [who] insists on finding what he calls truth; and it's either this or death." Will's search is well summed up by Louis D. Rubin's definition of the "quixotic journey," one that depicts "a man escaping from a version of reality that is not of his liking and going forth as an outsider in society, in search of another version that perhaps can be." Rubin goes on to say that "Quixote's quest represents another powerful modern urge: the effort to will oneself back into a Golden Age that has departed, through an effort of the moral intellect."[14] These defining traits are at the heart of Will's pilgrimage: flight from an unsatisfactory present and search for a higher truth, underlain by a fascination with the past and a nostalgia for a world in which standards were certain and unshifting. The search for self-assurance is Will's chief urge, and it is where he meets his most conspicuous failure. The Golden Age in which man's estrangement from the world was unknown has vanished, but his family's past provides him with a historical setting wherein to locate it.

The Percys had difficulty dealing with "everydayness," Wyatt-Brown observes, and this difficulty provides a clue to understanding Will Barrett's identity problems. The need for heroic striving runs in the family as well as the inability to deal with life outside the claims of honor and gallantry: "Unchallenged by monotonous routines of life and eager to meet the martial ideals of their heritage, Percys often found in political contest and war a way to stir blood and assert the family's claim to honor." These battlefields provided "expectations of manhood and bloody daring that peaceful circumstances thwarted." Wyatt-Brown observes that Walker Percy's ironic grasp of his family penchant for distinction is reflected in his protagonist's inadequate grasp of reality and that "a sense of inadequacy and dejection might arise when the warrior spirit had no legitimate outlet." He cites the Spanish Golden Age to illustrate how the relationship among honor, military life, and dejection was often a literary subject. As an example, he quotes Cervantes' *Don Quixote*, a favorite piece of Walker Percy.[15] Indeed,

14. James Atlas, "An Interview with Walker Percy" (1980), in *Conversations with Walker Percy*, 184; Rubin, "Quixote and Selected Progeny," 35–36.

15. Wyatt-Brown, *House of Percy*, 16–17. To the question in the New York *Times Book Review* about what work of literature he would like to have written Percy answered, " 'Don Quixote.' . . . If I had to choose—the first novel and maybe the best. What is so good about 'Don Quixote' is the happy conjunction of narrative and satire. . . . I can imagine how good

Spanish playwrights in the seventeenth century—particularly Lope de Vega, Cervantes's rival in literature and real life—produced a number of honor plays dealing with the feeling of dejection experienced by those to whom honor was unjustly denied. Honor heavily dependent upon the group, bestowed to the individual by the community, was the target of Cervantes' criticism and the cause of his irritation with many of the plots of his literary rival. Cervantes' prodigious knight represents a diametrically opposed option to the heedless acts of valor that these plays portray. Cervantes' debunking treatment of his hidalgo is a proof of the abyss separating him from Lope de Vega. It is not surprising, then, that Cervantes' ironic commentary on the excesses of chivalry may have supplied Walker Percy with a fitting literary representation to work out his own conflict with myth and history. Will Barrett, in his role of comic hero, a disinherited nobleman from a former Golden Age, is an attempt to come to terms with this conflict.

Will Barrett exemplifies Don Quixote's longings for all things heroic and for certainty in a time of vulgarity and mistrust. Above all, he represents many of Walker Percy's misfortunes. Jay Tolson's comment on the autobiographical content of Will Barrett's troubles fits well with the quixotic motif here discussed: "Williston Bibb Barrett may well be the person Percy might have become had he not made the commitments he made, a character who is always setting beyond his reach the very things he prizes." Will's longing for the fusion of action and belief is an abstract, even literary principle, always removed from the character's reach. As Michael Kreyling has rightly pointed out, "Certainty of action and integrity of character within a social order are accessible only on the printed page; [Will] reads *The Murder of Roger Ackroyd* for narrative closure and Freeman's *R. E. Lee* for the well-wrought model of heroic character in man." Will's ill-starred encounters with actuality bear the mark of Don Quixote's blunders: his intentions are invariably ill directed, and his attempt to live up to a code he

---

Cervantes must have felt to have hit on the two: telling a superb, funny, tragic adventure and in the very telling getting in the licks at what's wrong with society. Now there is a happy man. It would have been so easy to lose balance, slip over into sentimentality ('Dream the Impossible Dream') or get heavy-handed the way Mark Twain ruined 'Huck Finn' with Tom Sawyer. But Cervantes kept a lovely balance, had a very good time, gave us a very good time. I really wouldn't have minded writing 'Don Quixote' " (New York *Times Book Review*, December 6, 1981: 68, 70).

fails to comprehend earns him a punch on the nose on more than one occasion. "Will's groping toward certainty," notes Kreyling, "ends with the typical episode turned on its head: he is sucker-punched by a woman, a knight's nightmare of shame."[16]

Like Don Quixote, who in his delirium mistakes harlots for maidens and wayside inns for castles, this latter-day gentleman on his trip back to the South consistently jumps to the wrong conclusions and is constantly mocked by reality. Thus the "bevy of Virginia noblewomen," that picks him up while he is hitchhiking in Virginia turns out to be a noisy group of Texan women, "golfers from a Fort Worth club, fortyish and firm as India rubber" (*LG* 152), and the "Confederates" imprisoned during the celebration of the centennial are in truth blacks and rioters charged as agitators and kept behind the fence in Fort Ste. Marie (*LG* 336). The University of Mississippi riot scene provides a fine example of Percy's ironic gaze on Will's calamitous fortune. Will and his fiancée, Kitty Vaught, have arranged to meet after class to set off in search of the missing Jamie, the Vaughts' youngest son and Will's charge, who suffers from a terminal disease and who, they suspect, has gone to join his brother Sutter in New Mexico. As Will waits for Kitty, a protest march is already in progress. Will, unaware of what is going on, runs into a group of demonstrators. The encounter in which the engineer Will is knocked out at the foot of the Confederate monument is not unworthy of the Knight of La Mancha:

"What yall say," said the engineer amiably and stepped nimbly to the side, thinking they meant to go past him and down the path whence he came. But when they came abreast of the Confederate monument they turned toward the lights and the noise. They cleared him easily but what he did not see and they did not care about was the dark flagstaff behind them, which as they turned swept out in a wider arc and yet which he nevertheless saw a split second before the brass butt caught him at the belt buckle. "Oof," he grunted, not hurt much and even smiling. He would have sat down but for the wire fencelet, which took him by the heel and whipped him backward. He was felled, levered over, and would have killed himself if his head had struck the corner of the monument base but it struck instead the slanting face of the old pocked Vermont marble and he was sent spinning into the soft earth under an arborvitae. (*LG* 289)

16. Jay Tolson, *Pilgrim in the Ruins: A Life of Walker Percy* (New York: Simon and Schuster, 1992), 305; Michael Kreyling, *Figures of the Hero in Southern Narrative* (Baton Rouge: Louisiana State University Press, 1987), 172.

In this episode and elsewhere in the novel, Percy pokes fun at his protagonist's gaffes. However, he shows his sympathy for his character's frailty by carefully drawing our attention to the way Will maintains his composure at all times, particularly when his sense of honor and duty are at stake, even when those to whom he disinterestedly offers his help are persons of little moral fiber. Will's fortuitous encounter in Ithaca with Forney Aiken (the "pseudo-Negro" journalist he had met in Philadelphia) and his group of artist friends serves to illustrate this point. Will learns that one of the group, Bugs Flieger, has been arrested and thrown in jail. It is clear from what follows that it is not Will's bewilderment and naïveté that are being held up to ridicule but the pretensions of Aiken and his entourage:

> "Do you think you could prevail upon the local fuzz to do something for you?" the pseudo-Negro asked him.
>
> "What?"
>
> "Let Bugs out of jail."
>
> "Bugs?"
>
> "Bugs Flieger. They put him in jail last night after the festival, and our information is he's been beaten up. Did you know Mona over there is Bug's sister?"
>
> "Bugs Flieger," mused the engineer.
>
> The actor and the white girl looked at each other, the former popping his jaw muscles like Spencer Tracy.
>
> "Tell—ah—Merle here," said the actor, hollowing out this throat, "that Bugs Flieger plays the guitar a little."
>
> "Merle?" asked the mystified engineer, looking around at the others. "Is he talking to me? Why does he call me Merle?"
>
> "You really never heard of Flieger, have you?" asked the playwright.
>
> "No. I have been quite preoccupied lately. I never watch television," said the engineer.
>
> "Television," said the girl. "Jesus Christ." (*LG* 320)

Will's sympathetic portrait in the exchange is a result of his candor, which is thrown into relief against the snobbishness of the Aiken's party. His stance is enhanced when we learn that he helps Aiken and his friends to escape, not because of any ideological affinity, or any particular liking for them, but rather because his sense of honor tells him to do so. When the police burst into Sweet Evening Breeze's bar, where Aiken's gang has been hiding, Aiken and his friends have already fled through the back door.

Will had lent them his camper and remains behind to stall the police. One of them is the despicable town deputy, Beans Ross, "a realistic redneck version of the Shakespearean deputy of 'The Ku Klux Klan Comes and Goes' in *Lanterns on the Levee.*"[17] Without waiting for explanations, he lays Breeze out with a single blow. Will rebukes him for his brutality, but Ross bears down scornfully on Will and "snap[s] his middle finger on the engineer's fly," contemptuously asking, "Where's the poontang?" Overcoming this humiliation, Will at last finds an opportunity to act: "The engineer had time to straighten himself and to brace his foot in the corner of the jam and sill of the front door. For once in his life he had time and position and a good shot, and for once things became as clear as they used to be in the old honorable days. He hit Beans in the root of his neck as hard as he ever hit the sandbag in the West Side Y.M.C.A. Beans's cap and glasses flew off and he sat down on the floor." A gentleman to the last, Will delays his escape long enough to give Beans' sidekick, Ellis Gover, some assurance. "You bring charges against me to clear yourself," Will tells him. "Tell Beans the others got in behind you. You got it?" (*LG* 325–26). Later, when the police arrest the group, Will helps them by corroborating their story that he had indeed lent them the camper they were traveling in. It is Will's testimony that saves them from being locked up in Fort Ste. Marie. For once Will does not approach reality intellectually; however, it is ironic that he should at last act decidedly on behalf of precisely those who will not value the significance of his act. It is clear that Will cannot tolerate the deputy's brutality, and he responds to it out of his sense of moral uprightness. Will sets the artistic crew free for exactly the same reason that Don Quixote frees the galley slaves who cross his path. He has the opportunity to act as the savior knight and at last be one with his conviction, and this counts at least as much as his actual sympathy for their plight.

In almost every instance, the secondary characters of *The Last Gentleman* are key elements in Walker Percy's social satire. His treatment of Aiken and his friends as caricatures of the Yankee liberal, the new leftist of the sixties who claim to be free from bourgeois racial and sexual biases, is a good example. They are depicted as mere dilettantes of the African American cause whose cliché and paternalistic attitude provides no solutions to the grave problems confronting the South during those turbulent times. The Vaughts, in turn, whom Will describes as "rich Texas-type Southern-

17. Kreyling, *Figures of the Hero*, 172.

ers" or "Yankee sort of Southerners, the cheerful prosperous go-getters one comes across in the upper South" (*LG* 75, 54), are a parody of the affluent white southern family. In fact, much of the humor in the novel derives from the clash between the frenzied and somewhat farcical protagonist and the new emerging social and cultural values of sixties in both the North and the South. From this clash there results a satire on society; more particularly, as Percy has pointed out, the satire is "directed to events happening in the South." Although Walker Percy has remarked that "the reader is free to see [the protagonist] as a sick man among healthy business men or as a sane pilgrim in a mad world,"[18] there is no ambiguity about where the author's sympathies lie. Will Barrett suffers from amnesia and states of déjà vu. As a consequence, his experience of reality is seriously distorted, and his possibilities for leading a "normal" life or for establishing relationships are extremely limited. But in spite of his deep psychological disorder, and even though the author leaves us in no doubt about his character's mental illness, Will possesses a number of praiseworthy qualities that make us sympathetic toward him both as a human figure and as a singular type of misfit, so much so that the protagonist's formidable personal problem, when thrown into relief against the flaws of society itself, emerges as a case of social incompatibility as much as a personal disability.

The irony with which the author treats Will's ordeals reaches a very high pitch at times, but the humor is never entirely at the hero's expense. Most of the time it goes hand in hand with subtle social criticism facilitated by the situations Will gets involved in along the way. Walker Percy's sympathetic reference to Cervantes' fondness for the road over the inn, for "rotation" over "everydayness," can be seen as a vindication of his character's journey. If, on the one hand, his skepticism is directed toward Will's idealization of the past and his identification with a culture in decline, on the other, he feels deeply for his character's sense of alienation in modern society. In Lewis P. Simpson's opinion, "Percy's description of the cultural trauma, which is the psychic heritage of the educated southern youth like Will, derives . . . from Percy's own descent into the self."[19] Will's search in

18. Zoltán Abádi-Nagy and Ashley Brown interviews in *Conversations with Walker Percy*, 84, 13.

19. Walker Percy, "The Man on the Train," in *The Message in the Bottle* (New York: Farrar, Straus & Giroux, 1975), 89; Lewis P. Simpson, "Southern Fiction," in *Harvard Guide to Contemporary American Writing*, ed. Daniel Hoffman (Cambridge, Mass.: Belknap Press of Harvard University Press, 1979), 182.

The Last Gentleman is an existential search comparable to any modern hero's, but it is also the search of a dislocated white southerner from an old family of the ruling class, a man brought up according to traditional values who must now make a fresh place for himself in a society undergoing a process of creeping uniformity. Simpson's view that the author himself might have experienced a similar upheaval seems altogether accurate.

Walker Percy sends his hero to fight with windmills: the knight sets off in pursuit of a southern heroic model of conduct against a sanchopanzesque setting, exemplified by Mr. Vaught's "knack of getting onto the rhythm of things, of knowing when to buy and to sell" (*LG* 189). The world, as Will perceives it, is *easy* and *actual*, as "easy and actual" as the deltans he meets in the Vaughts' household. They are southerners of the Rooney Lee type in Will's estimation, "very much at one with themselves and with the dear world around them as bright and sure as a paradise" (*LG* 266). The savoir vivre that Will pursues so fruitlessly comes naturally to them. The contrast between Will Barrett and Rooney Lee (Robert E. Lee's son and Henry Adams' classmate at Harvard) underscores the irony of Will's plight. The concurrence of action and belief, which is at the core of the traditional heroic model, is natural to the mindless young southerner, "simple beyond analysis," "ignorant," and "childlike" (*LG* 57) like Rooney Lee, as described by Henry Adams in his *Education*. The irony of this counterpoint provides yet another indication of Will's quixotic quality.

More than any other character considered in this study, Williston Bibb Barrett is a literary descendant of Quentin Compson. Walker Percy explicitly stated that he wanted to start "where Faulkner left off . . . with the Quentin Compson who 'didn't commit suicide.' "[20] The divergence of these two characters is attributable to the differences in the personal and historical circumstances of the two authors, but more pertinently it reflects the authors' distinct attitudes towards the past and its legends. They both feared the homogeneity towards which the South was tending and despised the culture of materialism that challenged some its traditional values, but Faulkner's tragic vision springs from the assumption that the conditions of modern life no longer provide the opportunity for heroic action, whereas Percy's existentialist outlook suggests the possibility of rehabilitating the past in the present through a spiritual pilgrimage, a sort of ritual passage

20. Jo Gulledge, "The Reentry Option: An Interview with Walker Percy" (1984), in *Conversations with Walker Percy*, 300.

from myth to history undertaken by the man of faith. While Quentin Compson and Will Barrett have in common their profound estrangement from their respective times, they differ to the extent that each embodies the distinct outlook of his creator.

Will Barrett and Quentin Compson are highly sensitive, illusion-ridden young men, both touched with a strong sense of duty and honor. They have a craving for certainty and are unable to face reality without mental constructions of their own. They look for models and seek abstract aims that cannot be attained, incapable as they are of accepting the complexities of their worlds. Their search is futile inasmuch as they look for answers outside themselves. Although they each have a sharp eye and a clear perception of the ineffectual nature of their strivings, they are prone to mistake reality for their heart's desire and to be taken in by the events around them. Their emotional dysfunctions spring from their lack of proper father images, which might have bestowed upon them the unity of purpose and being and the identity each seeks so relentlessly. Both have a marked inability to reconcile romantic love with carnal love. In his quest for the ideal mate Will tries unsuccessfully to imitate the pattern of the southern male. Quentin, far more withdrawn than Will from any grasp on actual love, hides behind incestuous fantasies and ineffectual patterns of chivalrous honor. Both take up roles they are unfit to perform. Yet for all they have in common, there is one fundamental trait that sets them apart: Quentin's obsession with honor, role playing, and virtue finally undermines his life. Will's preoccupation with the same abstractions are much less agonizing, probably because the old code is far more removed from his experience; he is in fact baffled by it. (Ed Barrett is in a way closer to the character of Quentin Compson, insofar as he, like Quentin, internalizes the demise of his values system and can find no way out of his distress except by suicide.) Will is eventually able to settle his debt with the past and rebuild his life, thus avoiding Quentin's tragic fate. The essential difference between Will Barrett and Quentin Compson is evident from the beginning of *The Last Gentleman* in the author's detached and wry comic view of his main character and his tribulations. And in the end this difference is patently evident when Percy forces his protagonist to yield to the claims of reality and acknowledge the absurdity of his flight from the present. Will's visit to his old family home is a crucial milestone in his chimerical voyage.

After the Beans Ross episode, and having lost track of Aiken's group and the Trav-L-Aire, Will walks to his father's house. As he approaches, his nostrils pick up the ancient, unmistakable "ham-rich smell of the cotton-seed oil mill" (*LG* 328) that hung in the air the night his father took his life. The memory of that night, the brief, fateful exchange between him and his father comes back to him in every detail:

> "Don't leave."
>
> "I'm just going to the corner."
>
> But there was a dread about this night, the night of victory. (Victory is the saddest thing of all, said the father). The mellowness of Brahms had gone over-ripe, the victorious serenity of the Great Horn Theme was false, oh fake, fake. Underneath, all was unwell.
>
> "Father."
>
> "What?"
>
> "Why do you like to be alone?"
>
> "In the last analysis, you are alone." He turned into the darkness of the oaks.
>
> "*Don't leave.*" The terror of the beautiful victorious music pierced his very soul. (*LG* 331)

The unfortunate consequences of Ed Barrett's death for his son are a palpable demonstration of the great human cost of the quixotic act. The ideals that led to Ed Barrett's self-sacrifice "necessarily presupposed a former time in which men were better and wiser, more disinterested and virtuous than humans could ever be." The same distorted vision pictured a bygone society that was "more nearly free from all temptations to covetousness, avarice, lust and cruelty than had ever existed on earth." As a result, "falling away from perfection" and "the arrival of crass days" are inevitable with change and the passing of time.[21] (Ironically, Will inherits the same burden of nostalgia that drives his father to suicide and that mars his own life at a tender age. Will's obsession with the Confederate cause, which leads him to blow up a Union monument at Princeton and to wander about the battlefields of northern Virginia in one of his bouts of amnesia, and his fixation with Robert E. Lee, whose biography we see him reading throughout the novel, are instances of the appeal the past had for him.)

During Will's visit to his childhood home, he begins to understand the

---

21. Louis D. Rubin, Jr., "The Boll Weevil, the Iron Horse, and the End of the Line: Time and Change in Southern Literature and Life," in *The American South: Portrait of a Culture*, 386.

distorted world view that drove his father to suicide: "It was not in the Brahms that one looked and not in solitariness and not in the old sad poetry . . . but here, under your nose, here in the very curiousness and drollness and extraness of the iron and the bark" (*LG* 332). "The juncture of iron and bark" (*i.e.,* "the tiny iron horsehead in the hitching post . . . where the oak had grown round it") that Will's fingers explore in the dark as events both past and present rise up to meet him is a powerful metaphor for his inevitable acceptance of change and human vulnerability (*LG* 332). It reveals the absurdity of attitudes that insist on ignoring this ineluctable alternative. At last he is able to see the great falsehood concealed behind an apocalyptic concept of the world: "*Wait.* I think he was wrong and that he was looking in the wrong place. No, not he but the times. The times were wrong and one looked in the wrong place. It wasn't even his fault because that was the way he was and the way the times were, and there was no other place a man could look. It was the worst of times, a time of fake beauty and fake victory" (*LG* 332). As he stands among the water oaks close to the house, the scene Will contemplates contrasts starkly with his father's tragic fate as he relives it in his memory. From his vantage point, Will can see his aunts sitting peacefully on the porch watching television, reading "*Race and Reason* and eating Whitman's Sampler." They are "Christian ladies every one, four Protestant, Presbyterian, and Scotch-Irish, two Catholic and Creole, but long since reconciled, ecumenized, by bon appétit and laughter and good hearty hatred" (*LG* 328). Further on, in Shut-Off, Louisiana, Will observes Uncle Fannin and his black servant Merriam, "solid 3-D persons, true denizens of this misty Natchez Trace country," heartily enjoying Captain Kangaroo's "sad gags from Madison Avenue" (*LG* 346). Both instances illustrate how history mocks the nostalgic attitude. At the end of his journey, Will confronts the inescapable truth that the world of certainty is an impossibility, and the absolute truth implicit in his father's stoic vision gives way to the world of multiple interpretations, the world that Ed Barrett could never accept. Will's awakening has all the imprints of quixotic disillusionment.

In the world of William Faulkner, Quentin Compson cannot avoid his tragic fate. In a similar world a generation later, Walker Percy seems to suggest that there may be a place for his protagonist in the new order. Will Barrett finally comes to understand life as a continuous pilgrimage in which truth appears not as abstract, absolute, and definitive but concrete, personal, and perceptible only through contact with the real world. Will's departure for the Southwest to meet Sutter seems to imply that his search is not over but will now have a different quality. The lesson he learns does not differ from the one Don Quixote learns at the end of his life, and it brings to a close the chimerical phase of his journey. This statement does not speak of Bill Barrett's stance in *The Second Coming*. His problems are not solved—his nervous condition remains unremedied, his quixotic wanderings into the past have not ceased, and his father's stoical figure remains fixed in the background. We learn more details—or a different version of old ones—of what assails him and why, but the character's essential penchant for transcendence remains unchanged. Will Barrett's wanderings in *The Second Coming* are analogous more than complementary to the more exemplary quixotic quest of *The Last Gentleman*. It is the character of Will Barrett as portrayed in *The Last Gentleman* that remarkably combines the self-deluding Knight of La Mancha and the chaplinesque modern hero at the mercy of a world he fails to comprehend. Will Barrett's idealism and nobility of spirit, his clumsiness and his conspicuous failure consecrate him as the "last gentleman" of southern fiction, an existential Don Quixote of our times.

Some cultures and their literatures resonate, one with the other, because of similar dramatic historical experiences that generate the need for literary expression. The fate of Cervantes' Don Quixote resounds in the ubiquitous quixotic quests of southern literature. Each of the southern Quixotes examined in this study is a unique manifestation of the bemused knight, but they all share the old Hidalgo's endurance and persistence against impossible odds and immutable realities. Nor are the Quixotes of southern literature limited to these; there are others. There always will be, as long as people dream impossible dreams and insist on pursuing them.

BIBLIOGRAPHY

Aaron, Daniel. *The Unwritten War: American Writers and the Civil War.* New York: Alfred A. Knopf, 1973.

Adams, Henry. *The Education of Henry Adams: An Autobiography.* Boston: Houghton Mifflin, 1918.

Allen, William Rodney. *Walker Percy: A Southern Wayfarer.* Jackson: University Press of Mississippi, 1986.

Auerbach, Erich. *Mimesis: The Representation of Reality in Western Literature.* Translated by Willard R. Trask. Princeton: Princeton University Press, 1953.

Blotner, Joseph L. *Faulkner: A Biography.* 2 vols. New York: Random House, 1974.

Bradford, M. E. "Looking Down from a High Place: The Serenity of Miss Welty's *Losing Battles.*" In *A Still Moment: Essays on the Art of Eudora Welty,* edited by John F. Desmond. Metuchen, N.J.: Scarecrow Press, 1978.

Brashear, Minnie M. *Mark Twain, Son of Missouri.* Chapel Hill: University of North Carolina Press, 1934.

Brooks, Cleanth. *On the Prejudices, Predilections, and Firm Beliefs of William Faulkner.* Baton Rouge: Louisiana State University Press, 1987.

———. *William Faulkner: First Encounters.* New Haven: Yale University Press, 1983.

———. *William Faulkner: Toward Yoknapatawpha and Beyond.* New Haven: Yale University Press, 1978.

———. *William Faulkner: The Yoknapatawpha Country.* New Haven: Yale University Press, 1963.

Bunting, Charles T. " 'The Interior World': An Interview with Eudora Welty." *Southern Review* 3 (1972): 711–35.

Cabell, James Branch. *Beyond Life: Dizain des Demiurges.* Vol. 1 of *The Works of*

James Branch Cabell. Storisende Edition. 18 vols. 1919. New York: R. M. Mc-Bride, 1927.

———. *Chivalry: Dizain des Reines*. Vol. 5 of *The Works of James Branch Cabell*. Storisende Edition. 18 vols. 1909. New York: R. M. McBride, 1928.

———. *Figures of Earth: A Comedy of Appearances*. Vol. 2 of *The Works of James Branch Cabell*. Storisende Edition. 18 vols. 1921. New York: R. M. McBride, 1927.

———. *Jurgen: A Comedy of Justice*. Vol. 6 of *The Works of James Branch Cabell*. Storisende Edition. 18 vols. 1919. New York: R. M. McBride, 1928.

———. *Let Me Lie: Being in the Main an Ethnological Account of the Remarkable Commonwealth of Virginia and the Making of Its History*. New York: Farrar, 1947.

———. *The Letters of James Branch Cabell*. Edited by Edward Wagenknecht. Norman: University of Oklahoma Press, 1975.

———. *Preface to the Past*. New York: R. M. McBride, 1936.

———. *The Rivet in Grandfather's Neck: A Comedy of Limitations*. Vol. 14 of *The Works of James Branch Cabell*. Storisende Edition. 18 vols. 1915. New York: R. M. McBride, 1929.

Cash, Wilbur J. *The Mind of the South*. New York: Alfred A. Knopf, 1941.

Cervantes Saavedra, Miguel de. *The Adventures of Don Quixote*. Translated by J. M. Cohen. London: Penguin, 1950.

Chase, Richard. "Faulkner, The Great Years: *The Sound and the Fury*." In *William Faulkner: "The Sound and the Fury,"* edited by David Minter. New York: Norton, 1987.

Conley, Timothy Kevin. "Resounding Fury: Faulkner's Shakespeare, Shakespeare's Faulkner." *In Shakespeare and Southern Writers: A Study in Influence,* ed. Phillip C. Kolin. Jackson: University Press of Mississippi, 1985.

Cowley, Malcolm. Introduction to *The Portable Faulkner*, rev. and enl. Edited by Malcolm Cowley. New York: Viking Press, 1967.

Faulkner, William. *Absalom, Absalom!* 1936. Reprint, New York: Random House, 1964.

———. "Appendix: The Compsons (1699–1945)." In *The Portable Faulkner*, rev. and enl., edited by Malcolm Cowley. New York: Viking Press, 1967.

———. *As I Lay Dying*. 1930. Reprint, New York: Vintage, 1987.

———. *Faulkner at West Point*. Edited by Joseph L. Fant III and Robert Ashley. New York: Random House, 1964.

———. *Faulkner in the University: Class Conferences at the University of Virginia 1957–1958*. Edited by Frederick L. Gwynn and Joseph L. Blotner. Charlottesville: University Press of Virginia, 1959.

———. *Flags in the Dust.* (Unabridged version of *Sartoris.*) Edited with an introduction by Douglas Day. New York: Random House, 1973.

———. *Go Down, Moses, and Other Stories.* New York: Random House, 1942.

———. "An Introduction to *The Sound and the Fury.*" (*Mississippi Quarterly* version). In *William Faulkner: "The Sound and the Fury,"* edited by David Minter.
New York: Norton, 1987.

———. *Intruder in the Dust.* New York: Random House, 1948.

———. *Light in August.* 1932. Reprint, New York: The Modern Library, 1950.

———. *Lion in the Garden: Interviews with William Faulkner, 1926–1962.* Edited
by James B. Meriwether and Michael Millgate. New York: Random House, 1968.

———. *The Mansion.* New York: Random House, 1959.

———. "Mississippi." In *Essays, Speeches, and Public Letters,* edited by James B.
Meriwether. New York: Random House, 1965. First published in *Holiday* (April
1954).

———. *The Reivers: A Reminiscence.* New York: Random House, 1962.

———. *The Sound and the Fury.* 1929. Reprint, New York: Random House, 1956.

———. *The Town.* New York: Random House, 1957.

———. *The Wild Palms.* New York: Random House, 1939.

Ferguson, J. DeLancey. *Mark Twain: Man and Legend.* Indianapolis: Bobbs-Merrill,
1943.

Flaubert, Gustave. *Correspondance II, 1847–1852* (Correspondence II, 1847–1852).
Paris: L. Conard, 1926.

Fraser, John. *America and the Patterns of Chivalry.* Cambridge: Cambridge University Press, 1982.

Fuentes, Carlos. *Don Quixote; or, The Critique of Reading.* Austin: Institute of Latin
American Studies. The University of Texas at Austin, 1976. Originally published
as *Don Quijote o la crítica de la lectura* (Mexico City: Editorial Joaquín Mortiz,
1976).

Galligan, Edward L. *The Comic Vision in Literature.* Athens: University of Georgia
Press, 1984.

Harkey, J. H. " 'Don Quixote' and the American Fiction Through Mark Twain."
Ph.D. diss., University of Tennessee, 1968.

Hobson, Fred. *Tell About the South: The Southern Rage to Explain.* Baton Rouge:
Louisiana State University Press, 1983.

Holmes, Charles S. "*A Connecticut Yankee in King Arthur's Court*: Mark Twain's
Fable of Uncertainty." *South Atlantic Quarterly* 61 (1962): 463–72.

Howe, Irving. *William Faulkner: A Critical Study.* 1952. Reprint, Chicago: Ivan R.
Dee, 1991.

Huizinga, Johan. *The Waning of the Middle Ages: A Study of the Forms of Life,*

Thought, and Art in France and the Netherlands in the Fourteenth and Fifteenth Centuries. Translated by F. Hopman. London: E. Arnold, 1924.

Kreyling, Michael. *Figures of the Hero in Southern Narrative.* Baton Rouge: Louisiana State University Press, 1987.

Lawson, Lewis A., and Victor A. Kramer, eds. *Conversations with Walker Percy.* Jackson: University Press of Mississippi, 1985.

Llorens, Vicente. "Don Quijote y la decadencia del hidalgo," (Don Quixote and the waning of the hidalgo class) In *Aspectos sociales de la literatura española* (Social aspects of Spanish literature). Colec. España y los españoles. Madrid: Castalia, 1974.

Long, E. Hudson, and J. R. LeMaster, eds. *The New Mark Twain Handbook.* New York: Garland, 1985.

Longley, John Lewis. *The Tragic Mask: A Study of Faulkner's Heroes.* Chapel Hill: University of North Carolina Press, 1963.

McDonald, Edgar E. "Cabell Criticism: Past, Present, and Future." *Cabellian* 1 (1968–69): 21–25.

———. "Cabell in Love." In *James Branch Cabell: Centennial Essays,* edited by M. Thomas Inge and Edgar E. McDonald. Baton Rouge: Louisiana State University Press, 1983.

———. *James Branch Cabell and Richmond-in-Virginia.* Jackson: University Press of Mississippi, 1993.

MacKethan, Lucinda H. *The Dream of Arcady: Place and Time in Southern Literature.* Baton Rouge: Louisiana State University Press, 1980.

Maravall, Juan Antonio. *Utopia and Counterutopia in the "Quixote."* Translated by Robert W. Felkel. Detroit: Wayne State University Press, 1991. Originally published as *Utopía y contrautopía en el "Quijote"* (Santiago de Compostela: Pico Sacro, 1976).

Mencken, H. L. *James Branch Cabell.* New York: R. M. McBride, 1927.

Millgate, Michael. "Faulkner and History." In *The South and Faulkner's Yoknapatawpha: The Actual and the Apocryphal,* edited by Evans Harrington and Ann J. Abadie. Jackson: University Press of Mississippi, 1977.

Mixon, Wayne. *Southern Writers and the New South Movement, 1865–1913.* Chapel Hill: University of North Carolina Press, 1980.

Moore, Olin Harris. "Mark Twain and Don Quixote." *PMLA* 37 (June 1922): 324–46.

Moreland, Kim. *The Medievalist Impulse in American Literature: Twain, Adams, Fitzgerald, and Hemingway.* Charlottesville: University Press of Virginia, 1996.

Ortega y Gasset, José. *Meditations on "Quixote."* Translated by Evelyn Rugg and Diego Marín. New York: Norton, 1961. Originally published as *Meditaciones del Quijote,* Publicaciones de la Residencia de Estudiantes, Series 2, Ensayas (Madrid: Junta para ampliación e investigaciones de estudios científicas, Residencia de Estudiantes, 1914).

Osterweis, Rollin G. *The Myth of The Lost Cause, 1865–1900.* Hamden, Conn.: Archon Books, 1973.

———. *Romanticism and Nationalism in the Old South.* New Haven: Yale University Press, 1949.

Paine, Albert Bigelow. *Mark Twain: A Biography: The Personal and Literary Life of Samuel Langhorne Clemens.* 3 vols. New York: Harper & Brothers, 1912.

Percy, Walker. Introduction to *Lanterns on the Levee: Recollections of a Planter's Son,* by William Alexander Percy. Baton Rouge: Louisiana State University Press, 1973.

———. *Lancelot.* New York: Farrar, Straus & Giroux, 1977.

———. *The Last Gentleman.* New York: Farrar, Straus & Giroux, 1966.

———. *The Message in the Bottle.* New York: Farrar, Straus & Giroux, 1975.

———. *The Second Coming.* New York: Farrar, Straus & Giroux, 1980.

———. "A Southern View." *America* 97 (July 20, 1957): 342–44.

———. "Stoicism in the South." *Commonweal* 64 (1956): 428–29.

Percy, William Alexander. *Lanterns on the Levee: Recollections of a Planter's Son.* 1941. Reprint, with an introduction by Walker Percy, Baton Rouge: Louisiana State University Press, 1973.

Pettit, Arthur G. *Mark Twain and the South.* Lexington: University Press of Kentucky, 1974.

Prenshaw, Peggy Whitman, ed. *Conversations with Eudora Welty.* Jackson: University Press of Mississippi, 1984.

Rascoe, Burton. *Titans of Literature: From Homer to the Present.* New York: G. P. Putnam, 1932.

Reed, Walter L. *An Exemplary History of the Novel: The Quixotic Versus the Picaresque.* Chicago: University of Chicago Press, 1981.

Riemer, James D. *From Satire to Subversion: The Fantasies of James Branch Cabell.* Contributions to the Study of Science Fiction and Fantasy, no. 38. New York: Greenwood Press, 1989.

Robert, Marthe. *The Old and the New: From Don Quixote to Kafka.* Translated by Carol Cosman. Berkeley: University of California Press, 1977. Originally published as *L'Ancient et le nouveau: de Don Quichotte à Franz Kafka* (Paris: Grasset, 1963).

Rubin, Louis D., Jr. "Art and Artistry in Morgana, Mississippi." In *A Gallery of Southerners.* Baton Rouge: Louisiana State University Press, 1982.

———. "The Begum of Bengal: Mark Twain and the South." In *William Elliot Shoots a Bear: Essays on the Southern Literary Imagination.* Baton Rouge: Louisiana State University Press, 1975.

———. "The Discovery of a Man's Vocation." In *A Gallery of Southerners.* Baton Rouge: Louisiana State University Press, 1982.

————. "Don Quixote and Selected Progeny; or, The Journeyman as an Outsider." *Southern Review* 10 (January 1974): 31–58.

————. "The Golden Apples of the Sun." In *The Faraway Country: Writers of the Modern South*. Seattle: University of Washington Press, 1963.

————. "Mark Twain and the Post-War Scene." In *The Writer in the South: Studies in a Literary Community*. Athens: University of Georgia Press, 1972.

————. "Tom Sawyer and the Use of Novels." In *The Curious Death of The Novel: Essays in American Literature*. Baton Rouge: Louisiana State University Press, 1967.

————. "Two in Richmond: Ellen Glasgow and James Branch Cabell." In *South: Modern Southern Literature in Its Cultural Setting*, edited by Louis D. Rubin, Jr., and Robert D. Jacobs. Garden City, N.Y.: Doubleday, 1961.

————, ed. *The American South: Portrait of a Culture*. 2d ed. Forum series. Washington, D.C.: United States Information Agency, 1991.

Rubin, Louis D., Jr., and C. Hugh Holman, eds. *Southern Literary Study: Problems and Possibilities*. Chapel Hill: University of North Carolina Press, 1975.

Russell, Peter E. *Cervantes*. Oxford: Oxford University Press, 1985.

Salomon, Roger B. "Mark Twain and Victorian Nostalgia." In *Patterns of Commitment in American Literature*, edited by Marston La France. Toronto: University of Toronto Press, 1967.

Santayana, George. "Cervantes." In *Essays in Literary Criticism of George Santayana*, edited by Irving Singer. New York: Charles Scribner's, 1956.

————. "Tom Sawyer and Don Quixote." *Mark Twain Quarterly* 9, no. 2 (1952): 1–3.

Savater, Fernando. *Instrucciones para olvidar el "Quijote" y otros ensayos generales* (Instructions on how to forget *Don Quixote* and other general essays). Madrid: Taurus, 1985.

————. *La tarea del héroe* (The hero's task). Madrid: Taurus, 1983.

Serrano Plaja, Arturo. *"Magic" Realism in Cervantes: "Don Quixote" as Seen Through "Tom Sawyer" and "The Idiot."* Translated by Robert S. Rudder. Berkeley: University of California Press, 1970. Originally published as *"Don Quijote" visto desde "Tom Sawyer" y "El Idiota"* (Madrid: Gredos, 1967).

Simpson, Lewis P. *The Brazen Face of History: Studies in the Literary Consciousness in America*. Baton Rouge: Louisiana State University Press, 1980.

————. "The Chosen People." *Southern Review* 6 (1970): xvii–xxiii.

————. "Southern Fiction." In *Harvard Guide to Contemporary America Writing*, edited by Daniel Hoffman. Cambridge, Mass.: Belknap Press of Harvard University Press, 1979.

Smith, Henry Nash. "How True Are Dreams?: The Theme of Fantasy in Mark Twain's Later Work." *Quarry Farm Papers* 1 (1989): 5–23.

———. "An Object Lesson in Democracy." In *Mark Twain: The Development of a Writer.* Cambridge, Mass.: Harvard University Press, 1962.

Stein, Jane. "William Faulkner." *Paris Review* 4 (1956): 28–52.

Taylor, William R. *Cavalier and Yankee: The Old South and American National Character.* New York: Braziller, 1961. Reprint, London: W. H. Allen, 1963.

Templin, Ernest H. "On Re-Reading Mark Twain." *Hispania* 24 (October 1941): 269–76.

Tolson, Jay. *Pilgrim in the Ruins: A Life of Walker Percy.* New York: Simon and Schuster, 1992.

Torrente Ballester, Gonzalo. *El "Quijote" como juego (Don Quixote* as a game). Madrid: Guadarrama, 1985.

Turkevich, Ludmila B. *Cervantes in Russia.* Princeton: Princeton University Press, 1954.

Twain, Mark. *The Adventures of Colonel Sellers, Being Mark Twain's Share of "The Gilded Age."* Edited by Charles Neider. New York: Doubleday, 1965.

———. *Adventures of Huckleberry Finn.* Vol. 8 of *The Works of Mark Twain.* Edited by Walter Blair et al. Berkeley: Published for the Iowa Center of Textual Studies by the University of California Press, 1988.

———. *The Adventures of Tom Sawyer.* Vol. 4 of *The Works of Mark Twain.* Edited by John C. Gerber, Paul Baender, and Terry Firkins. Berkeley: Published for the Iowa Center of Textual Studies by the University of California Press, 1980.

———. *The American Claimant and Other Stories and Sketches.* New York: Harper & Brothers, 1917.

———. *The Autobiography of Mark Twain.* Edited by Charles Neider. New York: Harper & Brothers, 1959.

———. *A Connecticut Yankee in King Arthur's Court.* Vol. 9 of *The Works of Mark Twain.* Edited by Bernard L. Stein. Berkeley: Published for the Iowa Center of Textual Studies by the University of California Press, 1979.

———. *Life on the Mississippi.* 1883. Reprint, New York: Heritage Press, 1944.

———. *The Love Letters of Mark Twain.* Edited by Dixon Wecter. New York: Harper & Brothers, 1949.

———. *Mark Twain's Notebook.* Edited by Albert Bigelow Paine. New York: Harper & Brothers, 1935. Reprint, St. Clair Shores, Mich.: Scholarly Press, 1971.

———. *Mark Twain–Howells Letters: The Correspondence of Samuel L. Clemens and William D. Howells, 1872–1910.* Edited by Henry Nash Smith and William M. Gibson. Cambridge, Mass.: Belknap Press of Harvard University Press, 1960.

———. *Pudd'nhead Wilson: A Tale.* In *"Pudd'nhead Wilson" and "Those Extraordinary Twins,"* edited, with corrected text, full text of "Those Extraordinary Twins," and critical essays, by Sidney E. Berger. Norton Critical Editions. New York: Norton, 1980.

Twain, Mark, and Charles Dudley Warner. *The Gilded Age: A Tale of Today.* 2 vols. New York: Harper & Brothers, 1901.

Vandiver, Frank E. "The Confederate Myth." In *Myth and Southern History,* edited by Patrick Gerster and Nicholas Cords. Urbana: University of Illinois Press, 1989.

Van Doren, Carl, H. L. Mencken, and Hugh Walpole. *James Branch Cabell: Three Essays.* Port Washington, N.Y.: Kennikat Press, 1967.

Vargas, Llosa, Mario. "El último de los caballeros." (The last gentleman). *Quimera* 56 (1986): 12–15.

Vickery, Olga W. *The Novels of William Faulkner: A Critical Interpretation.* Rev. ed. Baton Rouge: Louisiana State University Press, 1964.

———. "The Sound and the Fury: A Study in Perspective." In *William Faulkner: "The Sound and the Fury,"* edited by David Minter. New York: Norton, 1987. Originally published in *PMLA* 64 (December 1954): 1017–37.

Vilar, Pierre. "El Tiempo del 'Quijote' " (The time of Don Quixote). In *El "Quijote" de Cervantes* (Cervantes' *Don Quixote*), edited by George Haley. El escritor y la crítica. Madrid: Taurus, 1980.

Wagenknecht, Edward. *Mark Twain: The Man and His Work.* Norman: University of Oklahoma Press, 1967.

Warren, Robert Penn. "Faulkner: Past and Future." In *Faulkner: A Collection of Critical Essays,* edited by Robert Penn Warren. Englewood Cliffs, N.J.: Prentice-Hall, 1966.

———. "Mark Twain." *Southern Review* 8 (1972): 459–92.

Wecter, Dixon. *Sam Clemens of Hannibal.* Boston: Houghton Mifflin, 1952.

Welsh, Alexander. *Reflections on the Hero as Quixote.* Princeton: Princeton University Press, 1981.

Welty, Eudora. "The Golden Apples." In *The Collected Stories of Eudora Welty.* New York: Harcourt Brace, 1980.

———. *Losing Battles.* New York: Random House, 1970.

———. *One Writer's Beginnings.* Cambridge, Mass.: Harvard University Press, 1984.

Williams, Stanley T. *The Spanish Background of American Literature.* 2 vols. New Haven: Yale University Press, 1968.

Williamson, Edwin. *The Half-Way House of Fiction: "Don Quixote" and Arthurian Romance.* Oxford: Clarendon Press, 1984.

Woodward, C. Vann. *The Burden of Southern History.* Baton Rouge: Louisiana State University Press, 1960.

Wyatt-Brown, Bertram. *The House of Percy: Honor, Melancholy, and Imagination in a Southern Family.* New York: Oxford University Press, 1994.

————. *Southern Honor: Ethics and Behavior in the Old South.* New York: Oxford University Press, 1982.

Zambrano, Maria. *España, sueño y verdad* (Spain, dream and reality). Barcelona: Edhasa, 1982.

Ziolkowski, Eric J. *The Sanctification of Don Quixote: From Hidalgo to Priest.* University Park: Pennsylvania State University Press, 1991.

INDEX